CONSUMER
BEHAVIOR OF THE
COLLEGE-BOUND
STUDENT

INTEGRATED
MARKETING
AND THE STUDENT
MARKETING PLAN

STUDENT
MARKETING
FUNDAMENTALS

STRATEGIC
PLANNING

MARKETING

D1568808

FOR **COLLEGES** AND **UNIVERSITIES**

AACRAO®

EDITOR

Richard Whiteside

**Vice President for Enrollment Management
Tulane University**

AMERICAN ASSOCIATION OF COLLEGIATE REGISTRARS AND ADMISSIONS OFFICERS

American Association of Collegiate
Registrars and Admissions Officers
One Dupont Circle, NW, Suite 520
Washington, DC 20036-1135

For a complete listing of AACRAO publications, visit www.aacrao.org/publications.

The American Association of Collegiate Registrars and Admissions Officers, founded
in 1910, is a nonprofit, voluntary, professional association of more than 9,300 higher
education administrators who represent more than 2,400 institutions and agencies in
the United States and in twenty-eight countries around the world. The mission of the
Association is to provide leadership in policy initiation, interpretation, and
implementation in the global educational community. This is accomplished through
the identification and promotion of standards and best practices in enrollment management, information technology, instructional management, and student services.

Library of Congress Cataloging-in-Publication Data

Student marketing for colleges and universities / editor, Richard Whiteside.
    p. cm.
Includes bibliographical references and index.
ISBN 1-57858-060-9
1. Universities and colleges—United States—Marketing. 2. College Students—Recruiting—United States.
I. Whiteside, Richard, 1947– II. American Association of Collegiate Registrars and Admissions Officers.

LB2342.82.S78 2004
    378.1'98—dc22

                                               2004002387

CONTENTS

CONTENTS

STUDENT
MARKETING
FOR COLLEGES
AND UNIVERSITIES

CONTENTS   III

PREFACE

RICHARD WHITESIDE
Vice President for Enrollment Management
Tulane University, New Orleans, Louisiana

The use of advanced marketing concepts and techniques is pervasive in contemporary society. These concepts along with their associated tools make it possible for providers of goods and services to formulate and execute plans, the intent of which are to make potential customers – prospective students – aware of the programs, services and benefits available at a particular institution of higher learning. Despite the almost universal adoption of marketing thinking in the early part of the 19th century, colleges and universities generally resisted the application of these techniques within the higher education environment. Critics often opined that higher education was not a business in the traditional sense and that the use of business tools was therefore inappropriate. Although the widespread application of marketing tools was resisted for many years within the academy, the use of these tools has now permeated even the most traditional and conservative institutions. Those responsible for recruiting and enrolling students at America's colleges and universities now understand that the complex task of achieving institutional enrollment goals requires the use of sophisticated marketing concepts and powerful business tools.

The body of literature on marketing comprises thousands of citations. These range from general texts on marketing as an academic discipline to more focused works that address the utilization of these principles in specific business situations. This book represents a collaborative effort between institutional enrollment managers and knowledgeable commercial professionals that assist some of us in determining how to provide a comprehensive framework for applying marketing concepts and techniques in the postsecondary educational setting.

The idea for this book surfaced at AACRAO's Strategic Enrollment Management meeting in 2002 (SEM XII.) During the course of that meeting, many attendees asked, "Is there a good book on student marketing for colleges and universities?" The answer I heard most often was "No." While there are many first rate works that address one or several aspects of marketing in the college or university setting, there does not appear to be a single authoritative source that interprets basic and advanced marketing techniques within the context of student marketing.

Higher Education is a major American industry. In 2001, our "business" served 15 million customers through more than 3,900 post secondary education entities. In that year, over 2.8 million individuals made their living working in higher education, and postsecondary educational institutions

STUDENT
MARKETING
FOR COLLEGES
AND UNIVERSITIES

made expenditures of more than $190 billion.[1] As in virtually every other industry, the competition for customers – students – has become more and more intense and the marketplace has become increasingly crowded with communication about the goods and services provided by the wide array of institutions and learning organizations. Today's prospective college student is an intelligent consumer with considerable latitude in college choice. The success of our industry in general and our own institution in particular is closely tied to our effectiveness in attracting and enrolling the kinds and numbers of students needed to make it possible for us to pursue our institutional missions.

The use of effective marketing techniques to advance our institution's interests is a requisite condition for flourishing in today's environment. Few institutions prosper without employing some level of marketing strategy. Even those select few whose enrollment position is secure can benefit from the application of marketing principles and tools as a way to help them determine why they hold such an enviable position in the marketplace and what they must do to retain that position.

The probability that an individual will enroll at a specific college or university is related to the level of congruence between three key elements as shown in Figure 0–1: Marketing & Recruitment; Admission Policy; and Financial Aid & Pricing.

When we seek to market our institutions, we attempt to create a greater overlap of these three "pre-conditions" for enrollment. Marketing an institution means more than simply mounting promotional campaigns designed to increase awareness and, hopefully, the desire to enroll. Effective marketing will also pay close attention to the quality of the product offered, the pricing for its services and the standards established to determine membership in the community of learners. While the enrollment manager may have considerable latitude in matters of promotion, such as pricing, he or she normally does not have the authority to act in the areas of academic programs and services (the products) or in the area of defining who is eligible for membership. Although admission staff members may make the actual decisions regarding who will be admitted, they are normally doing so in compliance with standards for admission that have been established by the faculty.

The organizational models used by institutions for arranging the functions related to recruitment, admission, pricing or enrollment management vary widely from institution to institution. However, they all have one thing in common: such models define the operations over which enrollment managers will have tight and immediate control. Typically, an enrollment manager's authority is limited to just a few functions selected from the many important functions that are part of the institution's enrollment equation. Those over which the enrollment manager has direct authority represent those that can be tightly "controlled." Those functions that are critical to enrollment managers but lying beyond the controlled functions represent arenas in which the enrollment manager must exert "influence" to shape

1   *Postsecondary Education Opportunity*, August 2001

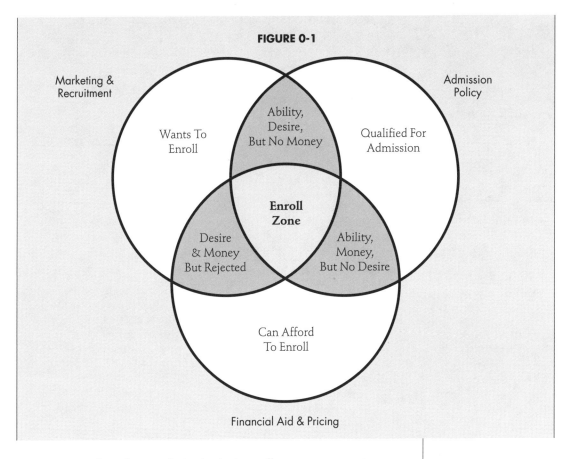

FIGURE 0-1

Marketing & Recruitment

Admission Policy

Wants To Enroll

Ability, Desire, But No Money

Qualified For Admission

Enroll Zone

Desire & Money But Rejected

Ability, Money, But No Desire

Can Afford To Enroll

Financial Aid & Pricing

action in a way that advances the institution's enrollment management program. As a result, successful college marketing is a complex task that requires the involvement of the entire academic community – those who fall into the controllable units as well as those who are reachable only through the use of influence.

Student Marketing for Colleges and Universities presents marketing theory and marketing techniques as they apply to our unique needs as leaders in higher education responsible for shaping institutional enrollments. This book includes chapters dedicated to both the theory and practice of marketing in higher education. It is intended for those in leadership positions who are interested in or responsible for marketing the institution to prospective students.

The basic paradigm underlying this discussion of marketing is the *"exchange paradigm."* Enrolling students exchange their time and financial resources for college programs and services. As long as both parties are satisfied with the exchange, both will derive the benefits they seek. However, when either party becomes dissatisfied, the free exchange between institution and student may be interrupted. Such interruptions exhibit themselves as enrollment declines and falling revenues. Marketing is a tool that enhances the probability that the exchange between institution and student occurs in a mutually satisfactory fashion and that the satisfaction level will be maintained or increased over an extended period of time.

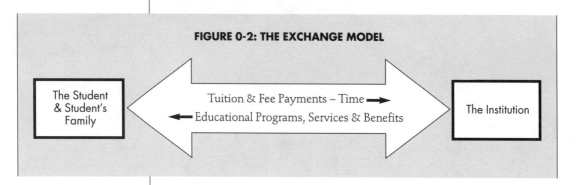

FIGURE 0-2: THE EXCHANGE MODEL

The Student & Student's Family

Tuition & Fee Payments – Time ⟶
⟵ Educational Programs, Services & Benefits

The Institution

Organization of the Book

Part I presents information related to the basics of marketing in the higher education setting. Chapter 1 provides an overview of marketing particularly as it relates to the job at hand – the recruitment and enrollment of college bound students. Chapter 2 addresses the fundamental need for a clear identification and delineation of institutional mission and vision to create an effective marketing program within the context of a particular institution. Chapter 3 addresses how to translate marketing techniques and institutional mission into a marketing statement unique to and appropriate for a particular institution. A discussion of brand and branding is presented in Chapter 4.

The materials contained in Part II of the book move the reader from general principles and practices of marketing into the more focused arena of applying these in the higher education setting. Chapter 5 describes how an institution can gain a clear understanding of its existing position within the marketplace by performing an assessment of its strengths and weaknesses. This chapter also presents valuable information related to conducting market research in the higher education setting. The identification of strategic options and priorities is addressed in Chapter 6. Identification of these options and priorities is requisite to setting the direction and determining the focus of the institution's marketing efforts. Having assessed the market position and identified strategic options, Chapter 7 focuses on how the higher education market can be segmented into the logical units required to effectively conduct institutional marketing. The last chapter in this section, Chapter 8, deals with the formulation and delineation of tactical interventions designed to make it possible for the institution to achieve its desired enrollment position.

Part III begins with Chapter 9, a discussion of the consumer behavior of the college-bound student. It details how the college-bound student population makes its buying decisions. Chapter 10 focuses on the use of direct marketing techniques designed to exploit what we have discovered about student decision-making behaviors. The last chapter in this section, Chapter 11, describes the kinds of systems support, both manual and automated, needed to support an aggressive student marketing program in today's highly competitive environment.

The final section, Part IV, comprises two chapters that are intended to integrate the work of the first eleven chapters of this book. Chapter 12 addresses the formulation of an integrated marketing orientation within the institution. The book's last chapter, Chapter 13, focuses on the compilation of the institution's student marketing plan – the document that delineates in relatively concise fashion what will be marketed, how marketing will take place and how the effectiveness of these efforts will be evaluated.

As a group, the chapters in this book provide both the theoretical and applied aspects of marketing in the college environment. The authors of the different chapters are individuals whose primary roles can be described as practitioners or whose primary roles are best described as providers of college marketing services. By calling on both populations for authorship, the editor is attempting to provide a balance between 1) what "ought to be" as described by those in a position to advise us on individual aspects of our marketing needs, and 2) what is "likely to happen" as related by those who labor in the recruitment field every day.

Acknowledgements

The authors of each chapter in *Student Marketing for Colleges and Universities* have freely contributed their time and talents in the compilation of this book. Their efforts provide insight that will advance the practice of our profession. For their commitment and dedication, they deserve the gratitude of the enrollment management profession. A publication of this magnitude takes more than the efforts of committed authors – it requires the assistance of trained and dedicated staff. In this regard, special thanks are also due to American Association of Collegiate Registrars and Admission Officers staff members who have worked diligently to ensure the high quality and broad dissemination of this book.

ABOUT THE AUTHORS

James Black is the associate provost for enrollment services at The University of North Carolina at Greensboro. His areas of responsibility include undergraduate admissions, financial aid, registrar's office, student academic services (primarily responsible for advising and retention initiatives), student success center, evening university, and the student information system (SCT Banner). Black is the founder of the National Conference on Student Retention in Small Colleges and cofounder of the National Small College Admissions Conference and the National Small College Enrollment Conference. He is currently serving as the director of AACRAO's Strategic Enrollment Management Conference. Black has published numerous articles and book chapters. Among his other published works are a monograph titled *Navigating Change in the New Millennium: Strategies for Enrollment Leaders* and a book he recently edited, *The Strategic Enrollment Management Revolution –*

STUDENT
MARKETING
FOR COLLEGES
AND UNIVERSITIES

considered to be a groundbreaking publication for the enrollment management profession. He has served as a consultant for more than sixty colleges, universities, professional organizations, and corporations and is currently one of only twenty-three IBM Best Practice Partners in the world.

Philip L. Cifarelli is the Chief Financial Officer of Exeter Group, Inc., an information technology consulting firm headquartered in Cambridge, MA. Exeter specializes in systems integration, custom software development, and IT strategy, and has a considerable practice in the higher education sector. As CFO, Cifarelli is responsible for Exeter's financial and risk management, contract administration, and internal systems.

Prior to joining Exeter in 2001, Cifarelli served for 18 years at Skidmore College in Saratoga Springs, NY. Skidmore is a private, coeducational, highly selective liberal arts institution with an enrollment of approximately 2,200 students. For the latter 16 years of his tenure, he served the College as its Director of Financial Services and Associate Treasurer, and in that capacity was responsible for all financial operations, treasury management, and capital finance. During his tenure at the College, Cifarelli played a key leadership role in the selection and implementation of the College's enterprise resource planning (ERP) systems. Prior to joining Skidmore, Cifarelli worked at Peat, Marwick, Mitchell, & Co. (now known as KPMG) as a Senior Accountant.

Cifarelli received his B.S. in Accounting from Utica College of Syracuse University. He is a licensed Certified Public Accountant, and a member of the American Institute of Certified Public Accountants and the New York State Society of Certified Public Accountants.

Elizabeth Clark is the Chief Strategic Officer of Royall & Company. She has been at Royall since 1993. Clark has won numerous awards for poetry and fiction (under a pseudonym), and has been the editor or ghostwriter of a number of successful nonfiction books. She consults on direct response with New York publishing companies. Clark has been doing *pro bono* consulting with families, on the matter of college choice, for the past eight years. Before joining Royall & Company, Clark was Editor for the Commonwealth of Virginia under Governor Lawrence D. Wilder, Jr.; she wrote policy during his campaign, and has also served as Wilder's Assistant for Clemency. Clark holds an MBA from the McDonough School of Business at Georgetown University, and studied Great Books/Classics at St. John's College (Md.) as an undergraduate. She divides her time between Richmond and Manhattan.

David S. Crockett is senior vice president of Noel–Levitz. His publications, consulting experiences, and conference/workshop presentations have led to his national recognition as an authority on enrollment management, academic advising, and student retention in colleges and universities.

Dave Crockett has devoted his career to teaching, campus/agency administration, and consulting for higher education s. For 18 years he served as vice president with the American College Testing Program (ACT). In that capacity, he planned and directed national marketing, public relations, service, operational, and consulting activities related to ACT's numerous programs and services. As a conference leader, he has designed and conducted hundreds of workshops, seminars, and campus presentations. He is also a former college director of admissions and financial aid, and he has held admissions positions at Kenyon College and Baldwin–Wallace College in Ohio. He has conducted the National Enrollment Management Survey for the firm and also founded and directed the initial and additional four National Enrollment Management Institutes held each summer.

Crockett is the firm's specialist in enrollment management practices at two-year community and technical colleges. Crockett has recently managed a multi-year enrollment management project with the Kentucky Community and Technical College System (KCTCS). He also has managed projects with the new Community College of Indiana and the Louisiana Technical College (42 campuses). Previously he directed a system-wide enrollment management project with the former Minnesota Technical College System. He also co-directed an enrollment management analysis project for the Louisiana Board of Regents for all public colleges and universities including the community and technical college campuses. Crockett is currently supervising the firm's enrollment management project with the nine Louisiana two-year colleges. He has also consulted directly with over 50 two-year community and technical colleges.

David S. Crockett has been selected for the 2003 NACADA Virginia N. Gordon Award for Excellence in the Field of Advising. This prestigious national award is presented to a National Academic Advising Association (NACADA) member who has made significant contributions to the field of academic advising.

Crockett is a native of Dayton, Ohio. After earning his Bachelor of Arts degree from Ohio Wesleyan University, he completed his Master of Arts requirements at the University.

Mark Cullen has been involved in the design, development, and implementation of higher education student systems since 1990.

Cullen was a co-founder of Exeter Educational Management Systems, where he was responsible for overall corporate management and the design of Exeter Student Marketing System and Exeter Student Suite, an integrated student system designed to help institutions attract, enroll, and retain high quality students.

Subsequent to Exeter Educational Management Systems, Cullen served as Chief Operating Officer of Sallie Mae Solutions, the software services division of Sallie Mae, where he was responsible for product design, systems development, general management, and outsourced administrative services for higher education. Cullen currently works as a Managing Director of Exeter Group, a higher education technology services consulting firm.

Cullen received his B.A. in Political Economy from Williams College.

STUDENT
MARKETING
FOR COLLEGES
AND UNIVERSITIES

Thomas Hayes recently stepped down as the chair of the department of marketing at Xavier University, a post he held for 13 years. Dr. Hayes has taught for the last twenty-eight years, and has also served as the director of institutional advancement. Before taking on the responsibilities of chair of the department, he served as Vice President of Research Services at Qualitative Associates, Inc., a full service qualitative research firm in Cincinnati. He is presently president of VisionQuest Marketing Strategy, a full service marketing consulting agency. He is a nationally recognized expert in services marketing, the marketing of higher education, and the development of ideas for new products and services, and consults in these areas on a national and international basis.

Dr. Hayes received a Bachelor's degree in psychology as well as an M.B.A. in marketing at Xavier University. He also received an M.B.A. in organizational behavior and a Ph.D. in marketing from the University of Cincinnati. Dr. Hayes sat on the Board of the Cincinnati Chapter of the American Marketing Association for ten years, including serving as its President in 1989–1990 and was voted Member of the Year for the period of 1991–1992. Tom served as Vice President of the Services Division of the American Marketing Association in 1994. He served as Vice President of the Marketing Management Council of the AMA in 1997–1998. In 2002, Dr. Hayes coauthored, with Philip Kotler and Paul Bloom, *Marketing Professional Services* (Prentice Hall.)

Thomas Huddleston Jr. earned a bachelor's and master's degrees from Texas A&M University Commerce and a doctorate from Oklahoma State University with a concentration in higher education and mass communication. He has held numerous leadership positions in higher education and industry. Within the private and public sectors, Dr. Huddleston's professional academic career has focused on strategic marketing and the development of student enrollment organizations within academic affairs and student affairs. He is recognized as a pioneer in the creation and development of the enrollment management concept that today is used by colleges and universities nationwide.

Dr. Huddleston's current assignment is the strategic management of a comprehensive division that focuses on student development and the enrollment of academically talented and diverse students. The division has increased student academic quality, improved student retention, developed student facilities, and fostered a productive environment for student learning.

In the industrial sector, Dr. Huddleston was responsible for the management of the Education Industry Worldwide Marketing program for the Sperry Corporation and Student Financial Systems, National Computer Systems. During those years, he managed the growth and development of computer software and hardware products used by higher education, federal government, financial institutions, and state agencies.

He has consulted at various colleges and universities within and outside the United States. Initially advancing and establishing a comprehensive enrollment model, his publications can be found in many books, journals, and magazines. He has presented nationwide in a variety of settings including collegiate and corporate institutes and conferences.

Dr. Huddleston is the Vice President of Student Development and Enrollment Services at the University of Central Florida in Orlando, Florida. The institution is a public metropolitan research university of approximately 42,000 students.

Olga Ivanova graduated with a Bachelor's Degree in Finance from South-West University in Bulgaria in 1998. She obtained a second Bachelor's Degree in Marketing in 2001 and a Master's of Business Administration in 2003 from the University of Central Florida (UCF).

As a teaching assistant, she has done extensive research in the area of global branding and prepared study materials and presentations on companies, including L'Oreal, McDonalds, Starbucks, and Wal-Mart.

As a research assistant, Ivanova has been involved in a project that required collecting and coding data on strategic alliances. The strategic alliances project examined companies that went public in 1996 and 1997 and the effect that the pre-IPO alliances had on the under-pricing of the Initial Public Offerings (IPOs). Ivanova has also tracked data on consumer behavior assessing the motives and reasons behind the purchasing decisions, and evaluating the level of satisfaction or dissatisfaction from a certain product or service.

Currently, she is working as a program assistant in the Marketing Department and involved in a market analysis project for a bio-medical company. The project requires assessment of the competition, collecting data on potential customers and revealing the marketing strategies of the major competitors.

Pamela Kiecker joined Royall & Company as Head of Research and Issue Analysis in January 2003. Dr. Kiecker retains her positions as Professor of Marketing and Executive Director of the Interactive Marketing Institute (IMI) in the School of Business at Virginia Commonwealth University. IMI offers a full array of educational programs and consulting services focused on direct and interactive marketing, including a graduate-level professional direct marketing certification, marketing research services, and cyberbranding and Web site usability testing. Dr. Kiecker founded IMI during her tenure as Chair of the Department of Marketing and Business Law at Virginia Commonwealth University and served as administrative head of the department from 1996 to 2002.

Dr. Kiecker has a Ph.D. in Business Administration from the University of Colorado at Boulder, an MBA from Minnesota State University, Mankato, Minnesota, and a B.A. from Carleton College, Northfield, Minnesota. Her areas of teaching expertise include consumer behavior, integrated marketing communications, and marketing research. Her research interests include communications effects, interactive marketing, survey research methods, and international marketing strategy.

STUDENT
MARKETING
FOR COLLEGES
AND UNIVERSITIES

Prior to joining the VCU faculty, Dr. Kiecker was on the graduate faculties of Texas Tech University, University of Calgary, Alberta, Canada, University of St. Thomas in St. Paul, Minnesota, and Minnesota State University, Mankato, Minnesota. Within her academic appointments, she also served as Research Analyst for the Business Research Division of the University of Colorado at Boulder, Research Fellow with the Texas Wine Marketing Institute at Texas Tech University, and Research Director in the Survey Evaluation and Research Laboratory, Center for Public Policy, Virginia Commonwealth University.

Dr. Kiecker has published more than 50 articles in academic and trade journals, including the *Journal of the Academy of Marketing Science*, *Journal of Business Research*, *Psychology and Marketing*, *Marketing Letters*, and the *Journal of the Market Research Society* and received research grants from the U.S. Department of Commerce, U.S. Department of Education, the World Bank, AOL, and the Virginia Center for Innovative Technology. She has won numerous awards for her research, is a frequent keynote speaker for professional business organizations and events, and has enjoyed diverse consulting relationships over the past twenty years with a variety of organizations including direct marketing agencies, retail businesses, financial, health care, and real estate services, non-profit associations, and consumer packaged goods firms. Dr. Kiecker has participated in academic programs and consulting projects in Scandinavia, Eastern and Western Europe, the United Kingdom, Canada, Mexico, Central and South America, India, Malaysia, and Australia.

Robert Lay currently serves as the Dean for Enrollment Management at Boston College. Lay has been a practitioner of enrollment management for over 25 years, and for over 20 years at Boston College, where he and his colleagues conceived many current enrollment management concepts and practices; the term "enrollment management" was first coined at Boston College in 1974.

Previously a university lecturer at University of Wisconsin, Madison and at Boston College, Lay has incorporated sociological research methods in developing the enrollment analytics for research-based decision making. Lay is a proponent of integrated student marketing communications closely coupled with programming for academic excellence. In addition to authoring many articles on enrollment issues, Lay has edited a volume with Jean Endo entitled *Designing and Using Market Research* (Jossey–Bass, 1987).

Past President of the Northeast Association for Institutional Research, now active in AJCU, AIR, AACRAO, NACAC, and CEEB, Lay currently serves on and is the former chairperson of the Deans' Advisory Committee to U.S. News and World Report.

Clifford Lull, president of the North Charles Street Design Organization, has played a leading role in the enrollment management, identity, and advancement programs of more than 60 colleges and universities. His area of expertise is developing strategic frameworks for online and interactive student recruitment communications. He has lectured on topics as varied as

Web site content and humor in higher education marketing at NACAC, CASE, and other professional conferences.

Robert J. Massa has served as vice president for enrollment, student life and college relations at Dickinson College in Carlisle, Pa., since July 1999. For 10 years prior to joining Dickinson, Massa was the dean of enrollment at The Johns Hopkins University. Beginning in 1974 he held various positions in admissions, financial aid and student affairs at Colgate University and Union College.

Massa received his bachelor's degree from the University of Rochester and a doctorate in higher education from Columbia University. He has published widely in books and journals in the field of college admissions and enrollment management and is active as an instructor and journal editor in national organizations for admissions and financial aid professionals.

Massa's Aug. 28, 2000, *New York Times* op-ed "Who Needs the SAT?", about restoring the male/female balance at Dickinson, and his January 2003 perspective piece in the NACAC Bulletin, "Early Decision – Fix It, Don't Kill It," have won him accolades from colleagues and inquiries from major national news organizations. He has also written and spoken extensively on the use of academic scholarships in student recruitment, tuition discounting and strategic enrollment management planning.

Bernice A. Thieblot, as co-founder of The North Charles Street Design Organization in 1972, has influenced practice and helped set standards for higher education marketing for more than 30 years. In addition to directing exemplary work, Thieblot has written for the NACAC *Journal of College Admission*, the College Board's *Admissions Strategist*, and CASE *Currents*, among others, and has spoken before national and regional meetings of professional associations in higher education advancement and marketing.

Richard Whiteside is Vice President for Enrollment at Tulane University. He has been at Tulane since July of 1993. Before joining Tulane, Whiteside was on the staff of the University of Hartford in West Hartford Connecticut for 14 years (Associate VP for Academic Administration), The Johns Hopkins University in Baltimore, Maryland (six years), the City University of New York in New York City (five years), and Pace College (University) in New York City (one and a half years.)

Dr. Whiteside is a graduate of Manhattan College in New York City and holds two graduate degrees from The Johns Hopkins University. He has done additional graduate work in counseling at the City University of New York and completed his doctoral level studies in educational leadership at the University of Connecticut. Whiteside was selected to participate in Harvard University's "*University's Institute for Educational Management*" during the summer of 1998 and the Center for Creative Leadership program "*Leadership at the Peak*" in 1999.

Dr. Whiteside is active in a number of professional associations including the College Board, the American Association of Collegiate Registrars and Admissions Officers, and the National Association of College Admission Counselors. He speaks frequently on issues related to Financial Aid,

Enrollment Management, Tuition Discounting, the educational environment, and the dynamics of change. He has served as a consultant on a variety of topics ranging from enrollment management to administrative information systems. His work in various enrollment management areas has been featured in *the Wall Street Journal*, the *New York Times, Kiplinger's Personal Finance* and on the "Today Show."

STUDENT MARKETING FUNDAMENTALS

PART ONE

OVERVIEW AND INTRODUCTION TO COLLEGE STUDENT MARKETING

ROBERT S. LAY
Dean for Enrollment Management
Boston College

DEVELOP YOUR OWN MARKETING IMAGINATION

College student marketing, as distinguished from other forms of marketing, seeks to manage those aspects of a college that condition and structure perceptions of a given campus community. Because most benefits and features of the student experience are intangible, college communications about an abstract notion such as the quality of a college will offer indirect evidence at best, and engender skepticism at worst.

A stressful decision is thus presented to prospective students, who cannot experience college life to gain a full appreciation of a particular college, but who must choose one based upon limited information. Colleges, on the other hand, must reinvigorate themselves every year by recruiting a cohort of new students who will fit well within a particular environment and contribute positively to the experiences of everyone in the academic community. Hence, good communications are vital as a shared objective for both students and colleges.

Only imagination fortified with a thorough understanding of the intrinsic benefits of a college or program will enable colleges to convey what is distinctive and valuable to individuals.[1] Creativity in the selection of messages and modes of communication is often required to convey credible information of highly complex benefits. Timing issues too are crucial in the effective communication of the positive elements of individual fit at each stage of choice, from initial awareness through program completion. It is important to reach prospective students when they are open and ready to hear about student success at an institution.

---

[1] *The Marketing Imagination* (Levitt, 1986) publication is something of a brand in mainstream marketing. Similar books fill airport bookstore displays and all purport to stimulate creative thinking. The demand for such books speaks to the difficulty most have in just stepping back from a company's market challenges, looking with an unbiased eye at what the company may offer that anyone might really want, and then developing innovative solutions.

Just as students are active participants in the life of a successful college, so too should be marketing professionals. The best college-marketing practitioners, because of their awareness of the expectations of entering students, may be among the strongest proponents for quality academic programs that actively engage students.

Now that the enrollment manager is aware of the important work she is doing for her institution, consider what is gained from marketing management concepts and techniques. Please keep in mind that while much of this introduction will present examples of traditional student markets, the marketing management approach described here is also effective when applied to nontraditional student markets.

College Student Marketing

College student marketing describes the organized efforts to advance a college's mission and goals through targeted communications and the recruitment, selection, and retention of students whose capabilities will contribute to their own development and that of others.

At many colleges, academic program managers may overlook the more expansive thinking required for good marketing. Part of the problem for academics may be that commercial marketers often exceed their own reach and try to apply mainstream thinking to student markets. It is true that many marketing writers do not seem to suffer from a shortage of hubris. McKenna (1991) described in the *Harvard Business Review* their tendencies with the characterization, "everything is marketing and marketing is everything." The other part of the problem is that many marketing techniques are so narrowly tailored for non-student markets that the technical arguments divert readers from basic marketing concepts. Do not be bogged down or intimidated by the narrow discussions over fine theoretical points, an example being the classic, "How many P's are in the marketing mix?" These discussions are often long on theory and technique, but belie any demonstrated empathy for unmet needs of the people whom marketers are trying to reach.

The danger in higher education may be in the application of similarly narrow approaches in college marketing as quick cures for poor institutional image or declining tuition revenues. Can integrated marketing or branding really solve an institution's problems without a realistic appraisal of whether the institution's educational programs will be successful over the next twenty years? The marketing imagination demands realistic vision through the eyes of future generations of students and a careful anticipation of the needs of select segments.

Higher education perhaps has been so open to a variety of unsuccessful management fads (Birnbaum, 2000) because of the unresolved tension that exists between building the best educational environments, and business principles of efficiency and control. Within a dynamic and thriving campus culture, high quality interactions emerge from shared academic values that encourage intellectual free inquiry, individual responsibility, and leadership among students and educators. Business principles applied without a firm understanding of an academic community may do more to destroy the

OVERVIEW AND
INTRODUCTION TO
COLLEGE STUDENT
MARKETING

4

PART ONE
CHAPTER 1

drivers of educational quality than any other management actions. College student marketing should balance the interests of the institution with the needs of prospective students in a fair educational exchange.

The Research Perspective

W.I. Thomas, *"What is perceived to be real, is real in their consequences."*

Marketing research is first and foremost a way of seeing the world by taking the viewpoints of students, parents, counselors, and other influential people in their lives. Research is a critical way of thinking, and without it, marketers are no better than salesman who seek the advantage in an exchange whatever the expense to the buyer.[2]

All good marketing should be based upon a detailed knowledge of the needs and desires of all those who in some way participate in the student's college search for *the right college*. Although it is natural to think about the students and their parents as the participants in college choice, remember that they are not the only persons whose needs and desires are of interest to enrollment managers. In addition to the other influential communication outside of the institution, from peers, college counselors, publishers, and the like, you must also factor in those already in the academic community – the faculty, the staff and other enrolled students. While influence may seem more indirect and less open to marketing control, colleges must perform research to understand the relative importance of the significant factors, and take each factor into account within their communication plans.

A word on probability ... students, with the many influencing factors, make their college choices in somewhat, but not completely predictable, ways. Their decisions are based upon what they perceive to be true about a college compared against alternative choices. While students may reveal their own interest in a particular college at each stage of their college choice, the goal is to maximize fit with an institution. Applicants should display patterns of growing interest in the programs available at the institution, and administrators should be tracking and managing meaningful relationships with prospective students and their families.

Demographic and survey research tools may be very efficient for describing large student markets, however, marketing imagination and the use of probing qualitative research techniques are also essential tools. Beyond the statistical profiles, campuses should practice "taking the place" of prospective students to understand not only their attitudes and perceptions, but also their hopes and dreams, and how they currently live. As we know, family situations vary widely, and each young person is likely to react differently to the image he or she has of your college. Some sympathy for how college may fit into their plans will go a long way towards understanding what prospective students may project of themselves into this new situation, your college campus.

---

2   Larry Litten has often described doing college marketing without market research to guide it as like driving with a fogged windshield on a crowded freeway.

There are no easy shortcuts to understanding the needs of students, their families, and everyone involved in college selection. Still, the techniques and analytics of marketing research are varied and adaptable to campus needs. Several chapters in this volume are dedicated to describing useful options for exploration and for developing a program of research-based decision-making.

The Core Educational Exchange Relationship

The so-called "value proposition" describes the organizational imperative to add sufficient fair value in exchanges that will produce net revenues to sustain institutional vitality. Put another way, if a college is not addressing the needs of students and families with educational programs and activities that are recognized as worthwhile, then a college will not and probably should not prosper.

Peter Drucker (1997), a management guru of the first order, famously predicted the demise of college campuses within the next 10 years. There is no question that new technologies have expanded the modes of educational exchange, yet we easily observe that college campuses continue to thrive in the midst of these varied learning options. But why is this the case, and more importantly, what is going to happen in the future? How long will college campuses thrive without significant changes?

The easy answer to this conundrum is to assert that the modes of learning on a college campus are not static, and that within ten years, the learning environment must change for campuses to continue to thrive. The task of enrollment managers is to understand and then communicate well how students with different learning styles will be accommodated and how learning will be enhanced during their college career at an institution. In some respects, smaller colleges may have advantages over large universities, in that virtual learning resources may be more easily highlighted as integral to undergraduate education. Research universities in particular must explain their more complex plans for phasing in new technologies that serve multiple goals. Whatever the institution, student marketing must include planning ahead for the incorporation of academic technologies, as well as for new modes of student communication, both internal and external.

College life is more like extensive participation in a voluntary association than it is about receiving services provided by some central organization. While a car wash may provide good service to its customers, the whole experience takes 10 minutes and the results only last until the next rain. Understanding the intensely personal nature of a college experience and the lifelong associational benefits is critical to marketing success.

Residential campuses are particularly powerful, as they succeed through shared living arrangements, curricular, co-curricular, and extra-curricular activities that may encompass a 24/7 lifestyle[3] over a student's college career. Commuter colleges may also be very successful in building relationships by carefully matching the full range of needs of the adult learner.

---

3   With some characteristics of a "total institution" (Irving Goffman, 1961)

Always keep in mind – students choose you before you choose them. Before colleges may select their class, prospective students must commit to attending a college. Students commonly seek immersion in a positive, challenging, and formative educational environment enhanced in quality by meaningful interactions with members of a community with shared academic aspirations. Fruitful and enduring relationships are central in achieving the mutual exchange benefits of attending college.

Student Market Concepts — Demand, Value, Segmentation, and Position

Understanding college student marketing requires that we gain an appreciation of some basic marketing principles as they apply to the higher education domain. Those involved in college student marketing will experience success only when mainstream marketing concepts and techniques are recast to fit the culture of the educational enterprise – a culture that shuns "operating like a business" but is involved daily in efforts to take its message to an increasingly consumerist-minded population of prospective students and their parents.

You may want them, but do they want you?

> Demand — *"the measure of desire, willingness, and ability to pursue a distinct educational experience"*

Colleges must work within limited budgets, often operating with a poor understanding or open distrust of marketing. By ignoring market analysis, colleges typically try to emulate what their peers are doing and hope that their admission recruiters and positive word of mouth will bring students to their campuses. If the college provides attractive programs and builds student success, then a college may be successful within a particular student marketplace (the institutional "niche") for some period of time. But what about when a college seeks to change its mission, or wishes to advance more aggressively, or is determined to seek new sources of students to increase diversity?

The anticipated level of student demand is an important consideration in the planning for any academic program. Unless demand is high and expressed directly, the sources and depth of market potential may be difficult to assess. When demand is low or the sources uncertain, early market research should explore potential for greater demand among existing student segments, and help prepare for the development and cultivation of new sources.

Every institution has primary, secondary, and tertiary student markets. Colleges vary considerably in the market intelligence that they have gained in understanding the nature of these markets (see Lay and Endo, 1987). Most college marketers have a fairly good intuitive feel for the primary sources of high demand, yet for the future vitality of the institution, it may be more important that they have an awareness of demand in secondary markets where demand is weaker, and in tertiary markets where potential demand is yet undeveloped.

Is it worth the investment?

> Value – *"realized benefits minus costs to attain"*

In commercial marketing applications, cost is generally regarded as the money that the consumer pays for the product or service. Costs are regarded as primarily financial in nature.

However, in the decision of a traditional college-bound high school senior, the person willing to pay for college is not usually the person who will experience the benefits. The reality is that for traditional undergraduates, parents bear most of the monetary cost and the student reaps most of the benefits. While the investment may be primarily financial from the parents' perspective, the investment from the student's perspective is often in their psychological commitment to program completion against other alternatives. The parent typically asks, "Is it worth my money?" Meanwhile, the student asks, "Is it worth my time and effort, and can I succeed?" Creating an effective *value exchange* requires that the college be attentive to these questions from both parents and students.

Students also may look forward to a wide range of experiential benefits associated with their attendance. While communications should articulate the *investment* benefits of attending a college and completing academic programs, the *consumption* benefits associated with the experience should also be conveyed to students. Student marketing therefore suggests that enrollment managers should be just as attentive to the consumption benefits that may or may not be associated with the campus experiences at their colleges. The importance of campus amenities, which typically appear as tangible to prospective students and parents, are to be ignored at an institution's peril. Residence halls, dining services, athletics, and extracurricular activities are seen by consumerist students and their families as "part of the package," and may directly influence the perceived worth of one campus experience over another.

In college choice, some consumption benefits are typically associated with the region and location of a college campus. A good first step, if the consumption benefits associated with what your college offers have not been explored systematically, is to detail the location advantages and disadvantages for each alternative listed by students in the choices set in the early stages of their college search. You may be surprised when confronted by the misperceptions or lack of knowledge of potential students, both of which may be minimized through communications.

Next, carefully examine the psychological costs and benefits that students at your institution realize on campus. One should be able to build upon simple location benefits by looking more broadly at the sources of satisfaction over four years. Word of mouth is most effective when consumption and investment benefits are both high and commonly recognized by students. Expanding communications to secondary or tertiary student markets with new messages are likely to connect better with students after the drivers of current and projected satisfaction are understood.

In summary, student demand is not shaped entirely by a college or your communications to prospective students. Parents and others add or diminish

OVERVIEW AND
INTRODUCTION TO
COLLEGE STUDENT
MARKETING

8

PART ONE
CHAPTER 1

that demand, depending upon the perceived investment and consumption benefits associated with a particular college against alternatives. Demand may vary widely, and develop naturally. Communications may be used to stimulate latent or undeveloped demand for the programs and quality of experience that a college offers. The largest impact of communications may be among prospective students whose needs and wants fit well with the programs and activities that a campus offers, but who may only be vaguely aware of the college's reputation or location.

Colleges that enjoy significant realized and potential student demand will be able to advance their cherished educational values and generate demand through clear and consistent communications. The real value of institutional branding, as it is known among commercial marketers, may be in the consistent communication over time of features that symbolize and summarize a complex range of benefits associated with a particular college name.

A simple illustration of the importance of name associations might be to look at colleges that suggest a location. What comes to mind when you hear these college names: University of Miami, New York University, University of Colorado, or Austin College? How would these institutions build consistent communications that extend an understanding of benefits or costs that may be associated with each? Do students know which are public, and which are private?

Perhaps it is obvious from this example that student-marketing successes often depend on past histories, and that student marketing should be a component of strategic institutional marketing. Thinking and planning should capitalize upon and support wider efforts. In many a college, administrators may need to seek a close alliance with institutional marketing, and advocate for greater integration of initiatives in pursuing multi-level objectives.

Does one message fit all?

> Segmentation – *"division of a heterogeneous market of students into groupings with relatively similar wants and needs"*

The segmentation of students is an analytical device of uncertain utility to the marketing manager. While all pools of prospective students exhibit differences, it is really a practical matter about whether a college decides to tailor its communications to each segment that it identifies. This management decision requires that research be done to determine the likely costs and benefits of differential communications, and whether these actions will help to advance enrollment objectives. In other words, jumping into doing expensive segmented communications is unwise unless the benefits will clearly outweigh the costs. Keep in mind that segmentation may reduce the clarity and consistency of communications, and also may carry an administrative overhead that distracts recruiting staff from individual attention to prospective students.

At larger, more complex institutions, perceived value to students may differ dramatically by decision segments (typically Geographic, Gender, Income, Race/Ethnicity, Legacy, Program Interest, and Applicant Strength). At many universities, carefully segmented communications may therefore be critical for communicating to all student segments that need to be reached.

STUDENT
MARKETING
FOR COLLEGES
AND UNIVERSITIES

PART ONE
CHAPTER 1

9

If communications should focus on distinct *decision segments*, it may be necessary to orchestrate the admission processes that fit the different choice and enrollment needs of students and parents. The options of early action, early decision, rolling admission, and common-date candidates reply are examples of how admissions may be tailored to match the needs of various decision segments.

If a campus is clear about its objectives for each student segment, it will want to track the changing size and characteristics of segments over time. Practitioners typically refer to the progressive focusing of interest — from larger pools of prospective students to the smaller population of enrolled students — as *the admission funnel*. Because the composition of the class is important in defining the character of your college learning environment, the marketing manager should remain focused on the desired class profile composed of students from each student segment. The marketing manager may monitor the effectiveness of communication efforts given the changing information needs of students, and thus ensure a smoother transition through each stage of college choice.

The image of a *funnel* is alluring to student marketers, but can be deceptive. The admission funnel metaphor suggests that colleges will be in more control of how students will make their choices than is realistic. Recall that students and parents have many options, and every college hopes it has the winning position; … competitive processes outside of the institution should keep us humble about the net effects of our marketing communications.

In summary, when significant variability among different subpopulations of students can be demonstrated through research, the use of market segmentation can prove to be a powerful and effective tool for stimulating and shepherding demand. Those elements that are judged to be of high value to a particular segment can be emphasized in activities and communication directed specifically toward that segment. Through each admission cycle, the marketing manager is able to monitor, enhance, and craft the desired class of entering students.

Is a more highly rated college always the best choice for the student?

> Position – *"the student-perceived ordering of an academic program or institution against peer colleges"*

Most college counselors lament the undue emphasis on rankings and the elevation of *name-brand* colleges in the continuous drumbeat of modern media coverage of admission issues. The concern is that students or parents may too easily take ranking position as a proxy for quality and academic fit with that institution, or worse, pursue the name brand solely for prestige and wider recognition. Colleges would do well to address with sympathy those students looking for easy answers, and good college communications should lead prospective students to look for issues of fit beyond what may be described in mass media.

College rankings have helped move positioning issues to center stage among college presidents and trustees. **Positioning** is now accepted in describing tactical actions to advance a college into a better position among institutions

OVERVIEW AND
INTRODUCTION TO
COLLEGE STUDENT
MARKETING

10   PART ONE
        CHAPTER 1

that compete for students, faculty, resources, or bragging rights within a state or region.

While the notion of competition is central to any positioning strategy, a common mistake is to plan for positional changes without a realistic (i.e., empirical) basis for what may be achieved with given resources. Expectations in these circumstances will be unrealistic because thinking may be aspiration alone. As stated earlier, marketing management offers a different and research-based perspective on strategic positioning.

The opportunity to manage internal expectations of what is possible is manifest in a student-marketing plan. The marketing plan should provide a realistic assessment of student market potential and an evaluation through the eyes of prospective students of the college's programs against viable alternatives. No marketing plan is complete, therefore, without describing in detail the resources that would be required to improve communications and a projection of likely returns to the college over time. Devising a marketing plan to be revised and updated annually is no guarantee that aspiring goals in strategic planning will not diminish your emphasis on market realities. Enlightened colleges often do better in achieving their mission objectives than those that rail against the market forces that they do not understand.

Communication Focus

Tell, Don't Sell!

> *"The aim of marketing is to make selling superfluous … the aim … is to know the customer so well that the product or service fits him and sells itself."*
> (Drucker, 1990)

As earlier sections show, student communication success depends as much on your creative ability to internally market your plans as on the marketing techniques you employ with external student markets. Now let's look at the great power that the educational community itself has in crafting effective communications to external audiences.

In a figurative sense, members of the college community write the story of the college. Each participant adds to and expands the story, which is part of the reason why collegiate word-of-mouth can be so effective. Colleges experiencing rapid change typically rely upon communications that will grow more effective with each graduating class.

In a more literal sense, student marketing would be wise to involve members of the college community in writing the story of the college that is told to families, friends, colleagues, and others. Each member adds to the story so that the word of mouth is authentic and credible, with the benefits that they enjoyed in their time at the college. Successful marketing plans usually dedicate resources to student, faculty, staff, and alumni volunteer programs as efficient ways to harness outreach efforts, to tell the story to visitors, and to "take the story on the road" to off-campus audiences.

Think about how you might define the limits and range of the college community. The more narrow the definition, the more potent the story. The wider the definition, the more diverse the stories, but the more extended the

STUDENT
MARKETING
FOR COLLEGES
AND UNIVERSITIES

PART ONE
CHAPTER 1

11

potential reach. Marketing research should provide regular feedback from students that will help to determine which activities are the most successful. Research should also stimulate your campus colleagues to develop marketing imagination that promotes the college's overall effectiveness.[4]

A crucial insight required in executing a successful marketing plan is to identify the need to achieve a deeper appreciation of what really takes place in an educational community, and of what people are saying about their campus interactions. An often overlooked technique is to simply ask members of the college community to write a short narrative on what they would say to prospective students in various market segments (geographic segments for example). Every college, in a natural process of self-organization, builds a unique sense of community within which most members are somewhat or very satisfied. The hard part is putting those distinctive features into words that prospective students will understand.

The objective is to find simple messages that resonate well with prospective students. While this may sound easy, the task may be obscured by the different voices that must be used for each different channel of communication that is available. The messages must be delivered differently for one-on-one, group, telephone, print, Web, letter, e-mail, community relations, public affairs and, advertising communications. A great deal of testing of different messages and modes of communication through various media is required over several years to refine communications. Information systems are critical for developing the level of detail needed for feedback and for tracking the trends in the aggregate that show what worked well in building relationships across each successive year.

One characteristic of relationship and contact management is that much of the perception of quality is affected by the intangibles of experiences. Does a reception at an expensive downtown hotel impart a more authentic experience of a college than an open house at the home of an alumni volunteer family in a nearby suburb? Neither provides the real college experience, however one or the other may be better for conveying the intangibles that students and families are seeking.

The more effectively that marketing can make the intangibles of a college tangible and credible, the higher the perception of quality among potential students. Be advised that overselling can have a dramatically negative effect for opposite reasons.

Most student marketing plans should keep current students and alumni at the center of their communication efforts about the distinctive nature of the institution. Prospective students often want to ask students and alumni the question, "How did the institution make your experience one that could not have occurred anywhere else?" The job of the enrollment manager is to provide opportunities for students to hear those answers.

---

4   Surveys of admitted students are particularly useful tools for assessing the effectiveness of marketing communications. A related benefit of distributing these results is that these data are easily understood and interesting to many people on campus who may support student marketing.

What will make a college's marketing efforts successful?

As good college student recruiters know, traditional promotion techniques often reduce the perceived value of a college. The commonplace "marketing mix" that is recommended to assist in the promotion of products and services needs to be carefully adapted and tailored for college student marketing. Consider the following elements that may be emphasized in some degree within marketing efforts:

Purpose – Clear, consistent, understandable goals that define the institutional mission and its core values.

Having a mission with which students identify, and that underscores the actions of a college's commitment to students is extremely powerful. On the other side of the coin, emphasizing a mission that excludes those with general interests will restrict primary demand.

Programs – Highlight mix of specific academic concentrations, quality, and student outcomes

Generic academic programs do little to distinguish a college in any meaningful way, unless the quality of instruction and learning is very high, or the level of student success, however defined, is very high. A program portfolio analysis helps to assess strengths and weaknesses among current academic and student development programs.

Flagship academic programs that add strength to the portfolio because of higher student demand or that support central mission goals will add meaning to all specific program opportunities at the institution. For example, although most colleges offer study abroad programs, a college that emphasizes area studies programs and that has a goal for every undergraduate to study abroad before graduation might position itself as distinctively different. More than *packaging*, a college must design program elements that work together in an understandable way to improve the overall academic experience.

Place – The location and surrounding area in which the campus is situated.

For some students, place may simply be a convenient destination. For others, place may offer freedom with the separation from parents and hometown. Some students may see a campus location as a refuge. Others may feel a mixture of fear and excitement about a campus location. Communications about campus location should be able to address each of these.

Some of the location benefits that students may see as available at a college have already been discussed. Many colleges now promote the city and area, especially in early stages of college search, more than they do the physical campus. Communication tools that use new technologies to stage some academic interactions with students wherever they are also afford new opportunities for conveying a sense of place to students who cannot visit the campus.[5]

---

5   Because students and faculty may interact virtually via new technologies, the online delivery of programs, services, and communications are likely to change perceptions of place.

STUDENT
MARKETING
FOR COLLEGES
AND UNIVERSITIES

Much of the advantage that some campuses that were early adopters of new technologies enjoyed seems to have dissipated, and tangible benefits of online learning options have been elusive. New technologies may now be perceived by many as critical in extending positive benefits through online learning options, and can be used to diminish limitations associated with location for many colleges.

Physical Factors (facilities and auxiliaries) – Campus physical plant, technologies, and tangible evidence of benefits.

Physical campuses lay out the tangible benefits that will be available to students better than almost any source of information about what students may expect. Classroom buildings, lecture halls, faculty offices, the libraries, study spaces, residence halls, dining halls, athletic fields, tech labs, and the like present a whole that is greater than the sum of the parts. Much of the identity of a college is represented symbolically through small and large elements of campus design.

Colleges themselves have expended many millions of dollars to improve facilities and to offer amenities to the point that many campuses are now small, self-contained cities dedicated to student life and learning. Few commercial enterprises provide this level of physical presence, with a few notable exceptions. Disney is often cited as the penultimate service provider, although many colleges are not far behind in their ability to constitute the physical elements that structure experiences on campus — perhaps colleges themselves are learning from the Disney approach.[6]

The implication for student marketing seems fairly straightforward as well: do whatever needs to be done to get students on campus. Some will slip through the cracks, yet the ones who can see themselves attending and being successful on a campus often have the best prospect of finding the college a good fit. Why? Because a good campus visit gives students the ability to project themselves into campus life in ways that are not possible any other way. A "random" interaction with a student to hear what he or she really thinks of a place cuts through all of the skepticism and often reduces dramatically the psychological costs that the student may have imagined. Never underestimate the importance of campus visits.

Commercial marketers describe the physical elements in a promotional mix as providing evidence of quality. The more intangible the product, the more elaborate the physical evidence that may be required to represent the quality.

People – The attitudes, skills, and other attributes of members of the academic community.

Being able to employ the volunteer efforts of various members of the community has already been discussed. Every college says that faculty care about students, so it is difficult to distinguish your communications from what prospective students see in publications, on the Web, and in video

OVERVIEW AND
INTRODUCTION TO
COLLEGE STUDENT
MARKETING

14   **PART ONE**
      CHAPTER 1

---

6   A review of what some colleges are now offering in the way of Disney-like amenities is described in Jacuzzi U, 2003.

presentations. At small liberal arts colleges, positive interactions between students and faculty who care are expected but do the faculty do research? At large research universities, faculty members are generally quite involved in research, but do undergraduates ever have an opportunity to work with faculty on research projects? Using creativity, a college can fill out portraits of people in its academic community, and demonstrate some unique qualities of its institutional environment.

Processes – Internally stepped and staged interactions

Student services organizations may build a strong customer-service orientation among staff with whom prospective students are much more likely to interact than faculty members. A well-run service organization also sends the message that a college is trying to control costs as it provides better service.

New technologies may significantly reduce bureaucracy and allow more self-service. By streamlining processes and allowing work to be done 24/7, students may assume responsibility for organizing their own lifestyles on campus.

Pricing – The stated financial cost of attendance and the net cost of full program participation.

The communication approaches used to describe the monetary cost of attendance should follow one of three strategies. First, emphasize that the value of education far exceeds the cost during the years of program participation. Some colleges offer detailed discussions of return on investment over a lifetime. More expensive colleges tend to select this approach. Financial assistance is offered to promote access for those who cannot cover the full tuition cost, and the same college may tout the advantages of diversity that derive from the college's investment in need-based financial aid.

Second, emphasize the selective awarding of financial assistance that will be a direct benefit to the student and the family. Merit scholarships are typically highlighted in communications in some detail, and students are flattered in thinking that the college wants them to attend once successful in winning scholarships. Mid-cost colleges tend to use this approach, and portray the scholarships as a reward and recognition of the student's hard work.

Third, some colleges offer low prices relative to more expensive alternatives. Communications may detail for students the advantages of saving money with a significant return on their investment. Colleges know that many students do not believe that they will receive scholarship support, and many parents do not want their children applying to places that they "cannot afford." Many students and parents may question a long-term commitment to a college so that neither feels that the choice of a more expensive college is worth pursuing very seriously.

Promotion – Publications, new media, sponsored events, recruitment travel, advertising, media relations, community involvement, and the like may be used to raise awareness and interest in the college or its programs.

Only a small group of colleges have large advertising budgets. These colleges tend to be located in urban areas and may use advertising to generate leads

STUDENT
MARKETING
FOR COLLEGES
AND UNIVERSITIES

PART ONE
CHAPTER 1

15

for continuing education or certificate programs rather than for the promotion of traditional academic degree programs.

Most colleges produce publications, do direct mail, offer a Web site for prospective students, travel to selected high schools, and participate in events that provide information to prospective students. Some colleges work with public affairs, alumni relations, and athletics as well to improve recognition among audiences off campus. Volunteers, as discussed earlier, are also typically used to meet, greet, and represent the college in telling an accurate story.

All of this hard work tends to payoff over time, although most prospective students would have found their way to their ultimate college choice anyway in a given year. Campuses should focus on building long-term **trust** through communications used to reach the students (and parents) that a college seeks to enroll.

Because of the stratified nature of American higher education, most colleges are competing within a limited stratum of similar institutions. The objective should be to enroll among these peers more students who value the college as their first choice against alternatives. Not only will a college enroll a more highly committed entering class that will bring enthusiasm to the student body, it will probably graduate a higher percentage of each successive entering cohort.

There is another reason too, usually referred to by mainstream marketers as seeking greater *market share*. Distinctiveness is hard won among similar institutions, but in expanding the share of the most desired students, colleges achieve recognition for steadily advancing as one of the best among the full stratum of institutions that compete for overlapping student markets. In a sense, all of the student marketing done by colleges in a stratum helps build a pool of prospective students, and the visibility gains to the leaders can be substantial.

Manage with Integrity and Deliver on Your Promises

The 1970s may have delimited the early days of modern higher education marketing as many institutions were facing rapid change and demographic shifts that portended shrinking markets and greater competition for scarce resources. A frequently asked question in higher education at the time was, "Is marketing a dirty word?" Marketing solutions were seen by many faculty members as a capitulation to business principles, to the diminution of educational mission, and were seen as undermining basic academic styles of collegiality.[7] Marketing was conceived narrowly as a set of techniques used to lure students to attending colleges that had lost their broader commitment to serve the best interests of students.

Enrollment management was conceived in the early 1970s at Boston College as an academic management approach that integrated communications and student recruitment activities with financial aid, student research,

---

7   This critique is still popular, as suggested in the book, *Shakespeare, Einstein, and the Bottom Line: The Marketing of Higher Education* by David L. Kirp, (Harvard University Press, 2003).

OVERVIEW AND
INTRODUCTION TO
COLLEGE STUDENT
MARKETING

16   PART ONE
CHAPTER 1

and retention functions to pursue broader institutional goals that promote student and institutional fit. Strategic enrollment management thinking replaced the notion that marketing concepts are inherently incompatible with student learning and outcome objectives. Enrollment managers used marketing to seek higher levels of student engagement, graduation success, and mission-defined formative outcomes to improve the quality of the core educational experiences for everyone in the academic community. The best institutions came out of the 1970s and entered the 1980s as more self-assured with the tools to chart their own futures as vital and dynamic organizations of human talent.

There is no substitute for institutional planning that brings together colleagues to respond to changes in a competitive environment and advance the institutional mission through long-term goals. Student marketing is a management function that can support institutional strategic planning 1) by providing objective and realistic perspectives on how the institution is performing and 2) by looking ahead for opportunities to develop new student markets. Student marketing should direct an institution-wide focus on student engagement and student-centered planning in admissions, financial aid, student services, academic affairs, information technology, alumni affairs, public affairs, development, and the president's office.

Specifically, student marketing brings the following outcomes to the planning table:

1. Meaningful content in communication with students and families

2. Greater diversity of talents and experiences that enrich the campus community

3. Reduced (or increased) demand for financial aid assistance

4. Matched program interests of students (matched with teaching and research objectives)

5. Interactivity and engagement of students with the institution on several levels

6. Student contributions to community and public service

7. Increased responsiveness to opportunities for enrolling students in the future

8. Student success in bringing recognition to the college

9. An involved and committed alumni base

10. A pool of highly satisfied graduates who want to support institutional advancement

11. Intergenerational ties with legacies

12. Role models for research, leadership, and humanitarian excellence

13. An educated electorate

STUDENT
MARKETING
FOR COLLEGES
AND UNIVERSITIES

PART ONE
CHAPTER 1   17

Contributions to student opportunities through the use of effective student marketing will reach far beyond any single college campus. The challenge will be to use marketing imagination creatively and with clear purpose so that the college or university will be able to be a contemporary force in the education of new generations of students.

OVERVIEW AND
INTRODUCTION TO
COLLEGE STUDENT
MARKETING

18

PART ONE
CHAPTER 1

MISSION AND VISION IN INSTITUTIONAL MARKETING

ROBERT J. MASSA

Vice President for Enrollment, Student Life & College Relations
Dickinson College

The relationship of mission and vision to marketing is best understood when viewed within the context of an institution's current reality and position. Without this context, appropriate connections between mission and vision and institutional action are not apparent. Very early in the new administration at Dickinson College, campus administrators recognized this and went to great lengths to connect mission, vision and action.

In the fall of 2002, Dickinson College embarked on the production of an admissions video for the first time in 10 years. It did so only after several years of strategic planning and with broad buy-in to institutional mission and vision. The video was planned to hit four areas that were critical to communicating what was distinctively Dickinson – a sense of place, a vibrant campus life, globalization and engagement with faculty and the wider world. What one sophomore said in his interview, however, convinced us that, after almost four years of defining and refining the message, we had succeeded: "It was heartening to come here," he said, "and find that Dickinson is what the brochures say it is."

Novices often confuse marketing with promotion. Promotion is advertising. It employs tactics to get the word out about an institution and its programs. Marketing, however, includes promotion but also incorporates the mission and vision of an institution in ways that convey a distinctive position. Sevier (1998) says that marketing must be consistent with mission and vision and that marketing is best seen as an extension of an institution's strategic plan.

Kotler and Fox (1985) define strategic planning as "the process of developing and maintaining a strategic fit between the institution's goals and capabilities and its changing market." It has also been defined as "a dynamic means of describing the organization, its goals, gaps to achieving them and ways to overcome the gaps for long-term viable success" (Stryker, 1997). Marketing, therefore, must flow from an institution's strategic plan, and mission and vision are at the core of that plan.

Institutional Mission

Sevier (1998) defines mission as a statement that describes founding and current principles and philosophies. Bryson (1995) tells us that a mission statement should clarify an institution's purpose. When the new administra-

STUDENT
MARKETING
FOR COLLEGES
AND UNIVERSITIES

tion took office at Dickinson College in 1999, the college entered into a strategic planning process by first discovering its past. In fact, the current mission statement, which serves as the cornerstone of its marketing plan, was derived directly from the college's 1783 charter – to provide a "useful" education and to produce citizen-leaders for the new nation. Tracing the founders' intent for the college helped to chart a course for the future. Dickinson's entire marketing plan today hinges on the notion of "usefulness" in the liberal arts and sciences, and on the global engagement with the wider world that its programs promote in order to prepare leaders for the nation and the world. Mission is the historical core of the institution – its reason for being. Without a clear statement of institutional purpose, institutional marketing is little more than the promotion of programs based on what is popular today.

Vision for Direction

There is no question that a clearly defined mission is essential for institutional direction in today's competitive environment. But without a vision for the future, a mission statement is pure rhetoric. An institutional vision gives future direction to the mission and is critical for building a marketing position. Sevier (1998) is clear on this point. Vision, he says, should clarify how an institution should behave as it fulfills its mission.

The vision of a college or university should be an aspiring statement that addresses what the college does to fulfill its mission. And here is where the major guideposts for marketing emerge. It is how a college undertakes its mission – and why – that can create a distinctive position for marketing. In Dickinson's case, it is clear that a useful education means hands-on learning engaged with the world. Its vision is to be a leader in this area as it is defined today. Globalization is at this heart of this engagement. A marketing plan that stresses this aspect of the Dickinson experience is consistent with both mission and vision and will position the college well as a leader in global education. And of course, the marketing position reflects reality, which is a priority.

The vision statement is an essential element of any marketing plan because it sets a direction for the future (Massa, 2001). It must also motivate faculty and staff, providing a reason for being that they can actively support. In this respect, a vision statement is a bold statement of ambitious goals meant to inspire all stakeholders. It must not be ambiguous. After September 11, 2001, if Mayor Rudy Giuliani had said, "I think we will try to clean this site up, and recover all we can, but I am unsure about the outcome and whether we have enough manpower, so we will just have to to see what happens," he would not have communicated a charge and a vision for what needed to be done in the aftermath of such a significant national tragedy. Instead, he was a confident leader, communicated what needed to be done and why, and provided a vision for the country to support.

A vision must be bold and set a tone that motivates all to achieve it. Sevier (1998) recommends that colleges broadly share the vision and involve stakeholders in the development of this future orientation. The vision must be future-directed, ambitious, consistent with mission, history and culture, reflective of excellence, clear in purpose and able to inspire commitment.

In his book, *Thinking Outside the Box*, Sevier (2001) talks about the role of leaders in the visioning process. He cites Karl Albrecht in *Northbound Train* as identifying four distinct leadership roles in the visioning process:

- The leader as a visionary who articulates the vision and direction of the institution;

- The leader as a team builder who hires the right people in key positions and develops them as a team;

- The leader as a living symbol who constantly reinforces the institution's position; and

- The leader as the "buck-stopper" who faces difficult issues and takes responsibility for them.

In order for a vision to take hold and to define an institution's market position, strong leadership is essential. A strong organization will have a leadership team, headed by the president, that is able to set a direction, serve as a catalyst for essential change and tell a consistent and compelling story. Each member of the team must share the vision widely and gain a commitment to "the story" from all campus constituencies. It is from this story that market position flows.

Enrollment Management Mission

The mission and direction of the enrollment management division must be linked to the institution's mission and vision. Through its own strategic planning, and in implementing the institution's plan, the Enrollment Management division must define and implement the institution's marketing plan in accordance with the mission and future direction of the college. Enrollment Management must translate the institution's vision into a position that will appeal to prospective students, parents, alumni and the general public.

Too often, enrollment managers try to convey a message that is complex – understood by its authors but not by the target audience. An institution is a complex organization with pressure from faculty and other stakeholders to highlight all programs in the college's marketing messages. That temptation must be resisted if the message is to be clear, direct, relevant and remembered. For Dickinson, this meant that all marketing messages must relate to the notion of a useful education and engagement with the world. Stories that demonstrate this position must be told again and again.

Beyond creating a marketing plan and communicating the college's position and its "promise," the Enrollment Management division is responsible for ensuring that promises are kept. At Dickinson College, for example, the Enrollment Management division includes the Student Life and College Relations units. With a clear understanding of its mission to develop citizen leaders and its position of engaging the world, staff members in the division do not "live in the viewbook." In fact, the admissions office works closely with College Relations to develop consistent marketing messages that can be used to recruit students and engage alumni. Staff in the Student Life area,

STUDENT
MARKETING
FOR COLLEGES
AND UNIVERSITIES

PART ONE
CHAPTER 2   21

meanwhile, provides feedback to those responsible for marketing the institution on a regular basis to assure the appropriate reality check – and vice versa.

The mission of Enrollment Management must include a commitment to the retention of students and a connection to alumni. In this regard, it is linked to the student experience and the ways in which alumni are connected to the institution through programs, the alumni magazine, mentoring current students and helping to identify and recruit new students. An Enrollment Management division that is integrated in this way can serve the institution well in fulfilling its vision and in marketing the institution to a broad audience.

Connecting Marketing, Mission and Vision

The last ten years have produced enormous changes in the way colleges compete for the attention of students, faculty, staff and alumni, as well as for financial support from alumni, corporations and foundations. Liberal arts colleges are particularly vulnerable to this increase in competition because the "big name" universities tend to control the market. Further, with their relatively low price, public universities have recently cut into the traditional student base of independent colleges. It is therefore important that colleges in a specific sector not only distinguish themselves from other colleges in their peer group, but from the broader representation in higher education.

If prospective students (and funding agencies) do not know what a college stands for, they will not respond positively to requests for engagement. Institutions must develop a position that conveys a "promise" to its internal and external audiences. Of course, this promise must be kept in order for the position to be effective. In the final analysis, developing and communicating an effective position is about "owning" an image in the minds of our target audiences. To be effective, the audiences must be aware of a college's position, and it must be relevant to them.

Once a mission and vision for an institution has been articulated with broad input from internal stakeholders, a process needs to be set to assure consistency of communication and delivery. At Dickinson, a task force was formed with broad representation to assess the effectiveness of publications and the Web in communicating the mission and vision of the college.

After the audit, the task force articulated a story with specific examples that related back to the mission, as written by Dickinson's founder in 1783, and by the contemporary vision of the mission. This story was communicated to staff that promote the college regularly and was told to all staff through an internal Web site. The task force also developed a list of themes and characteristics to support the college's mission. These themes would guide those who promoted the college and its programs to use certain key words and phrases in their publications. An internal Web site was created with these descriptors, and links to concrete examples of themes toward the fulfillment of the mission were provided for faculty and staff use in communication.

To assure the appropriate and accurate execution of marketing strategy, the task force set about the job of delineating a timetable for the formation of the positioning Web site. It also planned to send a regular reminder to all faculty and staff about the availability of the positioning Web site. It tasked the Publications Office with responsibility for the review of all submitted publications for consistency with the mission and vision. Further, the plan called for continued outreach to departments to discover and report new developments and how these relate to mission, vision and position. It also provided a mechanism for assistance offered by the College Relations unit to help faculty and staff craft the message – in print and verbally.

A Final Word

Sevier (2001) reminds us that, "Anyone can promote, but it takes a real master to communicate in such a way that audiences respond." Marketing messages must be *relevant* to the mission and vision and to the target audience. The message must be *remembered* – this is why it is critical that history, mission and vision explain how these principles apply today in programs and approaches to academic and student life. And finally, the message must be *repeated* in all venues. Every communication with prospective and current students and parents, and with alumni and funding agencies must reflect the same themes that support a college's position, mission and vision for the future. Only in this way will awareness take hold, and will marketing truly achieve its objective of promoting and strengthening the institution.

STUDENT
MARKETING
FOR COLLEGES
AND UNIVERSITIES

CREATING THE INSTITUTIONAL MARKETING STATEMENT

CLIFFORD LULL
President

&

BERNICE A. THIEBLOT
Founding Creative Director
The North Charles Street Design Organization

DELINEATING GOALS

To succeed, it helps to have a definition of success. Bob Bontrager (2002), in identifying the core concepts of Strategic Enrollment Management, mentions first "establishing clear goals for the number and types of students needed to fulfill the institutional mission." Unfortunately, many institutions stumble on the first step. As Bontrager points out, many operate on the simple premise that they need more students, without being able to state how many more, or which kinds.

In fact, most institutions are interested in more than enrolling greater numbers of students, and some are not interested in enrolling more students at all. Rather, they want to improve their cohorts of students on such measures as academic success or other talents, program interests, ethnicity, gender, home state residence, and ability to pay. But when such goals are stated, they are often more a list of wishes than a realistic assessment of possibilities.

Careful analysis of the enrollment landscape can help delineate the institution's enrollment opportunities and inform realistic goals. Bontrager recommends that this task be assigned to a high-level group with broad campus representation reporting to top decision-makers. The importance of this is all the more evident when one notes that all but a handful of the most selective institutions find they must make difficult choices among goals. For example, it might be desirable to have more students who are able and willing to pay full tuition, more students whose SAT scores raise the institutional average, and more students from disadvantaged backgrounds – but it is unlikely that the same students will meet all of these criteria. Success in any of these areas will tend to counteract success in another, so that revenue needs will have to be balanced against institutional prestige and diversity and the faculty's desire

STUDENT
MARKETING
FOR COLLEGES
AND UNIVERSITIES

PART ONE
CHAPTER 3   25

to teach more able students. But, finally, the enrollment enterprise will benefit from an informed statement of goals and their relative priority.

The Marketing Statement

Toward achieving enrollment goals, the marketing statement is the primary tool of communication. From it will flow those messages that are calculated to be most effective at attracting and enrolling the desired students. It will inform every aspect of recruitment outreach, from the character of campus visits and off-campus events to which media are chosen to reach students, to the content of Web sites and publications. It should also influence the character of the student's experience once enrolled, not only by establishing student expectations prior to enrollment, but also by shaping institutional decision-making regarding curriculum, teaching, advising, student life, and student support.

The need, then, is for a marketing statement upon which the institution can act – a statement that at least implies the institution's promises to its stakeholders, one that can guide and inform institutional decision-making in a host of areas, as well as shape marketing efforts. The enrollment manager may begin with existing statements.

The Mission Statement: The mission statement is not a marketing statement, of course, and chances are it is too wordy, too formal, and either too general or too specific to be immediately useful in a marketing context. Nevertheless, marketing messages cannot contradict it. A marketing statement must be true to the purposes of the institution it serves; it must have authenticity rooted in the institutional mission.

The Vision Statement: If a mission statement is about the fundamental purposes of the college or university – why it exists – a vision statement is the future-directed expression of the same idea – what it believes it can be. A vision statement may be the anchor of the institution's strategic plan. If the plan is a well-founded one – built on surveys of external conditions as well as internal strengths, weaknesses, and opportunities – then the vision statement can be foundational to the marketing statement, even though it probably is not market-ready.

Marketing statements can be called different things, depending on their intent or use:

- *A positioning statement* might assert a distinctive stance or establish a position for an institution within its competitor set. Such a statement may be more useful for internal information than for external communication.

CREATING THE
INSTITUTIONAL
MARKETING
STATEMENT

26   PART ONE
          CHAPTER 3

- *The "elevator speech"* is a useful term of recent years. This describes what one would say to make a persuasive case to another person in the time it takes to get somewhere in an elevator. Obviously, it matters who is on the elevator; a single elevator speech may not be suitable for all situations or constituencies. But short time and the need to be engaging are paramount, and the exercise of distilling refined messages to the most important audience is valuable. However the statement is framed, it must reflect a shared understanding of the position and purpose of the institution.

- *The communications platform* is a marketing statement with legs. It is built on the best statement about the institution around which there is at least functional consensus among key administrators and faculty members. The legs of the platform will be the deliverable promises made to each institutional constituency: students, parents, faculty, staff, alumni, donors, governing boards, legislators, or the public. These promises should grow easily and naturally out of the central statement.

It is a fine exercise to bring together internal groups to break down the marketing statement, positioning statement, or communications platform into its implied promises to each constituency.

Consensus

The process of developing a marketing statement – that is, the process of bringing key people together to focus on the essential purposes and goals, the "promise" of the institution – may be more valuable than anything the statement itself can accomplish.

The process should be informed by discussions that are rigorous and frank. It is not realistic to expect a unanimous outcome. An operational consensus is adequate to the purpose and may be the best for which the enrollment manager can hope.

It is prudent to keep in mind that many people may agree – and be wrong. Jim Collins (2001), in the fine best-selling business book *Good to Great: Why Some Companies Make the Leap and Others Don't*, describes the role of the "Council" in understanding and acting upon issues facing an organization: "The Council does not seek consensus, recognizing that consensus decisions are often at odds with intelligent decisions. The responsibility for the final decision remains with the leading executive." On that point, one might argue that the ultimate decision should rest with the one who has the most to gain or lose professionally from the outcome.

If the institution is trying to change its culture – once a decision is made – it will be important to draft the marketing statement/brand promise and the rationale for it, and share it with the campus community before going public with it. The goal of consistent orchestration and nurturing of shared values has a much better chance of being realized when the entire organization understands and supports it.

Once there is internal agreement on the salient benefits the institution offers, it will be necessary to delineate those benefits more fully. Every college or

STUDENT
MARKETING
FOR COLLEGES
AND UNIVERSITIES

PART ONE
CHAPTER 3   27

MAKING INSTITUTIONAL GOALS MEANINGFUL TO OTHERS

A public university's mission to keep the most talented students in its state from leaving to go to college may lead it to bring together from around the nation the best ideas about teaching, curriculum, campus design, and student services; the goal is to build a college comparable to the best, public or private, anywhere. This is an attractive position, but not because anyone else cares about the university's dreams of glory. The value of stating such a mission and vision in this instance is that it can explain and lend believability to the offer. To students: an excellent education and college experience. To faculty and staff: the stimulation of good ideas, gifted students, and institutional support for the best practices. To parents: excellent value for their tuition dollars. To alumni: increasing prestige for their degrees. To legislators and the public: increased value of the human capital within the state. Obviously, evidence of the truth of these claims must be part of the story.

university in America would say that it offers an excellent education. But the enrollment manager must be prepared to show what is different or better about the offerings of a specific institution. Often, the most powerful illustrations of real and important differences will be found in the ways the college meets the needs of those students it serves best. A good test of this idea might be, "We provide an excellent education for … (fill in here types of students and their goals), because … (fill in offerings and characteristics of institutional culture here)."

Care should be taken to avoid the sense that the process of making a marketing statement is an exercise in slogan writing. The marketing statement should be thought of as a tool for creative thought about communicating with publics, but not a public expression in itself.

Ultimately, it is high school students and their parents who will decide the merits of a college's marketing statement, as expressed by its brand messages. Whether or not the enrollment manager finds consensus difficult to achieve, recourse to these ultimate judges – via market research – may be the best way to inform the process of shaping public expression of the marketing statement. Everyone on campus may agree that certain good things are true about an institution, but that only makes for a good marketing position if those outside the institution who must be engaged – students or their families – actually care about those things. It is vital to find out which institutional promises matter. Too often, colleges act on the belief that some distinctive aspect of their organizational structure or their ambitions will be attractive to students. But students don't care how a college does business; they only care what that college can do for them, or help them do for themselves.

However the marketing statement and related promises are arrived at, testing the core ideas with target audiences is a valuable step. To take a somewhat offbeat example: A college may be committed to the goal of developing each student's capability of thinking and articulating ideas on his or her feet. Toward that end, the college may offer a great many classes in seminar format with dialogical teaching, and also may require that each student complete a public speaking requirement. The college expects that this skill will enable its graduates to move into positions of leadership in their communities and careers, and can present evidence that this is the case. However … many people fear the prospect of death less than the prospect of speaking in public. Can 16- and 17-year-olds be convinced that this is a good idea and something they want to do? And if so, how? At this stage, testing aspects of the desired student experience, and language to describe it, could prevent a costly meltdown later.

CREATING THE
INSTITUTIONAL
MARKETING
STATEMENT

28   **PART ONE**
      CHAPTER 3

DEVELOPING THE BRAND

CLIFFORD LULL
President

&

BERNICE A. THIEBLOT
Founding Creative Director
The North Charles Street Design Organization

THE POWER OF BRAND

The brand, essentially, is the sum of what people think of, and what they expect of, a named entity. Every product that can be named is a brand; each of our institutions is a brand; each of us personally is a brand.

A college or university – given certain attributes of location, reputation, cost, and programs offered – may expect a certain share of its market. Achieving a larger-than-expected share of the market is a function of consumer preference, and creating preference is a function of successful brand marketing. The consumer preference that results from successful branding has real value to both college and consumer. To the consumer, a college's brand can mean prestige, social cachet, or substantive advantages that pay off professionally and socially. To the college, it can mean greater selectivity and higher revenues. Fundamentally, it is why the cost of college attendance can vary so widely, even among institutions that would seem to be offering similar experiences and opportunities.

Defining the Brand

Marketing a brand, for higher education purposes, calls for shaping perceptions around the reality of an institution. For any number of reasons – because understanding is imperfect, because perception lags behind reality – there is usually a gap between how an institution is, and would like to be, regarded. Defining the brand is the first step in closing those gaps.

Because enrollment is the driver of marketing effort at most institutions, the enrollment manager is, in effect, the brand manager. For the enrollment manager, "the reality of the institution" has special meaning. Whether or not the job is specifically defined to encompass retention and promotion of successful outcomes for students, the enrollment manager has an obligation to the institution to take the long view of marketing. For the reason that institutional success is tied to student success, the interests of students must be integral to every part of the marketing plan. As the previous chapters point out, the mission and vision statements of an institution shape its enrollment management mission and are foundational to defining its brand.

STUDENT
MARKETING
FOR COLLEGES
AND UNIVERSITIES

In Creating Brand Loyalty, Czerniawski and Maloney (1999) list six elements of brand positioning that are adaptable to the higher education market. Paraphrased, they are:

1. Meet consumer needs, both functional and emotional.

The coffee at Starbucks meets a functional need (for caffeine), but the social atmosphere and presentation of the coffee meet emotional needs (for style and prestige). A college's programs, cost, and location may meet functional needs. Its campus atmosphere, culture, and reputation may meet emotional needs.

2. Target prospects with needs you can satisfy.

Those who sell lists of student names by secondary schools and by geo-demographic screeners make the task relatively easy for marketers seeking traditional undergraduate students.

3. Establish the consumer's frame of reference.

By what yardstick does the institution want to be measured? To some extent, it may be possible to shift the context. Jello went from being a gelatin product to a light dessert. A college might want to be seen as a certain kind of life experience, or as a means to an outcome; it might want to be seen as a "public ivy," a college of opportunity, a regional or a national resource, the top institution in one competitive cohort or the scrappy newcomer in another.

4. Identify your difference.

What point of difference from the competition does a college offer? The difference, of course, must be one that is meaningful to students.

5. Give a reason why.

Permission to believe is given when a college provides concrete evidence in support of claims, or the endorsement of credible sources: current students and their parents, alumni, media, ratings, and experts of various sorts.

6. Establish a personality or character for the brand.

Through language and visuals, a personality or character can be conveyed that, consistently applied, automatically evokes the institution in a stake-holder's mind. This brand identity, of course, should be consistent with the actual experience a student can expect to have with the institution.

Promoting the Brand

Books such as this one ordinarily do not acknowledge the role of creativity in developing the language, visual images, and character of engagements that define a brand and propel its messages. Perhaps that is because marketers are educated to think in the context of management science, and are not comfortable working with disciplines that rely so much on intuition and seem to have few rules. Yet behind any stunningly successful marketing campaign, there is a bit of magic, an individual inspiration. Usually, it is a well-informed inspiration, and often it is a thoroughly tested one. Successful marketing must at some point engage the consumer on an emotional level. One aim of this chapter is to help the higher education enrollment professional harness creative talent in the service of enrollment marketing goals.

An element of brand positioning that seems to present particular difficulties in higher education is that of differentiation – discovering and articulating a difference that will be meaningful and motivating to prospective students. It may be valuable for the enrollment manager to keep in mind that:

1. The institutional difference need not be unique.

If a college offers a benefit that resonates well with prospective students, and a competitor offering the same benefit is not exploiting it, the way is open to own that difference in the market. On this point, there may be an advantage to being realistic about the scope of the market; it is easier to be unique in a local or regional market than in the national market.

2. Combinations can create distinctiveness.

A college or university may have attributes and offer benefits similar to others that, in combination, create a distinct position. For example:

> Barnard College is not the only liberal arts college, the only women's college, the only college in New York City, or the only college affiliated with a major research university. But it is the only college that has all of those attributes, and can offer the benefits of them.

> The undergraduate college of Drew University is not the only one to have integrated technology into its teaching (although it was the first to issue computers to freshmen), or the only one to place high value on faculty mentorship of students, or the only one to encourage off-campus learning through domestic and international college-sponsored programs, or the only one to create partnerships with corporations and institutions in New Jersey and New York to provide experiential opportunities for students. But it is the only college in its market that does all of those things.

3. The most powerful differences can appear disguised as problems.

Many colleges find that their most interesting difference is at best ambiguous in the marketplace. Often, such a difference can be recast as a distinctive, even unique, benefit. To take two examples related to location:

> The University of Virginia's College at Wise, founded as a college of opportunity for the children of coal miners, is located in the far southwestern corner of the state, next to a national forest and 30 miles from the nearest restaurant with a tablecloth. Its mountain location is a turn-off for many students, but a turn-on for those who want that kind of experience. An active outdoors program, recruiting materials that emphasize the benefits of the location and campus culture, and a posi-

"Good design is good business," former IBM chairman Tom Watson famously stated in a Harvard speech in 1974. Was he right? A study designed by two Northeastern University business school professors, Julie Hertenstein and Marjorie Platt (2001), to test Watson's hypothesis is reported in the summer 2001 *Design Management Journal*. Indeed, the authors found statistically significant data confirming that companies that pay attention to design of their products and marketing financially outperform those that do not.

STUDENT
MARKETING
FOR COLLEGES
AND UNIVERSITIES

PART ONE
CHAPTER 4   31

tioning theme line – "Thomas Jefferson's dream … in the mountains" – have helped the college set enrollment records.

> Tulane University is about learning (and fun) in New Orleans. The work-hard/play-hard model thus evoked is a concern for those, especially parents, who fear the distractions of the city. Tulane has greatly strengthened its appeal by creating and marketing opportunities for students to learn things about architecture, engineering, history, law, culture, music that they cannot learn at first hand anywhere else. The idea is summed up in the title of the prospectus: "Only in New Orleans. Only at Tulane."

Creating preference by reaching a consumer on an emotional level is not necessarily an empty exercise in manipulation. Rather, as these examples show, it can involve revealing facts not known by the consumer, or looking at known facts in a way that reveals previously unrecognized benefits. Sometimes, it is just a matter of giving stakeholders another way of thinking, but often, as in these cases cited above, it takes institutional effort to enhance the difference that is to be the centerpiece of the positioning.

Although both UVA–Wise and Tulane's theme lines suggest a promise, neither is literally a promise or claim. Instead, both could be described as market-ready messages. Raw claims or promises are useful in research, but can be deadly in the market – for any number of reasons: they may be too complex, too particular, or just too uninteresting. In contrast, the market-ready statement may only hint at related promises and claims. It need not be as literal as a statement used in a planning or research context because, in actual use, it is possible to create context for a marketing message that makes its meaning clear. It may be worth noting that a theme line is not essential to a successful brand; only a point-of-view is.

4. Messages need not be identical to be consistent.

Bontrager (2002) notes that, "consistency of the content and visual representation of institutional image is critical in these times of intense competition and massive amounts of stimuli in the marketplace." More simply, Robert Zemsky (2003) has said, "Know your story. Tell it well. Tell it over and over."

In practice – just from the evidence of printed and electronic communications (leave aside the handling of campus tours and other personal contacts) – many institutions are either all over the place in their presentation, or so repetitive as to be tedious. It takes a great deal of thought and skill to present an institution consistently and engagingly to different audiences, or to the same audience at different times for different reasons. It is a bit like looking at something through different windows. To be consistent, messages need not be identical to one another, but they do need to cohere to a central idea about the institution. In fact, the acid test of a positioning is whether it can be expressed and supported in a variety of ways. Here is an institution that does this well:

> The University of Chicago, with its unparalleled liberal arts curriculum, offers a distinctive academic challenge to undergraduates who are intellectually talented and curious. Its publication for rising high school

juniors, titled "When I Was in High School," affirms the qualities that good Chicago candidates demonstrate early and helps them make the connection between their own proclivities and life at Chicago. The prospectus for rising seniors explores "The Life of the Mind" and offers humorous perspectives from students who are living it. A publication for students of color speaks to the benefits of an intellectual environment in which every perspective and every voice matters in the search for truth. "ChicagoLife," the comprehensive student handbook, is a friendly guide to navigating a complex urban institution. The common thread is the offer of a rich intellectual life.

The Creative Team

To develop materials for student recruitment, the enrollment manager ordinarily works with a team of creative people. The members of this team may be drawn from internal staff (perhaps from the institution's own publications office), or outside (from a consulting creative services firm or agency), or a combination of both.

At minimum, the creative team will bring to the task the skills of writing, photography/illustration, and design for print or digital media, and will be able to meld its work into a coherent program of appropriate materials. Use of the word "team" is purposeful here, as the value of having people from these different but complementary disciplines working together cannot be overestimated. The effort required to build and nurture a team of internal and external contributors who raise each other's level of performance is a worthwhile investment.

Optimally, one member of the team will have sufficient experience and domain knowledge to direct the others toward an outcome that is strategically powerful. In corporate environments, such as advertising agencies or creative services firms, the person who is charged with shaping the work of the creative team is called the creative director. Working with a creative director, or someone who carries out that function, can make the enrollment manager's task much simpler. Absent an experienced and talented creative director, the enrollment manager may be obliged to step into the role of coordinating and directing the work of designers, writers, et al., a job for which enrollment managers may not have the requisite training, experience, or time.

Having professional creative direction does not relieve the enrollment manager of the task of providing direction; it means only that his or her direction need not focus on the "how" of achieving the desired communications objectives. The enrollment manager must, however, clearly set forth the goals, conditions, and limitations of the program or project.

The Recruitment Marketing Plan

Clearly, it is better to have a complete plan for recruitment marketing – one that visualizes actions and outcomes on a continuum – than to chase prospective students from one stage of the process to the next with *ad hoc* ideas for engaging their interest. Yet, the latter happens surprisingly often.

STUDENT
MARKETING
FOR COLLEGES
AND UNIVERSITIES

PART ONE
CHAPTER 4   33

The recruitment marketing plan, essentially, is a plan to get the right messages to the right persons at the right times, while making efficient use of institutional resources. The plan may be informed by sophisticated tools that help the enrollment manager use staff and resources effectively, such as market segmentation, predictive modeling, and technology that allows personalization and tailoring of content even in the earliest stages of a relationship. At minimum, the plan should cover goals, audiences, media/activities, messages, timelines, and budget. In Chapter 13, Richard Whiteside discusses development of the plan in detail.

The recruitment plan is mentioned here only to make the point that it works with the goals and messages of branding on many levels. It is best to maintain a degree of flexibility in the plan – not only to allow for correcting course and taking advantage of opportunities that emerge along the way, but also to allow for the influence of strategic creative ideas on the development and execution of the plan. The main purpose of drafting the plan is to provide an orderly structure and a strategic reference point for recruitment activities; it need not anticipate every good idea, and it should not block out good ideas.

So many ideas and so many tactics are available to today's enrollment manager that it becomes easy to focus on tactics at the expense of brand overview and essential messages. The sheer force of a campaign that is designed primarily to move students from one step to the next in the admission process can have the effect of dragooning a student into a choice that is ill-considered and later regretted – even rejected – to the detriment of both student and college. Writing a plan that integrates messages and tactics, laying it all out and reviewing it critically, can help the enrollment manager guard against an inappropriate focus on the mechanics of recruitment.

Tools for Creative Direction

Once the foundational work of understanding an institution's mission and vision, marshalling its promises to stakeholders, and identifying its salient differences is done, there are tools and resources the enrollment manager and the creative team can use to stimulate fresh thinking about how to present the brand.

The creative brief. The enrollment manager acting in the role of brand manager must provide clear direction to the creative team while allowing freedom to explore. A document used to focus the efforts of the creative team, the creative brief can be used at the earliest stages of thinking about recruitment tools to guide work on the major themes, language, look, and tone of the materials, even on the shape of the recruitment plan. Later, more specific briefs can be drafted to cover the requirements of specific components of the program.

However the creative brief is structured, it should include these statements:

- The problem situation or opportunity;
- The goal/s of this task;

- Available media, limitations, essential requirements; and

- The specific responsibilities of creative team members.

The task of drafting the brief can, in itself, uncover and focus attention on the most pressing issues and best opportunities.

To allow room for creativity – for the unexpected flash of insight that can make all the difference – the brief should remain focused on end goals and not be unnecessarily prescriptive about details of execution. Using the available media and budget to excite and inform students who have characteristics that match well with the institution is a goal; producing a 36-page, four-color viewbook with a fold-out cover is not. The more open the creative brief and the earlier it is employed, the more likely that the response to it will reveal new opportunities and help shape the recruitment plan along distinctive lines.

Background research. The creative process may be fueled by insights and information gained from various sources.

Focused on-campus interviews of students. Enrolled students – particularly those in categories of greatest recruitment interest – may yield useful insights to the institutional culture and how students experience it. An interviewer whose work involves speaking with students on many campuses will find it easier to discern what is distinctive about what they say.

Audit of existing communications – with a fresh eye. Armed with a set of objectives and promises, the enrollment manager will find it useful to audit his or her institution's own marketing communications. It can be revealing to see how the current materials miss opportunities to make important points, or even unwittingly contradict key claims. Current students and prospective students can be helpful as critics of current materials, and marketing professionals may be able to spot missed opportunities or point to areas of weakness that may inspire something better.

Audit of leading competitors' communications. Competitors are competitors because they offer similar benefits. Auditing their materials will reveal what they claim and how they present it. Spotting their missed opportunities may furnish inspiration. Also, the enrollment manager will find a survey of competitors' marketing communications valuable as a way to avoid similarities.

Focused interviews of prospective students. Focus groups produce nothing creative; their participants are too grounded in the current paradigm for that. Still, there is nothing like the frankness of a high school junior to roil the creative juices. Focus groups early in the creative process may point to opportunities. Later in the process, focus groups of prospective students can be used to test ideas, copy, and proposed designs for materials.

Readings. The enrollment manager, cast in the role of brand manager, may benefit from familiarity with popular techniques for promoting creativity. Roger von Oech's book *A Whack on the Side of the Head* (1998) is a classic of its kind, as are two books by Michael Michalko: *Thinkertoys: A Handbook of Business Creativity* (1991) and the ambitiously-titled *Cracking Creativity: The Secrets of Creative Genius* (2001). All provide stimulating exercises that, at the very least, can bring a creative team together congenially. The University of

STUDENT
MARKETING
FOR COLLEGES
AND UNIVERSITIES

PART ONE
CHAPTER 4   35

Chicago psychologist Mihaly Csikszentmihalyi (pronounced "Chick-sent-m'haley") has written fine books on the understanding and nurturing of creativity, among them *Creativity: Flow and the Psychology of Discovery and Invention;* (1997) and *Good Business: Leadership, Flow, and the Making of Meaning* (2003). Csikszentmihalyi added to the language the word "flow," to stand for the joyful state of unconscious immersion in which persons find themselves when their work is going well.

Meetings. Bringing people together to trade ideas is an indispensable part of the creative process and can be made more valuable by the use of techniques designed to stimulate creativity. The most useful of these techniques are intended to encourage production of many ideas by stimulating unconventional thinking and withholding judgment, aiming for originality. Such sessions are often referred to as "brainstorming." A term borrowed from the field of architecture (and the French) is *charette* (pronounced shurETT), which can describe one of two kinds of meetings or meeting series, both of which are also important to the creative process: the initial input meeting/s where all requirements and agendas are covered, and the meeting/s to review, evaluate, troubleshoot, and solve problems in a proposed solution.

Time. As has been shown by various studies of the creative process, time for the informed subconscious to work is most valuable – but a deadline has a way of getting the subconscious cracking. Ideally, there will be a generous planned hiatus between the statement of a problem along with presentation of background information and the expectation of possible solutions.

Testing Brand Messages

Testing is not something that occurs only after a publication or a Web site – or a whole communications program – hits the street. Testing is, or should be, integral to the program from the first steps to the last. It can take place in the following ways:

Evaluation during the creative process. Members of a skilled and dedicated creative team will continually evaluate their own work, rejecting ideas and refining others many times before presenting them. Using a consultant creative firm adds to the mix not only the skills needed to produce competitive materials, but also insight from two different domains: the college or university being served and the wider world of marketing. And a specialist marketing communications firm may bring knowledge of the higher education marketing domain informed by engagements with hundreds of institutions. A list of suggested questions to ask before engaging a creative consultant may be found at the end of this chapter.

Feedback from staff. Counselors, those who engage with prospective students daily, should be part of the process, especially when evaluating materials they use personally, such as off-campus meetings and events.

Pre-testing with prospects. A market-ready message (or messages) at the hypothetical stage presents the opportunity to pretest an admission communications program (or any part of it) with end-users and get direct feedback. Here are two forms it can take:

Copy testing. A blind e-mail survey – one that comes from a source unidentifiable as the sponsoring college or university – can be an efficient technique for learning how various features, promises, or lines of copy resonate with pre-qualified students.

Formal focus testing of materials. Bringing prospective students together in the setting of a focus-group facility can be extremely valuable. It presents the opportunity to probe the thinking of pre-qualified students in a neutral setting. To create context, it is a good idea to exhibit the most coherent marketing statements – normally, key parts of the current viewbook or prospectus – of all institutions in the competitive cohort and to solicit impressions of those. When presenting new materials or ideas, it is crucial to present more than one option; students want to be helpful and, if asked, will critique whatever is put before them. Because focus groups can be difficult to interpret, it is useful to aim for a concrete finding, perhaps a measure of how students' impressions of the sponsoring and competitor institutions have been changed by exposure to the tested materials. For this purpose, in addition to the interview, each student might be asked to fill out a questionnaire form. These same principles apply to testing Web sites or other media.

In-market testing. The college admissions scenario offers distinct opportunities for testing ideas in actual conditions of use, particularly at the early outreach stage. Direct-mail search mailings can be split many ways to allow for tracking of responses to variations in message or presentation. E-mailings can be tracked in real time. Building response mechanisms into the communications program whenever feasible can provide a reading on which initiatives or messages were, or were not, effective – valuable information for the next cycle of planning,

Results measurement. Enrollment results are difficult to trace to particular activities. Even if careful tracking is done, it can be difficult to isolate variables, as most admission marketing programs evolve on several fronts in a given year. Yet, the thoughtful enrollment manager knows that enrolling a bigger and better class does not necessarily mean that everything that went into achieving the goal was right, or even necessary; falling short of a goal could indicate that everything done was wrong. Beyond enrollment numbers, there are ways to know the impact of a branding campaign and whether messages are on target. If morale is high and new students seem to fit well with the institution, if faculty members report they like teaching the new students, if freshman-sophomore retention improves, and if the language of the

THE MANY LIVES OF THE VIEWBOOK

Even though access to the Web is universal in the U.S. and institutional Web sites and e-mail initiatives are playing a growing role in engaging and informing stakeholders, the need persists for a core publication that states the case. For most institutions, one publication serves this purpose; it may be called a viewbook, a prospectus, or an admissions catalog, and it may be published in separate versions for use earlier or later in the admissions process. Although its days may be numbered, it offers coherence, portability, the authority and finality of print – and it plays an important role as a point of reference on the institution's positioning. Developers of marketing messages for other media can turn to it for inspiration and to audit their own work. Because faculty and staff should be familiar with the way the institution presents itself to prospective students – and the student expectations that are thus raised – these members of the campus community should be on the distribution list for any new viewbook or prospectus.

marketing program becomes part of the way enrolled students talk about their experience, success has been achieved.

Dealing With Creative Consultants

A creative consultant should be skilled in identifying institutional problems and opportunities – and in using communications techniques to help solve the problems and capitalize on the opportunities. A valuable partner in your marketing or advancement program, the right consultant brings to the relationship:

- Objectivity: the ability to examine strengths and weaknesses without bias
- Talent and refined communications skills
- Broad knowledge of the domain in which you must compete

From the start, you and the consultant should know what to expect of one another. Ask lots of questions up front, especially the hard ones. It is a good way to avoid misunderstandings on both sides, and a good way to test the chemistry of the relationship, a hard-to-define, but vitally important, consideration.

Ask Yourself

Before you pick up the phone or send out a request for a proposal, start by asking some tough questions of yourself and your staff as a first step toward building an internal process and getting buy-in to your program. We believe the following are good ones to consider at the start:

What services or expertise do you need?

You probably want an individual or a firm that can close certain gaps in your on-campus capabilities. Ask yourself what's missing: Time? Writing talent? Design talent? Do you need a marketing orientation for the Web, or Web design? Or knowledge of a specialized area of communication, such as graphic identity, high-end printing management, direct mail, advertising, special-events management? Or perhaps you need specific expertise in an area of concern, such as admissions, annual giving, or long-range fund-raising.

Are you open to new ideas?

If you know what needs to be done and how to do it, but need someone to execute your initiatives, you should seek an individual or a firm that has that capability. If you're looking for fresh insights and ideas, you need a person or a firm with analytical skills, original thinking, and the experience and diplomacy to help you "sell" the program your institution needs. As you know, that kind of support can be political as well as operational.

How much of a commitment do you want from a consultant?

Do you want someone to help you with a single project of relatively short duration, such as a major publication, a new magazine format, or a graphic-identity program? Or do you need ongoing support through all phases of a capital campaign, for example, or through several recruitment cycles of testing and experimentation with student recruitment techniques? Answers to these questions can help you determine whether you need the services of an individual or the more specialized and comprehensive services a communications firm can provide.

How much money can you justify committing to outside expertise?

If the cost of getting help means the difference between doing a job right or not, what are the consequences either way? Existing budgets are generally based upon historical costs. But zero-based creative thinking calls for zero-based budgeting. And remember, consultant-related costs are highly variable and usually subject to negotiation. You can avoid a false start at the outset if you have some idea of how much money your institution is willing to invest in the success of your program.

Ask the Consultant

Professional organizations such as CASE (Council for Advancement and Support of Education) maintain rosters of consultants in the higher education field and are a good source of candidates. The consultants' own Web sites and materials can help you winnow the field. Diligent homework and a clear understanding of your needs should enable you to limit to three the number you interview.

Expect a presentation focused on problems and solutions, and pay attention to the consultant's understanding of the more subtle or complex issues involved. Look for the kind of innovation that gives work impact. The work should communicate quickly and be persuasive and memorable. Above all, it should reflect a sense of each client for which it was done and not the style of the consultancy.

Some suggested questions:

What is your experience?

College marketing is a highly competitive enterprise. Mistakes can be costly in money, time, and reputation. Look for a record of success. Because good consultants work in partnership with their clients, none can claim total responsibility for either success or failure. Nevertheless, an orientation to results is a good sign. Ask about results, and don't be shy about checking claims.

Where did you come from?

What is the background of the consulting firm? Did it grow from an advertising agency or a printing company? The answer can be a useful clue to whether the firm can solve your problems. Remember that, to a person with a hammer, things tend to look like nails. Printing companies, or creative firms that have grown out of printing companies, tend to favor printing as the solution to marketing problems. Advertising agencies naturally lean toward advertising. Public relations firms believe in the power of the press. Make sure the culture of the firm you choose – how its people think about their work, how they spend their time, how they bill for their services – matches your needs and expectations.

STUDENT
MARKETING
FOR COLLEGES
AND UNIVERSITIES

PART ONE
CHAPTER 4   39

Can you show me samples of your work?

If you plan to depend on consultants to develop materials for your communications program, ask to see samples of what they have done for other institutions with similar goals. Look beyond the design, printing, and paper quality – to the ideas. Read the copy. Ask about the objectives … and the results. You might want to ask how recent the samples are. Companies have been known to cycle in and out of specialties, so you may be shown samples from an earlier, better era. Be wary of the mobility of talent in the industry. If you like what you see, and if you learn it was a team effort, try to find out if you'll be getting the same team – or at least the key players.

How many of our needs can you meet?

It takes time and effort for a consultant to gain a working knowledge of your institution. And not just the consultant's time and effort – yours, too. If you rely on multiple media, as most institutions do, your consultant should be able to help you ensure that messages are well integrated from one to another. To accomplish this, you may need a consultant with expertise in:

- *Graphic identity.* Design of visual elements that are true to an institution's largest vision, and that can be systematically applied to a wide range of needs, is a very special skill.

- *Web site development.* A consultant can help you develop a Web site consistent with institutional identity and positioning, as well as provide content development and design of interactive features that promise the greatest potential for marketing return.

- *Videotape/PowerPoint.* These media offer other ways to present the core branding messages – other windows through which to see the institution. Their tone and content should be consistent with other materials.

- *E-commerce.* E-mail is an essential part of today's enrollment marketing. E-mails should dovetail neatly with other marketing activities, and their tone and content should be consistent with core messages.

- *Advertising.* Print and broadcast advertising – including paid insertions in college guides – should present the same institution as other materials.

- *Mailing.* Mailing of a publication can easily cost more than its production. A knowledgeable consultant can help you navigate the regulations of the U.S. Postal service and provide reliable, cost-effective mailing services.

So, if you think you may have future needs in a variety of areas, get the whole story. Will the consultant who drafts your communications plan and follows through with insightful and effective work in publications, for example, be able to provide complementary work on your Web site? Or vice versa? What about a video or a CD–ROM or an advertising campaign for the same program? Finding and educating a string of consultants is hardly the best way to spend your time.

How can you help us save money or improve our return on investment?

There are many ways a consultant can help you save your institution money, starting with better planning, better targeting of messages, and getting things right the first time. Ask for examples of how to make the most effective use of available funds, and be open to ideas that may cost more but prove to pay proportionally higher dividends in effectiveness. It may be worth noting that a creative consultant who bills for services on the basis of time actually expended – rather than charging a flat fee for a finished project – creates the incentive for you to move things along and make efficient use of the consultant's time and resources, as well as the most constructive use of your staff.

What can you help us do for ourselves?

The best relationships with creative consultants are collaborative. Ask prospective consultants to give you examples of how collaboration might work within your institution. Some possibilities: guidance on setting up your own marketing studies, establishing formats and specifications for publishing internal periodicals, training an on-campus photographer, providing editorial guidelines for the catalog, handling mailings, budgeting publication inventories over a long period, or setting up databases to help you manage Web content more efficiently. If you want a creative consultant to take an interest in your entire program, be sure to raise this question at the outset.

May I speak with some of your clients?

You are not likely to hear much that's unfavorable, but you can get a sense of the consultant's scope – how the firm works, and strengths and weaknesses to look for – from someone in a situation similar to yours. Not that numbers necessarily matter, but it's reasonable to be impressed by consultants who are willing to supply a healthy number of references, from former as well as current clients. Ideally, a consultant or firm should be willing to give you a contact name for any client, past as well as present.

Would you work for our competitors?

This question is more sensitive in the area of admissions marketing, but it can be a factor in other areas as well. These days, it seems that if a consultant does good work for you, you can count on your closest competitors to try to hire the same consultant. How would you feel about that? (Believe this: the competitor's work will always look better to you.) Ask the prospective consulting organization if it has a conflict-of-interest policy – and how it works.

Who's in charge?

Generally speaking, the best relationships are predicated on the idea that the consulting firm knows its specialized area, while the in-house staff knows the institution. When there are disagreements, it is usually best to let the person whose turf it is do most of the talking. In the end, however, every consultant knows it's the people paying the bills who are in charge.

STUDENT
MARKETING
FOR COLLEGES
AND UNIVERSITIES

PART ONE
CHAPTER 4   41

How often do we review progress on a project?

Different firms have different procedures, but in principle you should be able to review the status of a project as often as you like. Experienced consultants will be able to share the schedule with you, noting the checkpoints along the way and the benefits of each. If you don't feel comfortable, ask for more. Beware of anyone who wants to surprise you.

What happens when we disagree?

This comes back to the control question above. The only reasonable answer is, "You win." If the consultant can't convince you, you get your way. Disagreement can be a good thing, so don't be shy about raising questions. A responsible consultant will be his or her own devil's advocate, putting ideas through a process of testing and questioning before presenting them to you. At the same time, your perspective from the institution's side is essential. An experienced consultant will be uneasy with a client who readily agrees to everything. It places a huge burden of responsibility on the consultant. Worse, it may mean that the ideas and plans aren't adequately vetted.

What will it cost?

Sometimes it's truly impossible to tell how much a prospective undertaking will cost, especially when you're buying creativity and expecting your consultant to break new ground. For large projects involving recurring expenses over time, such as an admissions marketing program that can have a life of four to six years, or more, it may be wise to look beyond start-up costs, which can be considerable. An experienced consultant should be able to look ahead and give you an idea of averaged annual costs based on cost histories for programs of similar magnitude.

What about billing?

How often do the bills come? Are they itemized? Will you be asked to pay a flat fee for a project, or will the consultant bill for actual time and expenses, so that your own efficiency as a collaborator can pay off? If a flat fee, how is that fee determined? Under what circumstances will you be asked to pay more than the contract amount? One good reason people hire consultants is to get a predictable result; billing is an important aspect of predictability.

What if we decide to cancel a project?

If you contract for a project and break that contract, you could be liable for the entire cost. Some consultants break large projects into incremental phases to which fees are assigned, so that you may contract for only one phase at a time. A consultant who bases billings on hourly rates and expenses may be willing to terminate projects for only those costs incurred up to the date of cancellation.

What happens if you make a mistake in our work?

We work in an inexact medium. Where there are few absolutes, experience and judgment count. That's what you're buying: time, talent, experience, and judgment. That said, a single typographical error can still ruin a project. Knowing that anyone can miss an error, ask what the consultant does to protect clients and what a client must irreversibly accept responsibility for. And you might want to ask the consultant's references about errors, and how they were handled.

What about deadlines?

If the deadline is important, and if the consultant is in total control of the project, then financial incentives or sanctions written into the contract are a simple way to help ensure on-time delivery. Usually, however, projects undertaken with consultants are collaborative, and the consultant would be foolish, indeed, to agree to a schedule unilaterally. On the other hand, when you are having trouble getting your own people to sign off in a timely fashion, you don't need a consultant who holds you to the letter. You need a cooperative spirit – someone who doesn't over-promise, but who will try to work with you. That's where references become useful: someone who has consistently kept promises in the past is likely to continue doing so.

Who owns what?

After a project is finished, who owns what? An established creative consultant with a reputation to protect may wish to retain an interest in the creative product (understandably, we think). This could mean that you may not revise electronic files, re-edit videotapes, or create recognizably similar spin-offs without the advice and consent of the creator. Read the fine print, so you'll know who owns the electronic files, the printer's film or electronic make-ready, the photography, the color separations, the illustrations, Web site designs, and any other components of the production process.

Who does the work?

One of the most frequent complaints from institutions that have worked with consultants is that the original contact person is never seen again. "Who will be doing our work?" is a good question to ask. Another is, "What else do they have to do at the same time?" The answers can tell you a lot about a consultant's orientation to clients. A sales-driven company may send someone who earns a commission for bringing in business, and who may or may not be responsible for seeing that your work gets done. Or, the big-picture consultant may have little to do with the actual crafting of messages and materials, with a resulting gap between intent and execution. Find out: it's another good question for references.

What will you expect of us?

There are things to know about your institution that no outsider can know – or can track down cost-efficiently. Hiring a consultant doesn't mean you can wash your hands of responsibility and involvement. You still have an important role. Some of the things a consultant may expect of you: background research materials, interview and photography arrangements, proofing, fact-checking, sign-off in good faith at various approval points, and protection from committees with mixed objectives seeking consensus. A consultant should respect your time, and some have established procedures to make your part of the job manageable. Ask the consultant what will be needed

STUDENT
MARKETING
FOR COLLEGES
AND UNIVERSITIES

from your end – particularly if your time is scarce or you would prefer to limit your involvement.

Will we have a written agreement?

The best-intentioned people can forget. Get everything in writing. An experienced and well-organized consultant will have consistent rules and practices and put them in writing as part of every contract. Read them, and question anything you don't understand.

Pay attention to the kinds of questions the consultant asks, as they are a good indication of interest and a predictor of thoroughness in the face of difficult problems. Remember that outstanding work comes from talent fueled by enthusiasm. And, finally, put the quality and appropriateness of the proposal ahead of the cost. Choosing primarily on the basis of price almost always results in a sacrifice of quality, service, and effectiveness.

STRATEGIC
PLANNING

PART TWO

ACQUIRING AND USING MARKETING INFORMATION FOR STRATEGIC DECISION-MAKING

CHAPTER 5

DR. THOMAS HAYES
Professor of Marketing
Xavier University

Information is the basis for any solid marketing program. However, in the world of higher education where Ph.D.'s abound and a high concentration of educated people can be found, "knowledge" may be one of the largest barriers to success. It is not what scholars and faculty know that is the "problem," it is what they "think" they know.

The most fundamental mistake one can make in the field of education marketing is to assume that one knows what the customer is thinking, be they students, parents, donors or faculty. The education "marketer" is different in thinking, background and viewpoints from one's typical customer base.

In the United States, only about twenty-two percent of the population that is twenty-one years old and above has a college degree. Chances are, those responsible for marketing within higher education institutions reside in this twenty-two percent. In fact, many may have multiple college degrees up to and including a Ph.D. This fact puts them in a minority within the United States. Furthermore, every institution of higher learning probably has its "own way of doing things." The school's mission, vision, values and day-to-day procedures guide one's behavior and shape one's thinking. Campus administrators learn how things are done in their schools by observations or through subtle rewards and punishments.

The following simple quiz is useful in seminars and is worth completing for the purposes of this discussion. The questions are:

1. How many years of education do you have?

2. Did you receive training in your organization when you began there?

3. How many hours a week do you work?

4. On your way into work in the morning, do you think about what is waiting on your desk?

STUDENT MARKETING FOR COLLEGES AND UNIVERSITIES

5. When you get in your car or ride the train home in the evening, do you think about what was left on your desk at the end of the day?

6. When you go on a week's vacation, what day of the week is it when you quit thinking about the messages, projects, and the reports that are left back on your desk, and what day of the week is it when you start thinking about them again?

Those responsible for marketing colleges and universities probably work more than forty hours a week. They probably fit into those categories of people who are thinking about what lies on their desks when they are heading to work in the morning and continue to think about it on their way home at night. They also think about work while on vacation and a few probably check in by phone when they are supposed to be relaxing with their families.

These indicators mean that not only are marketers of higher education more likely to be more educated than the average individual, they also know their own organizations quite well. They are aware of the benefits and limitations of their schools. In fact, it is this formal and informal education combined with a dedication and love of their schools that diminishes their ability to think objectively about what clients and customers want and obscures the ability to see things from their perspectives. What they know about their colleges and their capabilities is not likely to be known by customers unless they are told. Of course, even if prospective students, donors or employees know a great deal about a school, they still may not care. The fact that one's university was founded 175 years ago or has 45 majors does not mean much unless it can be related to customer needs. To reach students, parents or any other public in a manner that appeals to them, colleges must first understand what drives customers and determine their needs and expectations.

Knowing What We Do not Know

Larry Lauer, Vice Chancellor for Marketing and Communications at Texas Christian University at Fort Worth, Texas, likes to point out that while most universities and colleges have a very strong research agenda, they do very little research that allows them to understand their own business and market-place. Colleges often place a great deal of emphasis on the importance of research when a faculty member is up for tenure, but less on the use of research in making strategic decisions. Many believe that because they are surrounded on a daily basis by their primary customer base, students, they are in touch with the students' needs and desires. Formal marketing research is regarded as an expense that one cannot afford and is not needed. As a result, many decision-makers in colleges and universities fall prey to the "just talk to people" syndrome.

Although no one would argue that education marketers should not be talking with current and prospective students or their parents, there are some serious problems with relying on this method of gathering information. First, the individuals they speak with may not be representative of the customer group. Second, it is human nature to talk to people who are similar or to those with whom one feels comfortable. As a result, "just talking to people" is likely to support pre-conceived notions. Additionally, this technique is characterized

ACQUIRING & USING
MARKETING
INFORMATION
FOR STRATEGIC
DECISION-MAKING

48   **PART TWO**
CHAPTER 5

by biased interviewing processes. Finally, there are likely to be inconsistencies between how each individual is asked questions. A well-planned research program should eliminate these problems.

When gathering marketing data, a college should balance the information that it would like to have against what it really needs. The ideal first step is to determine exactly what it needs to know. The costs of obtaining, processing, storing and delivering information must then be determined. The university must decide whether the benefits of having additional information are worth the cost of obtaining it. By itself, information has no worth: its value comes from its use. Collecting information that is not used is a waste of money no matter how little one pays for it.

To effectively assess information needs to develop sound, strategic marketing plans, a thorough internal and external analysis should be conducted. Such an analysis requires that the university utilize its own internal records, search databases and public records for information about what is going on in its environment and utilize marketing research to answer specific questions.

The Marriage of Marketing Information and Strategic Decision-Making

In Chapter 2, the importance and development of the university's mission and vision statements were clarified. These statements, in essence, answer the questions, "What business are we in?" and "Where are we going?" The answers to these questions are part of the first step of strategic planning and are commonly called "the situation analysis." A third component of the situation analysis is the answer to the question, "Where are we now?" The answer to this question is typically not a short one. It involves a great deal of time and effort on behalf of the institution, especially if it is the first time the institution has embarked on completing the task. In essence, answering the question, "Where are we now?" is like taking a snapshot of the organization in time. It allows decision-makers to understand and "see" their institutional capabilities in relation to their competitors, environment, and needs and wants of each of their publics.

Virtually every university collects data for assessment purposes or accreditation needs. Unfortunately, much of the data that is collected is done on a decentralized basis across many colleges or divisions within the university. Even those organizations that have a position entitled "institutional research" may be using their data with the goal of accreditation fulfillment rather than strategic decision-making. The first step, therefore, of utilizing internal information is to centralize it in one location within the university. The type of information the university collects can be varied depending upon its needs. Typical questions might be:

- *What types of decisions are you regularly called upon to make?*

- *What types of information do you need to make these decisions?*

- *What types of information would you like to have that you do not have now?*

- *What information would you want daily, weekly, monthly or yearly?*

STUDENT
MARKETING
FOR COLLEGES
AND UNIVERSITIES

Examples of internal data that one might wish to collect would include: the number of students in each major over time, the revenue to expense ratio of each major, the number of hits to individual Web pages, trends in the number of inquiries for admission, the number of applications, the number of admits, and the overall enrollment. Other internal data that one would expect to collect would include trends in the development area such as annual giving, planned gifts, gifts per graduation year, or gifts broken down by alumni major even if the alums were dorm students or commuters.

Internal data is classified in marketing as "secondary data." Secondary data has usually been collected for another purpose and is normally easy to obtain and less expensive than other types of marketing information. Furthermore, obtaining secondary data is a good way for the researcher to determine a starting point in the strategic decision-making process.

While internal record systems supply decision-makers with the information about their own organization, especially information regarding the past, an important part of an institution's marketing information system are those sources of everyday information about developments in the environment beyond the institution. This information system should be designed to collect and analyze data concerning an institution's competitors, customers and environmental influences such as technological, demographic, economic and social/cultural influences.

Let us begin with an institution's competitors. Gathering information about the competition may conjure up images of "spy versus spy," but it is really not difficult or subversive. Most of the information an institution may need about its competitors is already available and accessible to the public. Some ways to learn about competitors are to read and carefully study their Web pages, observe competitor activities in the marketplace, and access third party information sources such as *The Chronicle of Higher Education* to collect needed information.

While some information is obviously proprietary, such as certain financial data or the exact amounts of alumni giving, much of what an institution needs to know is easily accessible. This includes information about majors, numbers of students, graduation rates, the ratio of endowment per student, and retention rates, as well as the competitor's strategic initiatives.

Two areas that must not be overlooked when assessing competitive information are the areas of leadership and future potential competition. One area of competitive analysis that is typically overlooked is the study of the decision-makers within the rival institution. Most individuals have certain predispositions in their behavior and thinking that they carry with them from post to post or institution to institution. Knowing types of initiatives and how aggressive or assertive a competitor's president or other administrative officers have been in the past will typically give a good indication of the type of behavior to be expected in the future. Secondly, one must remember to collect data on not just present competitors but those institutions that may be competitors in the future. For example, if the University of Phoenix does not presently have a market position within a community, the odds are that it

ACQUIRING & USING
MARKETING
INFORMATION
FOR STRATEGIC
DECISION-MAKING

will in the future. It is better to understand and anticipate the impact of such a competitor now than have to react to its presence later.

Environmental Trends

It is imperative that the university understand and track the environmental trends around it. While a college may not be able to directly impact these trends, they will certainly impact the college. It is therefore necessary to truly understand the character and impact of environmental forces upon the institution.

One of the obvious environmental trends that should be tracked includes the demographic shifts within the marketplace. It is no secret that the population of the United States is changing in its makeup. While much of the population, the baby boomers, are aging, the characteristics of the generations that have followed have progressively changed. The birth rate of Caucasian middle to upper-middle class people progressively dropped through the 1980s and 1990s and is not expected to recover. At the same time there has been an 18 percent increase in college-age men and women. This increase, however, is made up of predominantly African-American and Hispanic men and women. A commonly quoted figure is that by year 2010, one out of every five high school students will be Hispanic. These demographic shifts will have a major impact on institutions of higher learning throughout the United States. Many colleges will close in an effort to attract the "traditional" Anglo college student while others may wish to target "students of color." This type of strategic decision will impact an institution's procedures and structure.

Another fact of demography is that 22 percent of the population twenty-one and above already have a four-year degree; that means 78 percent do not. Knowing the demographic characteristics of those individuals in the 78 percent bracket has obvious implications for reaching out to "non-traditional students."

The impact of the economy needs to be tracked and taken into account. For example, federal cut backs in education have had major impacts on state universities and colleges. Public universities have experienced hiring freezes, tuition increases and lower graduation rates as a result of less federal dollars in their coffers. As a result, many public institutions are learning to behave and compete the way "privates" do. These institutions become more tuition-dependent as well as increasingly aware of fund raising necessities to offset the loss of federal dollars. Also, the strength or weakness of an economy can have obvious impacts on enrollment rates in graduate and professional programs. Many of these programs are dependent on tuition remission by employers that provide the benefit in stronger economic times and reduce it in weaker ones.

Institutions must be aware of social and cultural changes and trends that impact the university. One of the greatest over the past thirty years has been the number of women who have obtained and are obtaining their college degrees. In the 1960s only about 20 percent of college degrees went to women; today the figure is closer to 56 percent. This shift has had major implications for colleges and universities in that the needs and wants of female students are typically not the same as the traditional male student. Furthermore, colleges and universities have found the need to develop and hire faculty and staff to more closely reflect the current marketplace.

Another example of a social/cultural trend may be an increased emphasis on the teaching of values and ethics within the university setting. As newspaper headlines highlight the latest scandals in the business community and on Wall Street, such press may spark a boomerang effect in the classroom. Discussions in courses on the origin of these scandals and studying the issues surrounding them may be geared to avoiding them completely in the future.

Technology Trends

One of the greatest impacts on universities today is the rapid shifts in technology. These shifts not only affect how and where education and learning occurs, but also exert a tremendous impact on the cost of education. Technology shifts have enabled better educational tools to be developed. These include better communication between faculty and students via such programs as "Blackboard." Technology advances have also enabled multimedia techniques to be used in virtually every classroom in the college and university setting. Technology has allowed education to be delivered beyond the traditional classroom walls via online courses. This has allowed the university to access markets well beyond its traditional geographic area of competition. At the same time, it has allowed new competitors into the university's own backyard.

While technology has increased the university's options and potential level of quality it has not come cheaply. Universities now find themselves in a situation where the need for computer labs is increasing exponentially and at the same time the cost of these labs are greatly increased due to the rapid changes in software and hardware applications. With more and more technologically savvy customers, universities and colleges literally find themselves in a "technological arms race." It becomes imperative to provide students with the computer applications they need to learn and master in an effort to enhance their career opportunities.

Sources of Competitor and Environmental Information

As with information relating to a school's internal data, a great deal of what an institution needs to know about its competitors and environmental trends can be found in secondary data. There are numerous sources of existing (or secondary) information:

1. *Government.* The federal government publishes more marketing data than any other source in the country. Demographic information can be found in the census of a population, the census of housing, or the census of business. Special research reports issued by all levels of government can prove to be invaluable sources of data.

2. *Professional Associations.* Many well-known higher education professional associations regularly collect information about their members and about topics that interest their members. Organizations such as CASE (Council for the Support and Advancement of Education) or

ACQUIRING & USING
MARKETING
INFORMATION
FOR STRATEGIC
DECISION-MAKING

52

PART TWO
CHAPTER 5

ACE (American Council on Education) often obtain valuable information about target markets and competitor activities and trends.

3. *Firms.* Marketing research firms, marketing educational companies and media firms may possess old studies or syndicated data having considerable value.

4. *Published Sources.* Both the scholarly literature and the general business press can be helpful. Scholarly journals like the *Journal for the Marketing of Higher Education* can be useful for obtaining general ideas about marketing strategy and marketing research methods. Trade and business periodicals like *University Business* or *BIZ* also provide general ideas.

5. *Online Databases and Internet Data Sources.* By using commercial online data sources, marketers of higher education can conduct their own searches of secondary data sources. A recent survey of marketing researchers found that 81 percent use such online services for conducting research. Online databases are available to fill many marketing information needs. For example, a user can access a summary of the demographics of any zip code in the United States by using CompuServe to mine the *neighborhood report.*

In spite of the abundance of secondary data, there are limitations of which colleges should be aware. First, the specific information the higher education marketer needs may not exist. Second, secondary data must be carefully evaluated to be sure that it is relevant, accurate, current and impartial. It often becomes necessary to move beyond secondary data and collect primary data. Typically this is done through observational research or qualitative and quantitative methods. These techniques will be discussed in upcoming paragraphs.

Customer Analysis

Understanding an institution's customer is a basic tenet of marketing. This means knowing who they are demographically and behaviorally and their present needs and wants, as well as anticipating their needs and wants in the future. Much of the information a college may require about its customer base can be found through the same secondary sources the college used for taking its own internal snapshot as well as those of its competitors and the environment trends impacting it. Typical information obtained in this manner might be the age, gender and average income of its student population, or past perceptions and attitudes of an institution's student population obtained through standardized surveys like NCES (National Center of Education Statistics) or those done by the institution itself in past years. On the other hand, a college or university likely needs to go well beyond secondary data to truly understand its many publics. Collecting original data that addresses specific problems and answers specific questions is referred to as gathering "primary data." Collecting primary data is done through the marketing research process.

A useful definition of marketing research is as follows: the systematic design, collection and analysis and reporting of data relevant to a specific marketing situation facing an institution.

STUDENT
MARKETING
FOR COLLEGES
AND UNIVERSITIES

PART TWO
CHAPTER 5

53

A university will occasionally need to commission specific qualitative or quantitative marketing research. Qualitative research is designed to be exploratory in nature and cannot be projected for a larger population. Examples of qualitative research are focus groups and one-on-one interviews. Quantitative research is typically based on random samples and cannot be projected for a larger population. The most common type of quantitative research is surveys. For example, a university may wish to know what prospective students are looking for in their ideal educational experience or it may wish to understand the perceptions of the marketplace towards its institution in relation to competitors. Many studies can prove helpful to the school in such cases, but the organization must know how to choose the marketing research projects carefully, design them efficiently, and implement the results effectively, especially when working with the limited budget.

The responsibilities of marketing researchers in higher education include carrying out studies of market share, customer satisfaction, and image as well as market potential. While having an on-staff marketing professional offers certain advantages, very few universities have a full-service marketing research function. Instead, a person within the university may act as a liaison between the institution and the research firm that has the capabilities of designing and executing the research.

Working with external marketing research firms has several advantages, including gaining access to a level of expertise that is not available within the university, and maintaining objectivity in conducting research studies. Their expertise and objectivity can lead to higher response rates in surveys, more valid findings and more creative interpretations of results.

Employing a marketing research firm can be done indirectly or directly. Indirectly, a consulting firm or advertising agency that has already been brought to work on a particular project may suggest research and coordinate the project. There are a few drawbacks to the indirect approach. Using a consulting firm or advertising agency adds another layer of costs for the institution. Also, if an advertising agency has contracted with a marketing research company, it is likely that the solution to the problem under study will be promotionally based. It may be more helpful to hire a marketing research firm directly. Information about the existence and location of marketing research firms is readily available. The yellow pages, professional directories, conferences and an institutional representative's networking capabilities will locate many such alternatives.

In choosing a marketing research firm, however, the university should make sure the "fit" with the marketing research company is appropriate. This can be done by asking a series of questions which include:

- How well does the research firm understand the university's issues and requirements?

- How well do they answer questions?

- How do they do their research — for example, do they have a cookie cutter approach that they use for all of clients or is their research customized?

ACQUIRING & USING
MARKETING
INFORMATION
FOR STRATEGIC
DECISION-MAKING

54   **PART TWO**
CHAPTER 5

- How innovative are they?

- How easy is it to work with them? Are they responsible and flexible?

- What are the overall costs, including the cost of program development, implementation costs and the costs of the institution's reputation in the industry?

- Is there a comfort level and chemistry between the institution and the marketing research provider?

Collecting Market Research

Observational Research. One way to collect data is to carry out personal observations in various situations. For example, one may wish to observe students while they study to ascertain the types of resources and materials they use in the process. This may help to design learning spaces or library facilities. By visiting student dorms and observing how students work, interact and function, institutions may have a better idea of how to design the dorms of the future. Observational research is done to suggest issues to explore in more depth as well as qualitative interviews for more formal research studies.

Qualitative Research. Qualitative research can be used (1) to probe deeply into consumers' underlying needs, perceptions, preferences and the level of satisfaction; (2) to gain a greater understanding of marketing problems the causes of which are not known; and, (3) to develop ideas that can be further investigated through quantitative research. Qualitative research is not only a desirable first step, it is sometimes the only step permitted by limited budgets and can often help sharpen the marketing researcher's understanding of important issues.

Qualitative research typically takes one of two forms: individual interviews or group interviews called focus groups. Individual interviews, sometimes known as one-on-one or in-depth interviews, can be used to probe very deeply and are especially useful when the subject may be emotionally charged, because group conformity could bias the responses. For example, if the university was attempting to gain insights into a desired health and counseling center, some issues may not come up in a group of peers. In-depth interviews are also ideal for soliciting the viewpoints of experts because they allow for spending more time with each individual. For example, if a university is developing a new program or strategic initiative it may be helpful to interview an expert in the area to gain insights and avoid pitfalls during the process.

The second form of qualitative research, and probably the most common, is that of the focus group. A focus group consists of eight to ten people gathered for a few hours with a trained interviewer to discuss a program, a service, an idea or the institution. The focus group interviewer, or moderator, needs objectivity, some knowledge of the subject matter of the study, and an understanding of group dynamics and consumer behavior. Otherwise, the results can be worthless or misleading. A focus group usually starts with a broad question related to some research theme. For example, in a study that focuses on facility development students might be asked questions like, "What does

STUDENT
MARKETING
FOR COLLEGES
AND UNIVERSITIES

the ideal student center look like?" and "What services and facilities are provided within it?" Questions might then move to the subject of how well the present student center performs in providing the services discussed and what services it might provide in the future. As the focus group progresses, it is the job of the moderator to make sure that the discussion among participants is occurring freely and to focus the discussion on those issues the university wishes to better understand.

Within universities, focus group interviews have long been one of the major marketing research tools for gaining insight into student and other publics' thoughts and feelings. In many cases the results of the focus group interviews are used to guide the development of survey instruments for use in quantitative studies.

While focus group interviews are widely used, it is important that the university avoids developing a marketing strategy based upon information gleaned from focus groups alone. Participants in focus groups are not necessarily representative of the target market. This is especially true in universities that tend to select students who are most accessible and willing to participate. Furthermore, participants are typically paid for their time, offered refreshments and snacks and find the process entertaining. They may therefore be in a more positive frame of mind and more likely to give favorable answers than they would have otherwise given.

Quantitative Research. The purpose of quantitative research is to collect data that can be interpreted and projected to a larger population. This normally takes the form of surveys. Many within higher education take an overly simplistic view of survey work. They believe that writing surveys requires nothing more than asking a few obvious questions and finding the adequate number of people in the target market to answer them. Yet amateur research is liable to produce many errors and can waste anywhere from $5,000 to $100,000 of the institution's funds. Designing the reliable survey is the job of a professional marketing researcher. Issues and challenges that must be considered consist of:

- The construction of a questionnaire that obtains the information an institution desires and that cannot be misinterpreted by those answering the questions. Decisions revolving around questionnaire design would include: the choice of words to use, sequencing of questions, whether to use open or close-ended questions, and the type of scales to employ.

- Another important element of survey designs is the creation of a sampling plan. This includes identifying the sampling unit (who is to be surveyed), the sample size (how many people should be surveyed), the sampling procedure (how the respondents should be chosen), and the means of contact (how subjects should be approached).

The answers to these questions are not always obvious. As an example, consider the following situation to determine a sampling unit for the surveys as an example. If one wants to determine who influences student decisions in choosing a college, do they study peers, siblings, parents, guidance counselors, ministers, or all of the above?

In determining sample size, an institution must know exactly the objectives of the research and how certain it wants to be of the results. The more certainty required, the larger the sample size and the greater the costs.

With regard to sample procedure, whenever possible, an institution should achieve a random probability sample where all members of the population have a chance of being chosen. However, probability sampling is almost always more costly than non-probability sampling such as interviewing students in large class sections for the sake of convenience.

Finally, there are major differences between the means of contact used. While the choices are telephone, mail, personal, or electronic interviews, their advantages and disadvantages vary. Telephone interviewing is typically considered the best method for gathering information quickly and, in relation to the numbers and time involved, can be very cost effective. At the same time, many telephone surveys need to be relatively short. Mail questionnaires can be very inexpensive as a means of obtaining information, however, they are much more difficult to prepare and the return rate is usually low or slow. Personal interviewing is the most versatile of the methods available, however, it is also the most costly. Lastly, electronic interviews via the Internet can be very cost effective as well as fast, however, not all publics have access and are technologically savvy enough to fill out questionnaires online.

Types of Marketing Research Studies

There are a number of different types of marketing research studies a university or college may wish to consider. Among these are:

- Perception or image studies (probing how the university is viewed by current, past and prospective students).

- Competitive positioning studies (comparing the university to competing colleges on a range of quantitative and qualitative criteria by current, past and prospective customers).

- Performance evaluations (analyzing current and past clients' experiences with the university).

- Issues studies (examining customers' viewpoints regarding specific issues such as tuition, dormitories or the development of programs such as women's studies).

- Market demand/supply studies or trend analyses (investigating potential majors and/or programs for the university).

- Geographic studies (identifying locations for new branches of the university).

- Pricing studies (determining the impact of incremental tuition increases on enrollment).

- Benchmarking (comparing your institution's behavior and institutional procedures to those of competitors or aspirant institutions).

STUDENT
MARKETING
FOR COLLEGES
AND UNIVERSITIES

PART TWO
CHAPTER 5

57

- Media performance preference (determining how your publics prefer to receive information from you). Consider, for instance, whether prospective students prefer e-mail while alumni prefer print.

- Retention studies (investigating why students leave your institution before they graduate).

There are as many different types of marketing surveys that can be conducted as there are issues and problems facing the university. While each of these studies is helpful on its own or in any combination, each has its advantages and disadvantages. Once again, by using a professional marketing research firm, the university will increase its chances of using a survey technique best designed for its particular needs.

One tool that is particularly useful in identifying the university's strengths and weaknesses is the Importance Performance Matrix. The first step in this research technique is to identify those attributes that are important to an institution's clients in the delivery of a given service. Consider the case of a college seeking to identify attributes that potential students deemed as important when choosing a university or college. A focus group might yield the following factors: costs, location, academic reputation, personal attention, safety and quality intercollegiate sports programs among others. A quantitative study is then carried out through which prospective students are asked to rate the importance of each attribute as well as the university's perceived performance on each attribute. It is also helpful to assess the perceived performance of any competitors along the same attributes. Figure 5–1 shows an example of an Importance Performance grid for this fictitious university. (A separate Importance Performance grid should be prepared for each market segment.)

First, price is seen to be very important to this segment and this particular university appears to be on the expensive side. At the same time, the position of the location dimension on the grid indicates that this organization is not in an ideal spot in the minds of its prospective market. It would behoove the university in this situation to develop a strong argument for value over price and thereby move the price box into the right-hand top quadrant. Another potential strategy could be identified by the fact that personal attention is not that important to prospective students. Under these circumstances, the university will want to educate its publics as to the importance of personal attention in delivering a quality education, thereby positioning the institution in a stronger competitive light. Academic excellence is seen as something that is both important and an attribute of the university. This could be a differential advantage that the university wants to use in its communications, providing that its competitors are not seen as having an even stronger reputation.

Data Analysis and Report Presentation

The final step in the marketing research process is to develop meaningful information and findings to present to the decision-maker who requested the study. The words "meaningful information" are of key importance. The data must be gathered, analyzed, interpreted and reported in a manner that allows

ACQUIRING & USING
MARKETING
INFORMATION
FOR STRATEGIC
DECISION-MAKING

58   PART TWO
CHAPTER 5

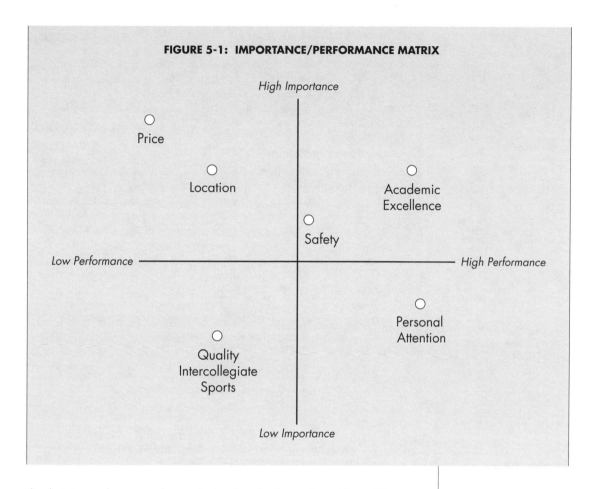

FIGURE 5-1: IMPORTANCE/PERFORMANCE MATRIX

High Importance

○
Price

○
Location

○
Academic
Excellence

○
Safety

Low Performance ——————————————————— *High Performance*

○
Personal
Attention

○
Quality
Intercollegiate
Sports

Low Importance

the decision-maker to use the newly developed information with confidence in addressing its strategic decision-making.

Marketing Research as an Investment and Not a Cost

One of the most common laments heard within universities is "I do not have a marketing research budget." Furthermore, marketing practitioners within colleges and universities may have a difficult time procuring a marketing research budget because those in higher levels of administration may not totally understand the value and necessity of solid marketing research and its impact on strategic decision-making. It is best to argue the need for marketing research as an investment rather than a cost.

Consider the following example: the average cost of tuition and room and board at a typical private university is somewhere in the ballpark of $25,000 per year. If the university is considering what by some may be considered extensive marketing research that totals $110,000 in costs, the enrollment manager must ask the question, "How many more students do I need to attract to pay for this research?" In other words, given the lifetime value of a

STUDENT
MARKETING
FOR COLLEGES
AND UNIVERSITIES

PART TWO
CHAPTER 5   59

student which includes four years of tuition and room and board as well as other fees and potential alumni dollars in the future, the marketer of higher education in this example would only need to attract one more additional student over the period of the first student's life to pay for the research. The question must then be asked, "What are the odds that professional marketing research will offer improved strategic decision-making to yield many additional students?"

Strategic Planning Revisited

These discussions clarify that developing a strong situational analysis can take time, effort and considerable amounts of money. However, the benefits of collecting this information far outweigh the costs. If this process is done correctly, the resulting strategic plan is infinitely stronger and can be followed with more confidence. Furthermore, based on the breadth and richness of the data collected in the situational analysis phase, the development of the following steps within the strategic decision plan should fall out of the data easily.

SWOT Analysis

The SWOT analysis answers the question, "Where am I now?" SWOT stands for Strengths, Weaknesses, Opportunities and Threats. The ultimate goal of SWOT analysis is:

1. To identify the institution's strengths in relation to their attraction to the marketplace and in comparison to competitors;

2 To identify and rectify weaknesses of the university in the eyes of its publics and in relation to its competition;

3. To identify, and have the ability to make informed decisions about, market opportunities as they are developing; and

4. To anticipate threats to the institution's wellbeing so that the university may be able to develop the strategies to minimize their potential impact.

The important thing for the marketer of higher education to remember is that a SWOT analysis must be developed and written from the perspective of an institution's target audiences. Furthermore, like many parts of the remaining strategic planning process, SWOT analysis may change depending on the target market being considered. For example, to a traditional undergraduate population, the perception that a university may have many social opportunities (or is known as a "party school") may be very attractive. However, a non-traditional student that is coming to campus at night may be concerned about his or her safety and see a "party school" atmosphere as being a weakness and something to avoid.

What the university places within its SWOT categories will vary with each institution and will likely change over time. Potential factors that may be included in a SWOT analysis might be:

ACQUIRING & USING
MARKETING
INFORMATION
FOR STRATEGIC
DECISION-MAKING

60   PART TWO
CHAPTER 5

- *Strengths* — a large financial endowment, located next to an ocean, a low teacher to student ratio, an excellence academic reputation, high name recognition developed through intercollegiate sports and/or academic programs and a large market share of an important market segment like the MBA.

- *Weaknesses* — high tuition in relation to competitors and a high level of tuition dependency for the institution's operating budget, a high dependence on adjunct faculty, antiquated facilities, and the opposite of anything found in the strengths category.

- *Opportunities* – some examples include: in a down economy a lower cost state university may be particularly more attractive than a private university with a significantly higher tuition, or the President of the United States visiting your campus during an upcoming academic year.

- *Threats* — the emergence of new competitors (both in traditional and online settings), continued unemployment in your geographical area, the potential of losing accreditation necessary for a competitive program, or lack of institutional will to enact necessary changes in an organization.

By creating a thorough SWOT analysis one can more accurately assess and prioritize, as well as articulate the next step in the strategic planning process: developing institutional goals and objectives.

Keeping Things Current

As discussed, by answering the question, "Where am I?" from the institution's market perspective as well as by facing the realities of its situation, the institution is essentially taking a snapshot in time of the university, its environment, competitors, and customer groups. This snapshot serves as a basis of the SWOT analysis as well as the remaining steps of a strategic planning process. It is imperative therefore that enrollment managers on a regular annual basis must take a new snapshot to determine where the university is now. One might ask if this is necessary assuming that a strong internal and external analysis should suffice for a number of years. In some areas such as demographic shifts that occur slowly and over time this may be the case, however, slow change is not universal, nor is it always perceptible.

Consider this analogy: If someone has grade school children, or nieces or nephews in grade school, one of the things that is part of school tradition is the annual school picture. It is not uncommon for a father to collect school pictures of his children in his wallet; as a new one is procured it is lovingly placed over the picture of the previous year or semester. During this process, he is likely to compare the picture from the present year to that of past years. At this time, he is likely to notice major differences in his child's appearance: he or she may have grown taller, thinner, more mature looking or some combination of the above. At the same time, over the course of that year he never noticed the changes occurring. Only when the snapshots are laid next to each other and compared do these changes seem obvious. The father is literally and figuratively too close to see the changes occurring.

STUDENT
MARKETING
FOR COLLEGES
AND UNIVERSITIES

Within the institution the same holds true. On a day-to-day basis, institutional administrators execute the tactics that make up the institution's strategic plan. Achieving one's goals is the primary objective, not focusing on the continual change in the environment, the institution and its publics. In the meantime, competition may have reacted to an institution's initiatives or taken the offensive themselves, its customer base may have become more educated and/or sophisticated in their decision-making process, or something may have happened in the environment that directly impacts the school (such as a chief competitor winning a national championship in basketball). Any of these changes, and hundreds more, may alter one's SWOT analysis and subsequent decision-making strategies. By regularly updating your internal and external data you are likely to stay abreast of changes and hold your lead on the competition.

The good news is that collecting and analyzing this information is easier the second and subsequent times in the future. Since the institution has already identified the sources of the information collected on a secondary basis, it simply needs to update the information. Any subsequent primary data collection is typically made faster and easier by the pre-existence of surveys already developed, research designs already in place and methods of analysis already determined.

ACQUIRING & USING
MARKETING
INFORMATION
FOR STRATEGIC
DECISION-MAKING

62   PART TWO
CHAPTER 5

IDENTIFICATION OF STRATEGIC PRIORITIES AND OPTIONS

DAVID CROCKETT
Senior Vice President
Noel Levitz, Littleton, CO.

A s author Lewis Carroll so aptly stated in his classic Alice's Adventures in Wonderland, "If you don't know where you are going, any road will get you there." So it is with marketing, recruitment, and retention efforts for many colleges and universities. This chapter is designed to explore the importance of clearly identifying institutional enrollment-related priorities, options, and goals. It is based on the premise that this is best accomplished in the context of a thoughtful planning process that includes annual tactical and longer-term strategic thinking, decision-making, and planning.

Planning does not ensure results, but it does provide disciplined appraisal, goal setting,prioritization, and strategizing that can minimize failure. A well-conceived plan is simply an organized thought process and communication tool that describes *what* the institution wants to achieve and *how* it will be accomplished. It has been said there are two excellent ways to fail: Do an equally good job of everything (because all things are not equally important), or do an excellent job of the wrong thing.

A thoughtful planning process helps to set meaningful enrollment goals and identifies the most important priorities and activities necessary to achieve those goals.

Strategic Enrollment Planning

The strategic enrollment plan defines the goals and key strategies that will guide the enrollment-related initiatives and activities for a period of the next three years. The plan should provide institutions with a thoughtful, clear, organized, and longer-term approach to more effectively managing enrollment. The strategic enrollment plan should be reviewed and updated annually as appropriate. Chapter 13 provides a description of creating an institution-wide marketing plan.

Why is there a need for engaging in strategic enrollment planning?

The central purpose of strategic enrollment planning is to influence the size of the student body and to influence the types of students that enroll. These issues are strategic issues. Strategic enrollment planning shapes the character, quality, and effectiveness of the institution. Enrollment must be planned. It must be planned not once, but continually as an institution and its environ-

STUDENT
MARKETING
FOR COLLEGES
AND UNIVERSITIES

PART TWO
CHAPTER 6   63

ment change. Because the annual and long-range strategic enrollment plans are both dependent on external environmental changes, it is constantly a "work in progress." So, while the end result is a written plan, it is continually evolving. Colleges and universities typically face a daunting list of issues and challenges that have the potential of impacting the desired enrollment state. Responding to these issues and challenges requires that the enrollment plan be under continuous review and modification. Following are some examples of these issues and challenges:

- Annual fluctuating enrollments

- Transfer and articulation issues

- Under- and over-subscribed majors/programs

- Mix of student body

- Admissions policies and practices

- Institutional image/position

- Long-term enrollment goals and strategies

- Preferred student profile and strategies for recruitment

- Identifying institutional vulnerability and development of recommendations for addressing issues

- Assessing institutional policies and procedures as they affect enrollment

- Defining minimal skills level for students to be successful

- Analyzing services needed to retain and graduate students with different experiences and learning needs

- Forecasting enrollment

- Cultivating programs for academically talented and under-prepared students

- Addressing organizational climate issues that are obstacles to achieving enrollment goals

- Strategizing to determine and implement a state-of-the-art enrollment program

- Reviewing/revising institutional missions

- Changing/shaping institutional image

- Changing the student profile (academic, geographic, demographic)

- Reviewing/revising the portfolio of programs and services

- Building involvement in commitment to strategic directions among the institution's constituents

- Developing appropriate growth strategies (e.g. product development or market development)

- Implementing strategies designed to improve the quality of student life and learning

- Target marketing and segmentation

What is the difference between annual tactical planning and longer-term strategic planning?

Annual enrollment planning should not be confused with long-range strategic enrollment planning. While they are obviously related and may use some of the same techniques, they are quite different in time frame, scope, and purpose. Tactical enrollment planning is performed annually and is concerned with the "here and now." Strategic enrollment planning is performed less frequently, is primarily the responsibility of senior management, and focuses on fundamental decisions and actions that shape the long-range nature and direction of the institution. The strategic enrollment plan is also generally less detailed and broader in scope and purpose than the annual enrollment plan. Both types of planning activity are important to enrollment success.

The following are differences between the annual enrollment plan and the strategic enrollment plan.

- The long-range strategic enrollment plan is driven by the overall institutional strategic master plan: Where does the institution hope to be in three-to-five years? How will enrollment affect this vision?

- The long-range strategic enrollment plan is broader in scope and is more abstract in terms of the strategies to achieve the goals and objectives.

- The long-range strategic enrollment plan incorporates longer-term strategies to achieve long-term enrollment goals of the institution (e.g. size, shape, quality, geographic make-up, and diversity).

- The long-range strategic enrollment plan places more emphasis on the external environment, product, and marketing strategies (e.g. local and national demographics, competition, SWOT, curriculum, and facilities).

Each type of plan is the result of a different type of planning process. The differences between the annual tactical enrollment planning and long-range strategic enrollment planning processes are best illustrated by examining the characteristics of the long-range strategic enrollment planning process. These include:

- Long-range strategic enrollment planning is a continuous process.

- The long-range strategic enrollment plan is more concerned with doing the right thing than doing things right.

- The long-range strategic enrollment plan seeks advantages from existing internal and external conditions, that is, synergistic effect.

- Long-range planning seeks to define an institution's mission, role, and scope.

- Long-range strategic enrollment planning emphasizes change through external and self-examination; hence it does not remain static.

Correcting deficiencies in tactical enrollment fundamentals is what generally results in short-term enrollment success and is typically the primary focus of the annual enrollment planning process. For many institutions, long-term enrollment growth and stability will require a more strategic approach that includes:

- Reviewing/revising institutional mission

- Changing/shaping institutional image

- Changing the student profile (academic, geographic, demographic)

- Reviewing/revising the portfolio of programs and services

- Building involvement in and commitment to strategic directions among the institution's constituents

- Developing appropriate growth strategies (e.g. product development or market development)

- Implementing strategies designed to improve the quality of student life and learning

- Target marketing and segmentation

- Product improvement

Concentrating on the longer-term strategic enrollment issues rather than tactical issues, generally involves a heavier reliance on market research, a more complex decision-making process, attention to organizational change strategies, and a longer lead-time with more patience for success. Longer-range strategic planning, while involving the campus community, is typically within the purview of the senior administration.

What are the steps in developing the strategic enrollment plan?

There are many different styles of long-range plans. The exact format adopted by an institution is of little importance. However, what the plan includes is crucial. There are four key activities associated with the compilation of a long-range strategic enrollment plan. These involve:

1. Conducting a situation analysis

2. Developing three- to five-year enrollment related goals

3. Identifying strategies to achieve goals

4. Assigning responsibility and estimating preliminary major costs to implement strategies

The product of each of these activities forms the core of the long-range strategic enrollment plan itself. Each activity leads to a narrative section of the plan addressing these key elements. The contents of the long-range strategic enrollment plan are the drivers for the annual recruitment or annual marketing plan.

Conducting a Situation Analysis

Conducting a situation analysis is a precursor to establishing enrollment goals and strategies. Chapter 5 also discusses situational analysis. Following is a brief review of the activities associated with situational analysis:

- Reviewing the institutional mission statement that describes the basic reason for the existence of the college/university.

- Reviewing the institutional strategic plan, if one exists: the strategic plan and desired enrollment state need to be consistent with each other.

- Assessing current strengths, weaknesses, opportunities, and threats, or driving forces (which combine *strength/opportunities*), and restraining forces (which combine *weaknesses and threats*). These driving and restraining forces represent many of the forces that must be overcome, and exploited, in order to achieve the enrollment goals.

- Compiling and reviewing historical enrollment, recruitment, and admissions data, both overall and by specific program, if available. Basic funnels should be included in the situation analysis, as well as appropriate research pertinent to the decision-making process (e.g. source code analysis, territorial analysis, conversion and yield analysis, campus visit analysis, ACT/SAT analysis, competition and market share analysis).

- Reviewing appropriate demographic trends and environmental data:

  — High school and other important markets

  — Graduation rates and projections

  — Migration patterns (percent expected to stay in-state or leave state for college)

  — Preferred majors by high school graduates

  — ACT/SAT test score analysis

  — Education attainment patterns of adults in the primary market

  — Job/industry trends in the primary market

- Evaluating any information from recent competition studies, to include:

  — Five-year enrollment patterns

  — Tuition and institutional aid of primary competition

  — Key recruitment themes and messages (as seen on competition Web sites, and in their literature)

  — Market share of your institution compared with primary competition

- Reviewing results of recent market survey research, to include:

  — Lost inquiry study

  — High school counselor survey

STUDENT
MARKETING
FOR COLLEGES
AND UNIVERSITIES

PART TWO
CHAPTER 6   67

— Admitted student questionnaire survey (for enrolled and non-enrolled students)

- Using data to confirm target markets

> **"If we could first know where we are, and whither we are tending, we could then better judge what to do and how to do it."**
>
> — Abraham Lincoln

What is a recommended individual program/major marketing/recruitment process?

In addition to the elements contained in a situation analysis, many colleges and universities could also benefit from a more systematic analysis and planning process particularly for under-enrolled programs/majors. The following model can be adapted to individual institutional situations and preferences.

Recommended Individual Program Marketing/Recruitment Analysis and Planning Process Model

1 Discuss program planning and analysis process with program area.

2 Collect and/or compile quantitative program data.

3 Determine/analyze program conversion and yield rates.

4 Hold a planning forum.

5 Conduct student focus groups.

6 Establish program goals.

7 Determine the program-specific strategies.

8 Integrate program-level plans with other existing enrollment plans.

9 Achieve program enrollment goals.

These nine steps are described in greater detail below.

Step One: Discuss the Program Planning and Analysis Process With the Program

This initial step secures the support and commitment of the program area and examines the goals of the process. It needs to be made clear that this is not an evaluation of either the program or its instructional staff. Instead, the purpose is to review the program from an enrollment management perspective.

The process is designed to accomplish the following objectives:

- To communicate the importance of instructional staff involvement in enrollment planning

- To give instructors ownership in marketing/recruitment plans

- To review past and current enrollment trends

- To review conversion ratios

- To conduct a marketing needs analysis

- To determine competitive features and benefits

- To establish enrollment goals

- To establish program-specific marketing/recruiting strategies and activities

- To determine instructor role responsibility in recruitment

- To communicate the importance of the instructor's role in marketing/recruitment

- To review program-related marketing/recruitment communications

- To reach a consensus on a program marketing/recruitment plan

Step Two: Collect and/or Compile Quantitative Program Data

The purpose of this step is to gather the necessary quantitative data to better understand the program from an enrollment-planning viewpoint. The following is typical of the types of information that should be analyzed:

- New student enrollment. New student enrollment (including transfers) is a measure of the effectiveness of the marketing/recruitment effort.

- Headcount enrollment. A headcount of students who have enrolled in a program during a three- to five-year period of time provides an overall measure of program popularity and viability.

- FTE enrollment. It is important to examine the historical trend line of FTE generation to determine whether growth, stability, or decline is evident.

- Retention rates. Student retention is one means of measuring a program's interest in, and efforts towards, encouraging students to remain enrolled in the particular program. Percentage increases or decreases in attrition are compared with institutional, system, or national standards.

- Program-related placement. A goal of almost all programs is to provide students with employment-related knowledge and skills or preparation for graduate school. One of the most effective measures of attaining this goal is the rate at which graduates of programs who seek graduate school entry or employment are successful.

- Number of graduates. Program enrollments that are stable or increasing will be reflected eventually as an increased or stabilized rate of degrees

STUDENT
MARKETING
FOR COLLEGES
AND UNIVERSITIES

PART TWO
CHAPTER 6   69

awarded. By examining the historical trend over a three- to five-year period, increases or decreases can be calculated.

- Student satisfaction. Students enrolled in specific programs should be surveyed on a periodic basis regarding their perceptions and opinions about major program elements.

- Average unit cost. If financial data are available concerning the yearly direct cost for each FTE enrolled in the program, these data can be used for a trend line analysis to pinpoint shifts in the average cost of the program. Any shifts can be studied in depth to determine the factors responsible.

Step Three: Determine/Analyze Conversion and Yield Rates for the Program

This step involves determining the number of inquiries, applications, deposits, and enrollees for the program. This analysis of the "program admissions funnel" results in a better understanding of the program's enrollment behaviors, strengths, weaknesses, and opportunities. The following rating scheme may be helpful:

MARKETING/RECRUITING NEED

Classification	Definition
A	A high-priority program that is consistently under-enrolled and requires special marketing and recruitment efforts.
B	A solid program that generally makes enrollment and requires continuing marketing/recruiting efforts to remain strong.
C	A low-priority program that consistently meets or exceeds enrollment: characterized by waiting lists and/or filling early in the recruitment cycle. A "C"-rated program needs minimal marketing/recruiting effort to maintain student awareness.
D	Insufficient information, or requires additional review before marketing/recruiting need can be determined.

CHAPTER 6

IDENTIFICATION OF STRATEGIC PRIORITIES AND OPTIONS

70

PART TWO CHAPTER 6

MARKETING/RECRUITING EMPHASIS	
Classification	Definition
1	Primary need is to increase the size of the inquiry pool with qualified inquiries.
2	Primary need is to improve the conversion rates between each stage of the admissions process from inquiry to applicant.
3	Primary need is to increase both the number of inquiries and the conversion rates.
4	Marketing/recruitment emphasis is not clear and further data or analysis is needed to classify.

The marketing concept inherent in the above rating scheme is that, with limited time and resources, institutions should first place marketing/recruitment emphasis on under-enrolled programs in order to strengthen their enrollment and viability. If they fail to respond to increased marketing and recruitment efforts, then obviously a decision needs to be made to eliminate or modify the program. This strategy is not intended to "starve" successful programs of marketing/recruitment emphasis, but rather to simply maintain awareness and enrollment in "healthy" programs while focusing limited resources on those programs that require special attention in order to achieve the desired enrollment position.

Step Four: Conduct a Program Planning Forum

This step gathers the input and recommendations of the program's instructional staff on a number of important enrollment issues. Some examples of topics that are typically discussed include:

- What should the enrollment goals for the program be?
- What are the best inquiry-generation strategies for the program?
- What program promotional themes and messages should be communicated to prospective students?
- What are faculty willing to do to aid the program marketing/recruitment effort?

Step Five: Conduct Student Focus Groups

Focus groups comprised of students majoring in the program can also produce useful insights and help to sharpen and focus the promotional themes and messages. Typical questions generally include:

- Where did you first hear about this program?
- What attracted you to this program?

STUDENT
MARKETING
FOR COLLEGES
AND UNIVERSITIES

- Do you have any concerns about this program?

- Where/how did you seek information about the program?

- Who influenced you to enroll in the program?

- What would you tell prospective students about this program?

- What are the strengths/weaknesses of the program?

- What are your perceptions of why some students do not complete the program?

Step Six: Establish Program Goals

The chief enrollment manager, in conjunction with other appropriate senior administrators, must establish enrollment goals for the program. These may be expressed as new students, headcount, or program graduation rate goals. Program-level goal setting may also identify qualitative as well as quantitative goals.

Step Seven: Determine Program-Specific Strategies

The chief enrollment manager, using the information obtained during the program planning process, must then determine the specific strategies and action programs that will be necessary to achieve the program enrollment goals. Each action plan should include the following:

- What is it that you are going to do? Provide a specific description of the activity that is generally quantifiable and measurable.

- When will it be done? Establish timetables that clearly show key dates and deadlines.

- Who will be responsible? Define clear assignments of responsibility for performing important tasks.

- How much will it cost? Include budget information showing the cost of implementation.

- How will you know if it has been accomplished? Define methods of evaluation or control that will be used to monitor progress or measure success or failure of the actions planned.

A draft of the program plan should be shared with the program staff for additional suggestions or modifications. Chapter 8 contains a discussion of how to identify, delineate and implement tactics.

Step Eight: Integrate Program Plans into the Institution's Marketing/Recruitment Plan

The individual program plans need to be integrated into the institution's master enrollment plan for implementation, along with appropriate control and evaluation measures. At this stage, the enrollment manager will have to allocate the resources required to pursue the program-level objectives. As the program-level tactics are integrated into the larger enrollment plan, opportunities for recruitment and promotional efficiencies may be identified. Some tactical objectives may be obtainable by "tuning" existing efforts while others will be entirely new outreach efforts.

Step Nine: Assess Progress Toward Program Enrollment Goals

The ultimate criterion of the effectiveness of the individual program's enrollment analysis and plan is whether they achieve the program's enrollment goals. The process described above can significantly increase the likelihood that the institution will successfully achieve the predetermined goals in under-enrolled programs. In this step, the outcomes are compared with the goals established in step six to determine if the intended results have been achieved. The results of this comparative analysis may indicate that "re-planning" is in order.

What is the appropriate role for instructional staff in attracting and retaining students?

The individual program analysis process described above invariably leads to questions pertaining to the appropriate role and responsibility of faculty in attracting and retaining students. This is a question thoughtful enrollment managers ponder as they seek to involve faculty in meaningful and appropriate ways in recruiting and retention. Virtually all studies of factors influencing college choice indicate the importance of availability and perception of quality of academic major/program. Likewise, a consistent finding in retention research has been that positive interaction with faculty correlates directly with whether students persist to graduation.

The faculties at institutions of higher education are tremendous assets. These people represent the very best of what the institution has to offer potential students. With this in mind, it is important to take full advantage of this strength in the marketing/recruiting process. Faculty involvement in campus recruitment programs nationally has been varied, somewhat fragmented, limited, informal, and not particularly well managed on many campuses. Some of the ways that faculty can be utilized in the marketing/recruitment process include:

- Participate actively in campus visits by talking with students interested in their programs

- Approve marketing/promotional materials pertaining to their program

- Telephone identified "Top" admitted applicants (personal marketing)

- Assist as necessary at special on-campus visit days

- Attend specific promotional activities identified by recruitment staff

- Volunteer to speak to high school classes

These are just a few of the ways that faculty can contribute toward a successful marketing/recruiting effort. These people are good representatives for the campus and they should be highlighted and utilized where appropriate without over-burdening them. A number of factors impact the role of instructional staff in marketing/recruitment activity:

STUDENT
MARKETING
FOR COLLEGES
AND UNIVERSITIES

PART TWO
CHAPTER 6   73

- Interest and inclination of individual faculty members in aiding and abetting the recruitment process

- Time limitations and competing legitimate priorities

- Enrollment status in their program

- Attitudes and beliefs about the appropriate role of instructional staff in marketing, recruitment, and retention

- Expectations for involvement communicated by the administration

- Clarity of requests for assistance by the enrollment staff

The following principles should govern faculty involvement in efforts to attract and retain students:

- First and foremost, faculty is primarily responsible for providing high-quality instruction.

- The faculty's on-campus role is more important than an off-campus role to the success of an enrollment program.

- Quality and availability of faculty can be a very important consideration in a student's decision to attend a college or university.

- Marketing/recruitment is a campus wide commitment and responsibility and, as such, must include faculty. This does not imply that faculty should be expected to become professional marketers or recruiters. In other words, let faculty do what they do best (teach!).

- Some defined part of instructional responsibility should be designed to support the enrollment effort (this arrangement needs to be negotiated and will vary by institution, program, and extent of other responsibilities).

- The support expected of faculty members should be clearly articulated and understood by the faculty, the enrollment team, and the administration.

- The faculty who will be involved need to be carefully screened. Some faculty members are highly effective in the enrollment process while others might be detrimental in the effort to reach enrollment goals.

On the following page is a sample survey helpful in discussing and clarifying the most appropriate role of instructional staff in recruiting and retention efforts.

SURVEY OF ROLE AND RESPONSIBILITIES OF FACULTY IN ATTRACTING AND RETAINING STUDENTS

	Strongly Agree	Agree	Disagree	Strongly Disagree
1. First and foremost, faculty is responsible for teaching and facilitating student learning.				
2. Attracting and retaining students is a responsibility of both instructional and student services staff.				
3. Faculty, recruiters, any student service staff have roles and responsibilities in attracting and retaining students.				
4. Instructional staff is important in a student's decision to attend an institution.				
5. Some defined part of faculty responsibility should be in support of the institution's recruitment effort.				
6. Faculty should represent the institution and their respective programs at off-campus recruiting events.				
7. Faculty should assist in the development of specific program information to be used in promotional activities.				
8. Faculty should organize program-related presentations/ workshops for high school teachers and students.				
9. Faculty should provide timely input and feedback on all program-related promotional materials (e.g. letters, brochures, media advertising).				
10. Faculty should support recruitment and retention planning by assisting in specific departmental strategizing.				
11. Faculty has a key role in identifying students who are experiencing academic or other difficulties.				
12. Faculty should be available during scheduled campus visit days.				
13. Faculty should be available to talk with campus visitors.				
14. Faculty should engage students outside of the formal classroom setting.				

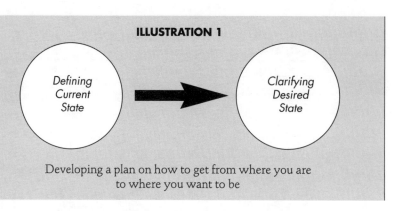

ILLUSTRATION 1

Defining Current State

Clarifying Desired State

Developing a plan on how to get from where you are to where you want to be

Determine the Desired Enrollment State and Establish Enrollment-Related Goals

Most colleges and universities need to clarify and sharpen their desired enrollment state annually and for a projected three- to five-year period. Specific and quantifiable desired enrollment states are not commonplace in higher education. Responses to questions about the desired enrollment state typically elicit the following general responses:

- More and better students
- More full-time students
- More day students
- More adult students
- Increase enrollment as far as facilities will permit
- Increase enrollment in under-enrolled programs
- More out-of-state students
- More high ability students
- More full-pay students
- More students of color
- More distant learning students

While the above statements represent a beginning in defining desired enrollment state, further refinement and specific annual and long-term enrollment goals are needed at most campuses.

Determining a *realistic* desired enrollment state requires that an institution consider a large number of interdependent variables. Some of these are:

- The financial needs and limitations of the institution
- The capacity of the physical plant
- The instructional capacity of the institution

- The political ramifications of either significantly increasing or decreasing enrollments

- The demands – and limitations – inherent in the market place

All colleges and universities need to:

- Determine a process for establishing the desired enrollment state – a process that assesses all of the interdependent variables noted previously

- Define the desired enrollment state for the year and for a projected three- to five-year period

The institution's desired enrollment state, once determined, must always be sanctioned at the highest administrative levels of the institution and shared institution wide. Setting clear and realistic enrollment goals is a key fundamental to achieving enrollment success. Overly ambitious enrollment goals greatly increase the probability of failure. Conversely, the establishment of less ambitious goals may increase the chances of success but also diminish the enthusiasm and commitment of those charged with the responsibility for achieving those goals. It has been said that a goal without a plan is a dream; a plan without goals is a listing of activities.

What are some possible categories of enrollment related goals?

Following are some possible categories of enrollment-related goals that a college or university might consider in defining the annual or longer-term desired enrollment state:

- Headcount

- FTE

- FTIC (freshmen)

- Transfers

- Concurrent enrollments

- Program/major

- Instruction sites

- Ability

- Day/evening/weekend

- Gender

- International

- Racial/ethnic

- Geography

- Graduate

- Special talent

- Continuing education enrollment

STUDENT
MARKETING
FOR COLLEGES
AND UNIVERSITIES

- Distant learning
- Retention and graduation rates
- Indicators of student success

Few, if any, institutions would establish goals in *all* of the above categories. For most institutions, the effort required to mount tactical level activities to effectively pursue goals in all of the areas identified above would overwhelm their capabilities. When too many goals are pursued it becomes difficult to pursue any single goal in a way that insures success.

How are enrollment goals best determined?

Enrollment goal setting is as much of an art as a science. The most common methods of determining goals include:

- Reviewing historical enrollment data
- Conducting an environmental scan to ascertain what external and internal factors could impact enrollment results
- Employing some old-fashioned "S.W.A.G." (scientific wild-ass guessing)

Goal statements should not be set unrealistically high. They should be challenging yet attainable. The institution should avoid setting just one goal that is used for the budget, as there is no room for contingency with this strategy. Instead, at lease two goals should be set:

- An internal budget goal that is known only to members of the president's cabinet and the chief enrollment officer (if he/she is not a member of the cabinet); and
- An external recruitment goal that is clearly articulated in the marketing/recruitment plan and can be shared with anyone who is interested in the recruitment effort for that particular admissions cycle (e.g. faculty, parents, high school counselors, prospective students, student phone team, and tour guides).

The internal budget goal will be lower than the external goal, building in some contingency. This type of goal setting assumes that goal setting is not occurring from the "top down" but jointly between admissions and the president's cabinet. Sometimes a third goal is set in the office of admissions that is slightly higher than the external goal but still realistic. If the institution chooses to set a third goal, it should be an internal goal known only to the admissions team. There is a tendency for the more ambitious admission office goal to "creep" into institutional budgeting systems. If this more ambitious goal is not achieved, the institution then finds that its revenues are below expectations.

How should goal statements best be written?

Following is a suggested way to formulate concise, results-oriented goal statements:

To <u>increase</u> <u>new student headcount enrollment</u> by <u>25%</u>
    (action)   (subject)   (standard)

no later than <u>Fall (year)</u> at the _____ campus.
       (deadline)   (site)

What are some examples of enrollment goals?

Following are some actual annual and longer-term enrollment-related goals developed by institutions of higher education.

Four-Year University

Overall goal – Enroll a total of 2,200 new students for Fall 2003, consisting of 1,500 new freshman and 700 new transfer students. This is compared to 1,862 new students in Fall 2002 (1,190 FTIC/672 transfer).

First-Year (FTIC) Students

The following table contains the recommended FTIC goals for Fall 2003.

EXAMPLE UNIVERSITY
FTIC Enrollment Figures: Fall 1997 through Fall 2001 and 2003 Goals

Stage	2003 Goal	2001	2000	1999	1998	1997
Inquiries	15,000	13,312	13,369	12,964	13,437	12,511
Conversion Rate	*22.0%*	*19.5%*	*18.7%*	*19.6%*	*16.8%*	*17.7%*
Applications	3,300	2,536	2,495	2,587	2,261	2,203
Acceptance Rate	*82.5%*	*83.0%*	*82.9%*	*85.9%*	*85.0%*	*87.4%*
Acceptances	2,725	2,106	2,068	2,221	1,921	1,925
Yield Rate	*55.0%*	*56.5%*	*58.6%*	*58.9%*	*55.2%*	*60.0%*
Enrolled	1,500	1,190	1,212	1,307	1,060	1,156

The proposed FTIC recruitment goals require the university to increase the inquiry pool to at least 15,000 and achieve a conversion rate of 22 percent (versus a five-year average of 18.4 percent). The acceptance rate is mainline and, as previously mentioned, we would expect the yield rate to decline slightly in light of a 30 percent increase in applications. Generally, when an institution increases the size of its applicant/accepted pool, it will experience a decline in the enrollment rate because growth in the applicant pool will occur among students with a lower level of initial commitment to the university. This is natural and to be expected. Example University has significant opportunities to increase the number of inquiries received as well as the

STUDENT
MARKETING
FOR COLLEGES
AND UNIVERSITIES

PART TWO
CHAPTER 6   79

quantity and quality of contact with students at this stage of the college-choice process.

In addition to the "funnel" goals, Example University recommended the following additional FTIC goals for Fall 2003.

- Seek an entering class with an average high school grade point average of 3.2 or better and an average ACT score (or equivalent) of 23 or better

- Seek 10 percent domestic-minority-representation in the entering class (150 students)

- Seek six percent out-of-state representation in the first-year class versus three to five percent in recent years

- Increase new student enrollment in the College of Arts and Sciences by 125 students

- To build an inquiry pool of 18,775, up from 15,684 in 2001, consisting of the following (with 2001 totals in parenthesis):

    — 4,775 solicited inquiries (3,984)

    — 7,000 travel initiated inquiries (5,850)

    — 5,000 student initiated inquiries (4,172)

    — 2,000 referral initiated inquiries (1,678)

Transfer Students

The following table contains the recommended transfer goals for Fall 2003.

EXAMPLE UNIVERSITY
Transfer Enrollment Figures: Fall 1997 through Fall 2001 and 2003 Goals

Stage	2003 Goal	2001	2000	1999	1998	1997
Inquiries	3,775	2,372	2,213	1,946	2,109	1,937
Conversion Rate	*45.0%*	*70.4%*	*73.2%*	*80.0%*	*78.1%*	*79.4%*
Applications	1,700	1,669	1,619	1,557	1,649	1,538
Acceptance Rate	*79.4%*	*78.8%*	*77.3%*	*79.4%*	*84.3%*	*69.8%*
Acceptances	1,350	1,316	1,252	1,236	1,391	1,073
Yield Rate	*51.9%*	*51.1%*	*54.0%*	*53.2%*	*54.4%*	*51.7%*
Enrolled	700	672	676	658	757	555

In light of the increased competition from Midstate University resulting from its ability to offer four-year degree programs in education and selected arts and science programs, Example University recommended far more conservative transfer student goals. In fact, Example University stands to lose as many as

100 students per year because of Midstate University's expanded offerings; therefore, staying essentially even in transfer enrollment probably represents a significant accomplishment. Example University projected an increase in inquiries resulting from some recommended inquiry-generation strategies (see next section) and improved inquiry-level data management. Other than that, the proposed transfer goals are very similar to what was accomplished for Fall 2001. No qualitative goals are recommended for the transfer population.

Territorial Goals

Example University is instituting a program of territorial management for the first time during the 2003 recruitment cycle. Under this model, members of the admissions staff are assigned responsibility for specific geographic market areas and the students each contains. The following table contains the territorial assignments and goals for 2003.

EXAMPLE UNIVERSITY
Territorial Assignments and Goals for Fall 2003

Counselor	Territory	Application Goal	Enrolled Goal
John	Service area	1,000	500
Nancy	Northern counties	450	220
Sue	Southern counties	425	205
Fred	Western counties	425	210
Mary	Eastern counties	750	275
Sam	Out-of-state	250	90
FTIC Sub-Total		*3,300*	*1,500*
Dean	Transfer students	1,700	700

Supporting Enrollment Goals

- To increase the positive image and awareness of the college as measured by baseline perception research of target markets.

- To improve and enhance the institution's market position and prominence.

- To increase new student enrollment of the direct-from-high school market by five percent for Fall _____ from the following "feeder" secondary schools (list high schools).

- To increase new adult student market enrollment by three percent for Fall _____.

- To achieve the following new student individual program enrollment goals for Fall _____ (list enrollment goals by program).

- To increase Fall _____ new student enrollment by 15 percent in the following under-enrolled programs (list targeted under-enrolled programs).

- To increase Fall _____ new student enrollment of students of color by five percent.

- To increase the number of high academic ability new full-time students for Fall _____ as measured by improved academic profile (e.g. assessment scores and high school rank in class).

Sample Retention Goals

Overall Goal: The overall goal is to improve the quality of student life and learning through improvements, modifications, and additions to the institution's educational programs, services, and facilities.

Goal One: Achieve an annual return rate of 58 percent for first-time, full-time freshmen entering the institution in Fall _____.

Goal Two: Increase the annual return rate by two percent each year for first-time, full-time freshmen entering in the fall in years _____, _____, and _____.

Goal Three: Achieve a cohort graduation rate (in five years) of 40 percent for new students entering the institution in Fall _____.

Goal Four: Increase the term-to-term persistence rate of part-time students effective with the _____ academic year.

Goal Five: Achieve a "performance gap" (i.e., the difference between importance/expectation and satisfaction ratings) of 7.5 or less for the college's programs and services as measured by results of the Student Satisfaction Inventory (SSI).

Some final thoughts on enrollment goal setting

The following points are important to the goal setting process:

- Goals are a clear expression of the important outcomes of the marketing, recruitment, and retention program.

- Goals are derived directly from the enrollment planning process.

- Effective enrollment plans begin with a clear understanding of the goals that must be achieved in order to succeed.

- Generally, marketing, recruitment, and retention plans contain no more than one overall and six to eight supporting goal statements.

- Goals should be stated as simply and concisely as possible.

- Goals are most often, but not always, expressed quantitatively and relate to desired enrollment outcomes. If a goal is not measurable, it should at least be recognizable and qualitative in character.

- Goals must always be supported by one or more strategies (enabling objectives).

- Goals should be mutually agreed upon by those who must achieve them.

- Goal setting is important and necessary but not a complicated or time-consuming task.

Identifying and Selecting Key Strategic Priorities and Options

The next step in the planning process is to formulate appropriate key strategies. Like goals, these key strategies should be hierarchical, measurable when appropriate, clear, specific, and realistic. Spend the necessary time to ensure the formulation of the key strategies that will produce the best results.

Strategies are broad statements of something that is important to do but does not identify how it will be done. Some people prefer to think of enrollment strategies as enabling objectives, enrollment fundamentals, or critical success indicators (CSI's). Regardless of what they are called, the failure to identify and implement key enrollment strategies will prevent institutions from achieving their full enrollment potentials.

Use the 80/20 rule to make the enrollment plan a truly effective document. Remember, the 80/20 rule states that 80 percent of the results generally are derived from 20 percent of the effort. The challenge is to know which "key" 20 percent to focus on to produce 80 percent of the results. Identifying key strategies, however, is not sufficient: they must be implemented to be effective. Key strategies, by definition, deserve the lion's share of attention. On a day-to-day basis, it is very easy to be diverted from the key 20 percent. One of the most important functions of the enrollment manager and the enrollment plan is to keep staff attention focused on the actions critical to determining enrollment success or failure.

Further, avoid the temptation to develop too many "key" strategies. An effective marketing, recruitment, and retention plan might have between 15 and 20 key strategies – more than 20 could mean that staff may divide their attention indiscriminately and limit their effectiveness.

Listed below are some key strategies critical to most successful marketing, recruitment, and retention programs at colleges and universities. This list is not intended to be exhaustive. A college may select appropriate strategies from this list and include others that are unique to the institution. The examples are not necessarily in order of importance. In constructing key strategies it is helpful, but not necessary, to quantify them whenever possible and appropriate.

Common Key Marketing/Recruitment Strategies

- Increase image and awareness of the college in targeted markets.

- Generate a sufficient number of inquiries of the right type and mix to achieve enrollment goals. The inquiry program will include student-initiated contacts, student referrals, travel inquiries, and all forms of solicited inquiries.

STUDENT
MARKETING
FOR COLLEGES
AND UNIVERSITIES

PART TWO
CHAPTER 6

83

- Implement an expanded and sequential written and out-bound electronic communications system with prospective students from inquiry to enrollment to achieve targeted conversion and yield rates.

- Expand the number and quality of the college's promotional publications that support the marketing and recruitment programs.

- Automate the admissions office to manage the communications flows, support telecounseling, track inquiries, and produce management reports to monitor progress towards enrollment goals.

- Implement a systematic and ongoing state-of-the-art telecounseling program (using trained and supervised student callers) designed to enhance conversion and yield rates. This program will also utilize professional staff, faculty, and other volunteers.

- Conduct special events and on-campus visit programs that include the use of current students, alumni, and faculty. The number and type of programs should maximize the number of campus visitors and the conversion and yield goals.

- Compile and maintain a comprehensive enrollment database management information system to support enrollment planning, decision-making, and monitoring progress toward goals. The database should help monitor and evaluate all activities of the enrollment program.

- Develop an effective volunteer recruitment program that includes the use of current students, alumnae, faculty, and parents.

- Administer a financial aid program that supports the achievement of new student enrollment goals.

- Design and conduct an ongoing program of staff development/training and foster a recruitment and admissions climate that is goal-oriented, rewards achievement, is physically attractive, and provides an opportunity for professional growth and development by individual staff.

- Implement a program of relationship management in the college's recruitment effort.

- Develop a college wide system for capturing and coding all inquiries.

- Systematically qualify the college's inquiry and applicant pools in order to concentrate time and resources on those prospective students targeted by the college and most likely to enroll.

- Develop special marketing and recruitment initiatives to increase enrollment and/or strengthen demand in the following under-enrolled programs. (List programs.)

- Develop and execute an internal communication plan directed at faculty, staff, and administration to better inform them of marketing/recruitment issues, enrollment targets, efforts and activities, and outcomes.

IDENTIFICATION OF
STRATEGIC PRIORITIES
AND OPTIONS

- Develop and maintain relationships with key influential individuals or groups (e.g. high school counselors, teachers and principals, social agencies, area employers, advisory committees, parents/spouses)

- Establish an organizational structure for recruitment that ensures adequate staffing, authority, responsibility, and accountability for achieving enrollment goals.

- Conduct modest market research to obtain information on how the college is perceived in its primary market and to identify more clearly key marketing messages and themes.

- Evaluate the effectiveness of the annual marketing/recruitment plan and make necessary modifications for the next recruitment cycle plan.

Common Key Retention Strategies

- Improve delivery of freshman intake services

- Improve academic support services

- Improve effectiveness of the academic advising program

- Improve classroom instruction

- Integrate individuals into the educational and social life of the institution

- Respond more systematically to the needs of "at-risk" students

- Conduct retention/attrition research

- Address major areas of student concern and dissatisfaction

- Make improvements to physical plant

- Encourage wider participation in extracurricular activities

- Provide faculty/staff development programs

- Revise admissions materials and procedures to improve student/institutional fit

- Mandate assessment and course placement

- Increase frequency of out-of-class contact among faculty, staff, and students

- Implement an "early-alert" system

- Modify the delivery and timing of financial aid

- Provide enriched or accelerated academic experiences

- Implement an extended orientation program

- Provide special services for adult learners

- Implement an institutional quality service management strategy

- Develop a comprehensive approach to undecided/exploratory students

- Involve college community in effort to improve the quality of student life and learning (retention)

Moving From Current to Desired Enrollment State – A Final Word

Moving a college or university from current to desired enrollment state involves a three-step process as depicted in Figure 6–2.

1. *Developing the Fundamentals of the Enrollment Program:* Successful enrollment programs are driven by sound fundamental strategies, systems, and procedures, just as are successful athletic teams, musicians, and businesses. The fundamentals of a successful marketing, recruitment, and retention program include:

   - Exceptional enrollment leadership (e.g. enrollment champion, commitment of executive management team, board)

   - Image- and awareness-building strategies

   - Clear and realistic goals

   - A comprehensive written enrollment plan (marketing, recruitment, and retention)

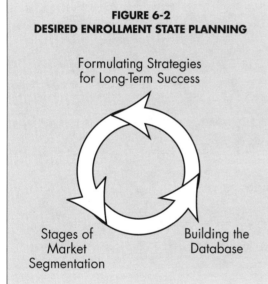

FIGURE 6-2
DESIRED ENROLLMENT STATE PLANNING

Formulating Strategies
for Long-Term Success

Stages of
Market
Segmentation

Building the
Database

   - An effective organizational structure

   - A trained and talented enrollment team

   - Adequate resources (e.g. budget, staff, technology, facilities)

   - Effective operational processes (e.g. data entry, file processing, internal communication, recruit-back program)

   - Powerful management information systems

   - Development of an adequate inquiry pool

   - Effective and efficient methods of managing the enrollment funnel (e.g. qualifying and grading)

   - Purposeful written, telecounseling, electronic, and personal communication systems and programs

   - Management reporting and monitoring of progress towards goals

   - A competitive scholarship and financial aid program

   - An institutional service philosophy and student-centered policies and procedures

   - Organization and delivery of quality academic programs

   - Quality and availability of student support services and programs (e.g. career services, advising, first-year student programs)

- Faculty commitment to student success and supportive teaching styles

- Programs that serve targeted at-risk populations

- Individualized intervention programs (e.g. early-alert, mentoring)

The first step in the transition process is to address the deficiencies in enrollment fundamentals and to do so quickly and effectively as possible to maximize short-term enrollment results.

2. *Building the Comprehensive Enrollment Management Database:* While building and refining enrollment fundamentals can lead to short-term success, long-term enrollment growth and change will result from improvements in *product* – not *process*. The enrollment database is composed of primary and secondary research that will support institutional enrollment planning and decision-making. The components of a comprehensive enrollment database include:

- Historical admissions, financial aid, and enrollment data

- Operational admissions and financial aid data

- Demographic and population trends and projections

- Environmental scan data

- Competition information

- Attitude, belief, and perception data, including:

- Focus-group interviews

- Formal survey research (telephone/mail)

- Retention and attrition research studies

- Student satisfaction data

The market research component of the transition process is designed to assist an institution to assemble a comprehensive database that will aid and abet enrollment planning and decision-making.

3. *Formulating Strategies for Long-term Success:* For many colleges and universities, long-term enrollment growth and stability will require repositioning the institution among its competitors and establishing a distinctive market niche. At this stage, the institution is able to build upon the experience of improving the enrollment fundamentals combined with the data available from the research study to facilitate or participate in an institutional planning process that might include:

- Reviewing/revising institutional mission

- Changing/shaping institutional image

- Changing the student profile (academic, geographic, demographic)

- Reviewing/revising the portfolio of programs and services

STUDENT
MARKETING
FOR COLLEGES
AND UNIVERSITIES

PART TWO
CHAPTER 6   87

- Building involvement in and commitment to strategic directions among the institution's constituents

- Implementing strategies designed to improve the quality of student life and learning

- Target marketing and segmentation

- Product improvement

The Growth Strategy Matrix

The following *Growth Strategy Matrix*, common to most introductory marketing courses, can prove to be a useful tool for thinking about enrollment-related strategic options within the context of colleges and universities:

Marketing theory suggests that all types of organizations, including colleges and universities, can select from among the four possible growth strategies described briefly below:

Market Penetration relies on capturing a larger market share by penetrating current markets more deeply with existing programs and services. Success is achieved by improving the communication systems and promotional messages, and by innovation in the form of more aggressive marketing and recruitment strategies and tactics. Most colleges and universities have growth potential on which they can capitalize by increasing their market penetration through more effective implementation of enrollment fundamentals. Market penetration is the least costly and the least risky of the four growth strategies.

FIGURE 6-3
GROWTH STRATEGY MATRIX

	Existing Products	New/Modified Products
Existing Markets	Market Penetration	Product Development
New Markets	Market Development	Diversification

Market Development relies on developing new geographic or demographic markets – students who are not currently being served by the institution. Distance learning, multiple learning site strategies, and new market development are typically market development strategies. This strategy obviously has cost implications and is more risky than market penetration. Nonetheless, it continues to be a viable long-term growth strategy for many institutions.

Product Development relies on product enhancements – developing new or modified programs or services – to attract students from the same general market area and to achieve higher retention rates as a result of increased student satisfaction. Product development strategies generally are directed at current markets and are best driven by the institution's knowledge of and expertise in the market it serves best. Product modifications, enhancements, or innovations require time for development and implementation before they can be promoted to new students or have an impact on the satisfaction levels of current students. In the field of higher education, the time required for product development can be excessive: two years or longer may elapse before students enroll specifically because they are attracted by improved products/services. Product development should be an important and continuous long-term enrollment growth strategy at virtually all institutions of higher education.

Diversification involves developing a new product that appeals to a new geographic or demographic market. This strategy usually involves the greatest combination of cost and risk. Diversification is not, in general, a highly viable growth strategy for higher education.

While market and product development should remain important long-term strategic growth approaches for most institutions, market penetration represents the best short-term tactical growth strategy.

It should be noted that identifying and selecting strategies to pursue often involves more than the growth strategies described above. Institutions should consider a wide array of other strategic approaches such as:

- Maintaining the enrollment status quo

- Downsizing enrollment

- Changing price and net revenue performance

- Enhancing the quality of student life and learning (retention)

- Changing admissions selectivity criteria

The planned change structure/diagram implies that organizational change results from a series of carefully planned transitional steps that lead systematically towards a clearly defined enrollment state. Only after assessing present state in relation to some desired enrollment state can an institution establish which strategies will move it most effectively and efficiently towards the desired condition.

Enrollment is a multi-variant phenomenon and does not lend itself to a one-time, casual analysis. Change in the desired enrollment state requires multiple strategies implemented effectively over several years. It is important to note that there are generally no "quick fixes" or "silver bullets" for complex enrollment problems.

Moving a college/university towards its desired enrollment state begins by building and refining the fundamentals of a successful enrollment program. Enrollment fundamentals, supported with market research data, can be developed into research-based enrollment and institutional strategic enrollment strategies and plans. The strategies and plans are then implemented and evaluated before the entire process recycles with necessary and ongoing modifications as the institution moves toward its desired enrollment state.

In closing this chapter, it is wise to heed the admonition of nineteenth-century English essayist and reformer John Ruskin:

> "What we think, or what we know, or what we believe is, in the end, of little consequence. The only consequence is what we do."
> — John Ruskin
> *19th Century English Essayist and Reformer*

STUDENT
MARKETING
FOR COLLEGES
AND UNIVERSITIES

MARKET SEGMENTATION

THOMAS HUDDLESTON
Vice President, Student Development and Enrollment Services

&

OLGA IVANOVA
Research Assistant
University of Central Florida

CHAPTER 7

The universe of higher education comprises various market segments. These segments could include alumni, business leaders, affecting agents, and prospective students. Each segment has certain needs, motivations and defining characteristics. In reality, the fundamental marketing concept is based on an exchange relationship. This relationship is based on a "value perceived: value received" standard. If "student costs" are equal to or less than what attendance at a particular university requires, the chances of strengthening the prospective students' interest is enhanced.

Prospective student "costs" may include not only net tuition but also psychological and social issues, such as campus appearance, unfamiliarity with other students enrolled, distance to the college from home, etc.

The marketing literature distinguishes between two major types of markets: homogeneous and heterogeneous markets. Within the homogeneous markets, a large proportion of students have similar requirements for a product or service. The type of strategy applied to homogeneous market is undifferentiated strategy, which means that the market is considered as one aggregate whole and no segments are distinguished within the market.

Heterogeneous markets are recognized as containing students with different characteristics. Classifying the buyers as part of one group or another depending on the similarities among them in terms of product needs is called *market segmentation*. Students and potential students are now considered more and more as consumers and the market for higher education is recognized as being heterogeneous (Tonks, D.G. & Farr, M., 1995).

There are two types of marketing strategies applied to the heterogeneous markets: undifferentiated and differentiated targeting strategy. Undifferentiated targeting strategy means that an organization does not divide the market into meaningful segments and addresses the total market with one or more strategies. As an example, there would be no different market strategies for student segments that attend different secondary schools, ethnicity background, place of residence, or intended area of study in college.

However, differentiated targeting strategy means that an organization targets two or more segments by designing a separate marketing program for each of them (Pride/Ferrell, 1999). Thus, an organization can attain greater revenue and a deeper position within each market segment. Separate marketing

STUDENT
MARKETING
FOR COLLEGES
AND UNIVERSITIES

programs might focus on selected characteristics including test scores, income levels, gender, ethnicity or community college students.

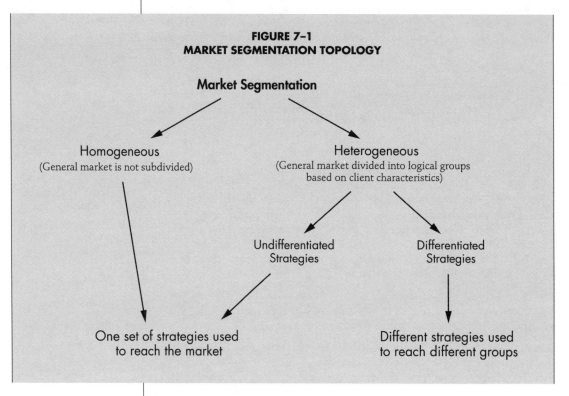

FIGURE 7–1
MARKET SEGMENTATION TOPOLOGY

Segmentation Variables

Marketers differentiate among four major categories of segmentation variables: demographic, geographic, psychographic, and behavioristic (Pride/Ferrell, 1999).

Demographic Variables.

Traditionally, the demographic variables are the most frequently used segmentation variables. Students' wants, preferences, and usage rates are very often associated with demographic variables. Demographic variables are easier to measure than many other variables. Often when a non-demographic variable is used, it is very likely that it will be linked back to demographic characteristics (Kotler, P., 1982). For example, when using benefit segmentation, such as learner needs, it is very possible that marketers will relate to the age and income level of the learners to segment the market of higher education.

The market should be divided into different segments on the basis of demographic variables, such as age, gender, family size/life cycle, family lifestyle, income, occupation, education, religion, race, and nationality.

Age. Age is a very important segmentation variable in the marketing of higher education because students' wants and capabilities change with age. For example, many colleges introduce evening programs to meet the needs of the continuous adult learners seeking higher education who are unable to attend day classes.

Gender. In the area of higher education, gender segmentation is applied in terms of gender-specific colleges: female and male. Within a single gender, further segmentation can be used. With the increasing gender gap between men and women, and with women earning more Bachelor's, Master's and Ph.D. degrees than ever before, colleges are becoming more involved in marketing efforts to attract more men to their campuses.

Income. This segmentation variable plays a very important role because income level determines the accessibility of a certain school and/or a program. The availability of financial assistance and introduction of pricing strategies are important factors that can impact the effect of costs on the decision-making process of prospective students.

Religion. In the United States, there are many higher education institutions with religious affiliation, i.e., the 28 Jesuit Catholic colleges are examples of institutions with religious affiliation. The religious affiliation plays an important role when deciding on what marketing tools should be used to successfully reach the target audience. In the above-mentioned example, students of Catholic parents become a key market in the selection of prospective students.

Race. This is an important demographic variable because it is often used to promote the local state government or the Federal government policy. For example, Florida's Governor Bush adopted the "One Florida" plan into his official admission policy, thus ending the formal race-based admissions within the public universities.

Nationality. This demographic variable is appropriate when an educational institution emphasizes the diversity of its campus community. For example, even though only 3.3% of the student body at University of Central Florida (UCF) comprises non-resident aliens, the university tries to accommodate the needs of the international students by creating an International Students and Scholars Services Center. This department is specifically designed to address the problems of international students and help them understand and comply with the rules and regulations of the university, the state and the country. In addition, to facilitate the financing of their education, the university offers some scholarships, fellowships and other types of financial assistance.

Demographic Trends When demographics are used to segment the market for higher education, the demographic trends have to be analyzed in order to anticipate and prepare for the possible changes in the content of the student body. The American families are changing in terms of the fact that there are fewer marriages, fewer students, higher divorce rates, working spouses and aging parents – the so called "sandwich generation" where the person is pressured by taking care of both his or her children and parents at the same time. In addition to these trends, there are more non-family couples; there is a geographic shift from north to south, more demand for higher education and an increase in the proportion of the ethnic population.

STUDENT
MARKETING
FOR COLLEGES
AND UNIVERSITIES

Many college administrators are concerned with their enrollment because the states with the most colleges, such as Massachusetts, New York, Pennsylvania, Ohio, Michigan, Illinois and Indiana, will have practically no population growth through 2010. They will be looking for students from the states with high growth rates, such as California, Florida and Texas. Conversely, students are becoming more demanding in terms of the quality of the academic programs offered, the faculty expertise, location, campus life and future professional placement (Michelle, M.L. & Brent, C.D., 2001).

Another important demographic trend is the new gender gap. According to a recently published article in *Business Week*, "... in every state, every income bracket, every racial and ethnic group, and most industrialized Western nations, women reign, earning an average 57% of all Bachelor's Degrees and 58% of all Master's Degrees in the United States alone." If this demographic trend continues, there will be 156 women per 100 men earning degrees by 2020 (M. Conlin, 2003). As mentioned above, the colleges and universities might change their recruitment policies in order to adjust to the demographic change, attract more male students and reinforce their respective missions.

Geographic Variables.

When geographical segmentation is applied, the market is divided into different geographical entities, such as nations, states, regions, counties, cities, zip codes or even neighborhoods, based on the notion that consumer needs vary geographically. For example, a university in Florida has five branch campuses offering programs adapted to the needs of the nearby inhabitants. The students who chose these campuses may be "place bound," or, the university may be willing to increase its diversity by being involved in numerous diversity programs. Also, adopting geographic variables to segment the market for potential students provides an opportunity to target the needs and interests of out-of state students better and eventually attract more of them to the university campus.

Geo-demographic Segmentation. This is a type of market segmentation that clusters people in zip code areas and smaller neighborhood units based on demographic information and lifestyle (Pride/Ferrell, 1999). The latter includes income level and purchasing power. Geo-demographic analysis is widely used for recruitment of students in the United States. It is a powerful tool for identifying, locating, and attracting suitable potential students. Many vendors now employ geo-demographic analyses to not only identify market segments across the potential student body, but also to communicate with the selected target segments through both conventional media and more personalized methods. (D. G. Tonks & M. Farr, 1995).

In geo-demographics, a common assumption is that students of families with certain lifestyle characteristics will be more likely to respond to those universities comprised of students and families of similar life styles. Generally, these findings are more prevalent in smaller clusters. Today, these findings can be identified more easily through zip codes and high school graduate enrollment analysis.

When geo-demographic segmentation is used, approximately 40 different cluster groups can be identified. These cluster groups are segmented and eventually become target groups based on the institution's needs. It will not be productive for a university to try and use all the available cluster groups nor to apply strategies for each group. Eventually, the university uses targeted clusters to identify prospective students, understand inquiries, select applicants, and retain students. The university usually employs strategies to support all the steps of the process. In addition, the cluster groups should fit the university's strategic profile.

Cluster groups, once identified, can be sorted by zip codes and by neighborhood block areas. Communication is one way to deal with the target groups. Different messages would be tailored to the lifestyle of the target market. For example, the high socio-economic group will have great appreciation of tradition; they are more mobile; distance is not an issue; and they are interested in studies abroad. Another example of a strategy that uses cluster groups is that used to reduce tuition.

Psychographic segmentation.

According to Philip Kotler, in psychographic segmentation, buyers are divided into groups on the basis of their social class, lifestyle, or personality characteristics.

Social Class. This is defined as relatively stable and homogeneous divisions in which individuals or families sharing similar values, lifestyles, interests, wealth, status, education, economic positions, and behavior can be categorized. Targeting various zip or postal codes facilitates social class segmentation. Zip codes give information on the social status without the need to collect additional information from respondents other than addresses (Blackwell, *et al.* 2001). There are six social classes in the United States:

(1) upper uppers (less than 1%);

(2) lower uppers (about 2%);

(3) upper middles (12%);

(4) lower middles (30%);

(5) upper lowers (35%); and

(6) lower lowers (20%).

Social classes show distinct consumption preferences in the nonprofit area, including the area of higher education (P. Kotler, 1982).

Lifestyle. Within a social class, different lifestyles can be found. By collecting information on people's activities, interests and opinions, marketers have found that they can categorize different lifestyles and cluster them in different groups.

Behavioristic Segmentation.

In behavioristic segmentation, students can be divided into groups on the basis of their knowledge, attitude, use, or response to an actual product or its attributes. Many marketers believe that behavioristic variables are the best starting point for constructing meaningful market segments (P. Kotler, 1982).

STUDENT
MARKETING
FOR COLLEGES
AND UNIVERSITIES

PART TWO
CHAPTER 7   95

Benefit Segmentation. In the context of higher education, benefit segmentation is the division of the market that sees a benefit in pursuing higher education.

One type of benefit segmentation is learner-based segmentation, which is based on learner's needs (Rogers *et al.* 2001). This type of segmentation is an attractive alternative to the conventional method of segmenting the market using demographic or geographic variables. Learner-based segmentation studies the individual differences of the student body in terms of expected benefits, expected educational outcome, and types of needs.

According to the segmentation scheme of Rogers, Finley and Kline, there are six learner segments:

1) *Career-Oriented Segment* – Learners who are attending an educational institution in order to prepare for future career changes.

2) *Curiosity-Driven Segment* – Students whose quest for knowledge represents their ultimate goal.

3) *Socio-Economic Advantage* – Learners seeking the status of obtaining a university or college degree

4) *Stepper* – Learners who want to build on their first degree with more education (i.e., a graduate degree or post-graduate degree).

5) *Undecided* – Individuals not knowing specifically why they are attending university or college; often motivated by external factors, such as peers or family.

6) *Dual-Purpose Segment* – Learners that are interested in pursuing their primary interest in athletics or performing arts while obtaining a university degree.

If an organization adopts the learner-based segmentation approach, there are several institutional areas that will be affected, such as organizational image, recruitment techniques, curriculum policy, student services and fund raising.

Loyalty Status. An educational institution might study those loyal to it to find out the basic satisfactions they derive from affiliation. Afterwards, it should try to attract others who are seeking the same satisfactions (P. Kotler, 1982).

Figure 7–2 presents a high level approach for segmenting markets within a complex university offering academic programs throughout the full range of degree levels. Without additional segmentation, it is in reality a homogeneous approach to market segmentation in that a large proportion of students in the post-secondary learning population have similar requirements for a product or service – a baccalaureate or master's degree.

The model presented in Figure 7–2 implies that all individuals in a cell will be recruited using the same strategy. Thus, all prospective students in the baccalaureate degree market regardless of individual characteristics would be approached in the same fashion. Figure 7–3 shows how individual heterogeneous segments can be derived for each of the larger markets shown in Figure 7–2.

FIGURE 7–2
HOMOGENEOUS MARKETS FOR HIGHER EDUCATION
BY TIME STATUS, LEVEL OF STUDY & DEGREE

| | Continuing Education & Certificate | Undergraduate | | Graduate | | | |
		Associate	Bachelor's	Master's	Doctoral	Professional	Other
Full-time							
Part-time							
Virtual							
Other							

FIGURE 7–3
SAMPLE HETEROGENEOUS SEGMENTS FOR HOMOGENEOUS GROUPINGS

| | Continuing Education & Certificate | Undergraduate | | Graduate | | | |
		Associate	Bachelor's	Master's	Doctoral	Professional	Other
Full-time							
Part-time							
Virtual							
Other							

Demographic	Geographic
Age Sex	Region State
Income etc.	ZipCode etc.
Behavioristic	**Psychographic**
Benefits Learner Based	Life style Social Class
etc.	etc.

Definition of Target Markets

After the process of market segmentation is completed, each segment is being analyzed and evaluated on the basis of its attractiveness and potential profitability. One or numerous segments may be selected as target segments. This means that the organization will direct its marketing efforts toward these particular segments. Those market segments will comprise the *target market* of the higher educational institution.

Target Markets Versus the Universe

Focusing on the most attractive market segments as opposed to targeting the market as a whole has important advantages.

Gibbs and Knapp recognize the process of market segmentation and selection of target markets as having three basic attributes:

- Increased value, which can lead to higher realized profit since the marketing effort will be specifically directed to the segments that show higher profitability potential;

- A better match with customer needs, by developing a different marketing mix tailored to specific segments so that marketers can satisfy the customers' needs and better meet their expectations; and

- The ability to exclude those segments that do not match the requirements of the students and/or programs, which affects the bottom line of each marketing campaign.

Understanding Primary, Secondary and Tertiary Markets

The Primary Market. In the context of higher education, the primary markets are defined as high-yield in terms of the number of applications received over a particular period of time from one or a number of high schools, community colleges, or other educational institutions. The primary markets can be looked at as given geographic areas within a certain radius of the university (W. Ihlanfeldt, 1980). Careful analysis should be given not only to the applications received but also to the yield of those applications to accepted, and eventually to enrolled, status. Too often institutions continue to focus on high application areas that have low yields and high recruitment costs.

Usually, the primary markets of an institution are within a five-hour drive of its location. Few institutions, if any, are "national," which means that they attract students from throughout the nation in significant numbers. An institution should continuously cultivate its primary market even if it yields a constant flow of students without any significant effort on the part of the institution. This condition may not persist over time, and the institution may have to place greater reliance on its primary market in the future to offset a serious enrollment problem or to achieve desired growth in enrollment. Moreover, the competition should be analyzed and the actions of the major competitors within the institution's primary market must be thoroughly evaluated. The rule of thumb is that an additional investment in the primary market should always yield a greater return than a similar investment in a secondary market.

The Secondary Market. The secondary market is typically a lower-yield market in terms of the number of applications and enrollments. In a geographic sense, the secondary market is usually larger than the primary market. Even though the secondary market is a low yield market, an educational institution may redirect its resources to enlarge it for strategic reasons including greater diversity of students from different locations and secondary schools. This strategy becomes less difficult when the institution's academic reputation becomes more prestigious or if new programs are offered that reflect better the market demand from different locations and secondary schools (W. Inlanfeldt, 1980).

The Tertiary Market. In the geographic sense, tertiary markets usually include random students from educational institutions and geographic regions without a discernable pattern. For a small college or university, the tertiary market may be larger than the primary and secondary markets combined. Within the same educational institution, the primary, secondary and tertiary markets may differ among the different colleges, majors, programs, etc. For example, the primary market for the School of Optics (CREOL) at the University of Central Florida is comprised of mainly international students, most of which come from Asia and Europe.

In addition, the primary, secondary and tertiary markets are very dynamic and they can change drastically over time. For example, since the end of the Cold War, the countries from Eastern Europe produce an increasing number of students that come to the United States to pursue their Master's or Ph.D. degrees. Today, for some colleges and majors, particularly graduate-level programs, those students comprise their primary markets.

Identifying Target Markets

The easiest way an institution can identify its primary target market is to analyze the patterns of applications and enrollments of the current student body by general demographic characteristics. If simple records have been preserved showing the number of students submitting applications, the number accepted, and the number enrolling by high school within a particular geographic area, identifying the primary market should be a relatively simple task.

The process of identifying the secondary markets has to be cost-effective since the return on investment is lower in comparison to the primary market. Thus, very often when identifying secondary markets, the school's alumni, small family receptions and focused communication programs are the main resources used, and the time spent should be directly related to the expected return. The amount of staff time devoted should increase proportionately to the success of the strategies employed. Success could be defined as increasing the number of applications and matriculations within an area.

For most educational institutions, it is not financially feasible to identify the tertiary market and spend significant resources on targeting them.

Tailoring the Marketing Mix

After the market for higher education has been segmented and the target markets have been identified, the tools for communicating with the target audience have to be properly selected and used. The traditional marketing mix includes the four P's – ***product, price, place, and promotion***. Today, the traditional mix has been expanded to include the four C's – ***costs, convenience, customers, and communications***.

Product leadership in the area of higher education can be achieved when a college or university offers a unique combination of location, top quality

STUDENT
MARKETING
FOR COLLEGES
AND UNIVERSITIES

PART TWO
CHAPTER 7   99

faculty and a prestigious reputation. Again, understanding the fundamentals of the exchange relationship is important.

The actual tuition rate charged and paid is the **price** element of the marketing mix. In certain occasions, higher education is viewed as commodity when the students decide to attend a particular educational institution based solely on price. Sustainable competitive advantage can be achieved when an institution has "relatively" low price and "comparatively" high quality of product offering. The price to be paid may be compared with the expected value, time to be expended, perceived faculty expertise, and the quality of the academic facility. The expected value should exceed the price paid in order for the prospective student to matriculate.

Price represents one of the most controllable of the P's for most institutions. Colleges and universities manipulated this dimension through the careful application of student financial aid. In many institutions the "published price" bears little relationship to the actual costs paid by the majority of its students.

When discussing the price element of the marketing mix, price elasticity plays a very important role. Price elasticity measures the sensitivity of potential or current students to changes in the tuition price. Low price elasticity means that the change in the price will have almost no effect on the decision making process of potential or current students. Low price elasticity is very often positively correlated with the loyalty of current students.

One example of a pricing model is the process in which the college or university decides to allocate financial funds to a small proportion of its students that have the best secondary school academic records. The college or university provides scholarships or other rewards for their good academic performance. The funds for this target group may be taken from students with low price elasticity or less mobility.

The **place** where a certain educational institution is located is very important in terms of student mobility. Many prospective students want to attend an institution within a predefined distance from their primary residence. Institutions beyond this radius will have a difficult time attracting this kind of student. Other students, however, have no predefined parameter with respect to distance. These individuals exhibit a tendency to be highly mobile, that is, they will often travel great distances to attend a college or university that provides the program or educational experience they are seeking.

Promotion is a tool for communicating with the target audience. It prohibits capturing the reaction of the targeted segment. Promotion, in the classic sense, is a one-way effort. The institution seeks to make more of its products and services known to the prospective student through outreach efforts like radio, television and newspaper advertising. The primary characteristic of classic promotional campaigns is that they do not have a built-in feedback mechanism – they do not involve a two-way exchange of information.

As noted earlier, the marketing mix today incorporates the so-called "four C's" approach, including customer, cost, convenience and communication. The **customers** are the potential students willing to attend a particular educational institution and pay certain tuition, or **cost**. **Convenience** is related to location and academic schedule, ease joining the academic community and the other factors including such basics like parking and the availability of public transportation.

Communication may include two basic forms: conventional media and direct or personalized tools. The conventional tools include telemarketing, mailings and announcements on the radio, television or cable, magazines and newspapers, billboards, etc. In addition to the conventional media, many colleges and universities employ a personalized approach in order to reach their target audiences. An example is the personal mailing sent to selected business graduates from the public universities in Florida. Thus, the Florida university promotes its business school in general and the graduate business program in particular.

Admissions offices use several other communication formats. At the forefront are college Web sites and e-mail programs. The use of these electronic media varies from a static Web page to an interactive portal to the development and communication of a personal viewbook. Automated e-mail and personal call phone promotions are also used.

Often, communication tools can be segmented into mass, direct, small group and person-to-person. Each of the segments has a particular focus that fits best the stages involved in a college choice process. Figure 7–4 portrays this segmented interaction:

FIGURE 7–4
SEGMENTATION OF COMMUNICATION TOOLS

Confrontation Strategies	Student Understanding			
	Awareness	Comprehension	Conviction	Commitment
Mass Confrontation: Publicity, Press Releases, Feature Stories, Advertising, Public Addresses, Web	40%	10%	5%	5%
Direct Confrontation: Case Statements, Viewbooks, Posters, Magazines, Direct mail, Web Segment, E-mail	40%	50%	20%	10%
Small-Group Confrontation: College Nights, HS visits, Receptions, Campus Visitations	10%	20%	35%	15%
Person-to-Person Confrontation: Phone calls from staff, Volunteers, Interviews, Meetings with faculty	10%	20%	40%	70%

The market for higher education is broad and diverse. Segments within the market have different needs and wants and respond to different messages.

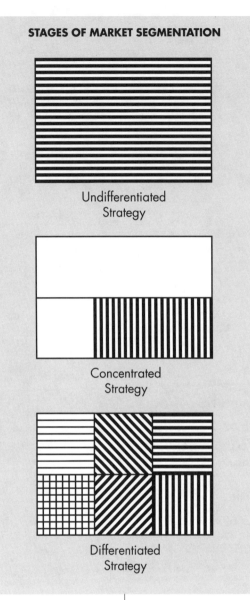

STAGES OF MARKET SEGMENTATION

Undifferentiated
Strategy

Concentrated
Strategy

Differentiated
Strategy

Any college or university can identify a large number of target markets that might prove beneficial as it attempts to create the size and kind of student body it desires. The identification and selection of target markets is, however, more than an academic exercise – it is a decision that must be implemented if it is to have any benefit at all. The selection of a large number of target markets may in itself create a problem in the effort to mount an effective institutional marketing program. Most institutions have limited resources and if these resources are spread too thin across segments, little of value will occur. The key is in the identification of those target markets, and only those target markets, that are within the limits of the institution to engage successfully. If the institution seeks to communicate with too many or the wrong target markets, the effort will fail.

Summary

There are two major types of markets: homogeneous and heterogeneous markets. Homogeneous markets comprise students with similar requirements for a product or service while the heterogeneous markets contain students with different characteristics and needs. It is incumbent upon the institution to strategically pursue the markets desired.

The stages of market segmentation are chosen from an undifferentiated approach, concentrated or differentiated strategy.

The market of higher education can be segmented using four major types of segmentation variables: demographic, geographic, psychographic, and behavioristic.

Demographic segmentation is based on age, gender, income; and race; geographical segmentation divides prospects into different geographical entities. The geo-demographic segmentation clusters people in zip code areas and smaller neighborhood units based on demographic information and lifestyle. Psychographic segmentation segments persons on the basis of their social class, lifestyle, or personality characteristics. Behavioristic segmentation, divides persons or groups on the basis of knowledge, attitude, use, or direct response. Market segmentation is appropriate for use in primary, secondary and tertiary markets.

Market segmentation strategies are useful in "targeting" desired consumers. The development of the segmentation strategy is dependent upon careful analysis and differentiated approaches appropriate for the markets desired.

THE DEVELOPMENT OF TACTICS & PLANNING FOR EXECUTION OF TACTICS

RICHARD WHITESIDE

Vice President for Enrollment Management
Tulane University

Earlier chapters address a number of key marketing issues and concepts including: the nature of marketing in the college and university environment; the importance of brand; strategic marketing options and priorities; approaches that can be utilized to position the institution; target market segmentation; and approaches to integrated marketing. This chapter addresses the development of tactics – actual actions – to make the changes (market position, enrollment, etc.) that an institution wants to make. The identification and execution of tactics represents where the "rubber meets the road" in a marketing program. All of the preceding activities, while necessary, would be of little value to the institution if it decided not to produce results with the information.

The enrollment picture at an institution will change whether or not enrollment managers choose to intervene. The choice is between deciding whether or not to manage that change through the application of marketing principles and activities. Sitting on the marketing sideline will eventually lead to unplanned changes that may be favorable or unfavorable. Engaging in a marketing effort provides the opportunity to plan the nature of the change and increase the probability that the changes accomplish desired goals. These planned and desirable changes will not be realized until interventions that are well-designed and executed take place. Without these interventions, all of the efforts to effectively market the institution will remain solely in the theoretical dimension. It is only through the implementation of tactics that the action intended to modify the enrollment status quo actually occurs – even if the desired outcome is limited to simply securing the institution's current market position.

Tactics Defined

The textbook definition of tactics is "a procedure or **set of activities** engaged in to achieve an end, aim or goal." The emphasis here is on a "set of activities." In other words, tactics comprise sets of actions taken to reach a desired end. Simply put, tactics are the means to an end.

STUDENT
MARKETING
FOR COLLEGES
AND UNIVERSITIES

PART TWO
CHAPTER 8   103

Much of the language of marketing is taken from the vocabulary of the military. Long before marketers were a significant factor in American business, the military understood and utilized the powerful concepts related to the delineation of mission, objectives, strategies and tactics to give meaning to and control over the problems they were expected to resolve. Successful military engagements have always been those that featured a clear mission, defined goals, articulated strategies for achieving those goals, and the successful execution of those activities, or tactics, necessary to achieve the strategic intent. The adoption of this schema provided the military with a powerful tool for managing situations of extraordinary complexity and for increasing the probability of a successful outcome.

In military campaigns, those charged with the responsibility for managing the overall effort are keenly aware of the relationship of each activity to all others, and how both individual activities and sets of activities relate to strategic initiatives and overall goals. However, this level of understanding is typically not a part of the daily lives of the foot soldier – the individual charged with the responsibility for a discrete set of activities. Anyone who has ever served as an infantryman in a combat situation and been ordered to secure what appears to be a meaningless object ("Take hill number 339") has had serious doubts about the sanity of the generals. The individual task – "Take hill number 339" – is just another meaningless exercise likely to put the individual at risk. The individuals charged with the responsibility for achieving the tactical objective are left wondering, "What's it all about?"

Those engaged in college and university marketing run the same risk as those in the military – the risk of experiencing less than adequate performance because the individual responsible for executing a tactic sees it as simply another meaningless activity. Unless some effort is expended on educating those responsible for the execution they may not understand that their task is important, perhaps critical, to the realization of a strategic objective. In other words, they need to know where this task fits in and why it needs to be accomplished. In the college setting, an environment with a culture that values rational problem solving, the desire to comprehend meaning is elevated from mild to extreme. In large measure, the college decision-making process is an attempt to create context, consensus and meaning.

A tactic or a tactical objective has no meaning in and of itself and cannot be evaluated in isolation from the goal, strategy or end to which it is directed. For example, if an institution employed the tactic of awarding greater amounts of financial aid, this tactic could not be judged with regards to either appropriateness or effectiveness until the reviewer understands the strategy and goal toward which this tactic is directed. There is an interdependent relationship between goals and means that is highly relevant in the design and selection of tactics.

The Relationship of Mission, Goals, Strategy and Tactics

Writers in areas of marketing, planning and change utilize many definitions, sometimes conflicting, of mission, goals, strategies and tactics. A discussion of which set of definitions is correct inevitably evolves into a lively debate. It is not the intent herein to resolve these differences. Instead, the reader is only

THE DEVELOPMENT
OF TACTICS
AND PLANNING
FOR EXECUTION

104   PART TWO
CHAPTER 8

asked to subscribe to the understanding of these terms as outlined and defined in Figure 8–1. The important element here is the realization that there is a hierarchy and that those items lower in the hierarchy are derived from and must be consistent with the intent and values contained in those items that precede them in the hierarchy. In other words, vision is derived from mission, goals from vision, strategies from goals, and tactics from strategies. Adopting the hierarchy as illustrated makes it possible to develop a framework for determining whether a possible course of action is an appropriate course of action. Given the limited resources available to those charged with building or maintaining enrollments, the avoidance of inappropriate tactical forays represents a major concern.

When designing tactics, the tactician assesses the suitability of a particular tactical intervention by evaluating the tactic relative to its relationship to a strategic objective that is linked to a goal that is derived from the vision and mission of the institution. Any tactic that cannot be easily linked "upward' through the hierarchy is likely to be an inappropriate tactic for the task at hand. In the final analysis, the tactician should be able to easily demonstrate the relevance of each tactic used to the mission. If it takes considerable effort to make this linkage or if the linkage itself is weak, the tactic is most likely of marginal value and could be a target of justifiable criticism. Mission-relevant tactics are more likely to be defensible, effective and embraced than those that are not.

FIGURE 8–1
VISION, MISSION, GOALS STRATEGIES & TACTICS
A WORKING SCHEMA

Term	Definition/Explanation
Mission	A statement of the institution's purpose and philosophy – its reason for being (e.g. train society's future leaders)
Vision	The ability to "see" the applicability of the mission in the present and the future – to understand how the philosophy, values and principles expressed in the mission will be used now and in the future to meet the needs and desires of the institution's constituents (e.g. realization of the institution's leadership mission is dependent upon training highly capable individuals drawn from culturally diverse populations for leadership responsibilities.)
Goals	The major achievements that are related to mission and vision that the institution desires to achieve (e.g. improved representation of underrepresented populations)
Strategies	Broad sets of activities (e.g. creating greater institutional access) the institution adopts to achieve its goals
Segments	Logical groups of individuals for whom tailored messaging may be appropriate
Tactics	Discrete activities the institution implements as a part of its strategy objectives (e.g. lower net cost of attendance by applying larger amounts of financial aid)

While mission, vision, strategy, goals, segments and tactics are frequently discussed as individual items, they are tightly coupled. It is this clear and powerful relationship between the elements that makes it possible for marketing efforts to be sustainable and successful. When the relationship between the elements is tenuous, the marketing effort will be less effective and less well coordinated than necessary to establish a favorable position within the market.

Where do tactics originate?

As in any complex organization, the formulation of collegiate goals and strategy is normally within the purview of those charged with the leadership of the institution. In Chapter 6, Dave Crockett identified the differences between the institution's long-range strategic enrollment plan and its annual enrollment plan as well as the differences in the processes used to develop each type of plan. Senior institutional leadership bears the primary responsibility for the formulation of long-range goals, objectives and strategies. However, the achievement of the desired goals and objectives is dependent upon the activities executed by those lower in the organizational hierarchy. Those charged with the day to day responsibility of executing tactical activities may not even be fully aware of the strategies that a particular tactical maneuver is intended to support. For example, the staff of the mailroom may not understand the relative level of importance of getting a particular mailing accomplished on the designated day. To them, it is just another job that needs to be done.

The task of identifying and designing effective tactics that are consistent with institutional goals and strategies falls to functional managers – individuals capable of translating goals and objectives into programs of action. In this role, the functional manager is the lynchpin between the institutional architects and those responsible for achieving the design coming from the architects. Such functional managers are likely to be those who hold director-level positions. As directors they have a broader perspective on the situation at hand and they are expected to comprehend the intent of senior staff implicit in the goals and objectives contained in the long-range enrollment plan. In their capacity as functional managers, they assume the primary responsibility for translating goals and objectives into programs of action comprised of meaningful and effective tasks.

The relationship between Goals, strategy, tactics and level of leadership is shown in Figure 8–2.

Characteristics of Well-Defined Tactical Interventions

As discrete sets of activities, tactics can be described using who, what, when, where, how and why language. For example, an individual tactic can be delineated by describing it in terms of what activity is to be undertaken, when that activity will take place, where that activity will occur, who is responsible for the activity, how it will occur and why – that is, to what purpose – the activity will be undertaken. Using this language in the formulation of tactics is a good beginning but not the total set of considerations that must be addressed when designing tactical interventions. If the designer stops

THE DEVELOPMENT
OF TACTICS
AND PLANNING
FOR EXECUTION

106 **PART TWO**
CHAPTER 8

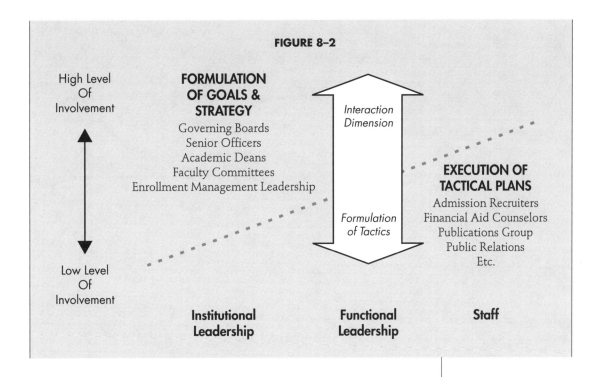

FIGURE 8–2

High Level
Of
Involvement

**FORMULATION
OF GOALS &
STRATEGY**

Governing Boards
Senior Officers
Academic Deans
Faculty Committees
Enrollment Management Leadership

*Interaction
Dimension*

**EXECUTION OF
TACTICAL PLANS**

Admission Recruiters
Financial Aid Counselors
Publications Group
Public Relations
Etc.

*Formulation
of Tactics*

Low Level
Of
Involvement

**Institutional
Leadership**

**Functional
Leadership**

Staff

at this point, there is no agreed upon methodology for determining if the intervention is effective. Likewise, the tactician has little information relative to what the intervention will cost. Effectiveness and cost are always important considerations – more so when the resources available to pursue tactics are limited. Therefore, a carefully constructed "tactical description" must delineate both the assessment technique that will be used to determine effectiveness and the costs associated with implementing the tactic.

Figure 8–3 presents a sample format for defining a tactic that includes the key elements for an individual tactic. Individual tactical descriptions are designed for each strategy. Any given strategy is likely to involve more than one tactic and any long-range enrollment plan is likely to involve more than one strategy. As a result, the annual activities, from a tactical sense, will typically involve the simultaneous and highly coordinated execution of many individual activities designed to reach the overall goals contained in the long-range enrollment plan.

Additionally, tactical activities must relate to the market segments that have been identified by the institution as target markets. The introduction of market segmentation into the process of designing and defining tactics is required because a tactic that promises to be highly successful in one market segment may be a dismal failure when applied to a different segment. For example, an effort to promote the institution to part-time and continuing education students using drive-time radio may be highly effective. However, using drive-time radio to recruit full-time graduate students could prove to be a wasted effort. Likewise, a single tactic may be effective for more than one

STUDENT
MARKETING
FOR COLLEGES
AND UNIVERSITIES

PART TWO
CHAPTER 8

107

FIGURE 8–3
TACTIC DESCRIPTION REPORT

Tactic Description Report
Identification Number 2.1

Strategic Intent: *Increase number of applications*

Tactic 2.1 consists of a series of e-mails to prospective students that describe Main College's student financial aid program, our majors, internships and student housing options

Tactic Category	Electronic Recruiting
Target Market Segment	Inquiries for the Fall 2004 term
What	E-mail campaign
When	Four e-mails, one per month in September, October, November and December on the 15th of each month
Where	Posted from Admission Office Server
Who	Bill Smith author and coordinator with data services
How	Listserve of "inquiries" from admission file
Why	Research indicates that prospective students feel that they do not know enough about these topics
Cost	No incremental cost
Assessment	Track number of responses and incremental "hits" on Web site pages within 72 hours of distribution
Follow-up notes	The e-mail strategy was well received, more than 300 prospective students responded to the invitation to visit the Web site; office received 135 e-mail responses

segment but the content of the message sent may vary by segment. For example, a college may have identified three market segments with regards to academic ability: those who demonstrate high ability and clearly demonstrate eligibility for academic merit scholarships, above average students who are highly desirable but not necessarily candidates for academic merit scholarships and the remaining prospective students. If the college decides to use e-mail to distribute information regarding its financial aid programs, it would most likely want to tailor the message about the aid program so that it is relevant to the target audience.

In the Figure 8–3 example, the institution might want to emphasize its merit scholarship programs to the students in the high ability segment, but only its need-based aid programs for those falling into the average ability segment. In this example, the institution is employing the same tactic: direct mailing of financial aid information but varying the message by market segment.

THE DEVELOPMENT
OF TACTICS
AND PLANNING
FOR EXECUTION

108   **PART TWO**
CHAPTER 8

The relationship between market segment, tactics, strategy, goals, vision and mission is shown in Figure 8–4.

Categorizing Tactics

The number of tactics used in a comprehensive institutional marketing effort is likely to be large. The number increases dramatically and is largely dependent upon the number of market segments that have been targeted, the number of strategies being pursued and the number of goals that have been defined. The sheer number of tactics likely to be developed makes it desirable to develop some form of classification system for tactics. The precise nature of the schema adopted by a particular institution is unimportant. The focus should be on developing a classification system that is suitable for the institution and which makes the classification of tactics relatively simple and straightforward.

Figure 8–5 shows a classification system presently in use at a comprehensive research university. It identifies seven categories of tactics. At this institution, all tactics are assigned, sometimes arbitrarily, to one category. Such assignments make it possible to assess the costs associated with a major category of tactics and to track them for purposes of assessment with respect to effectiveness and comprehensiveness.

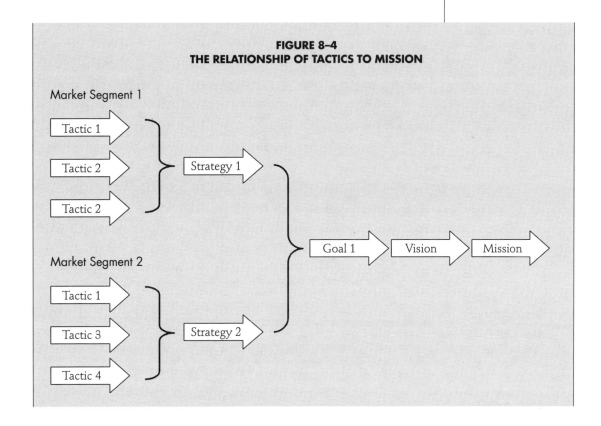

FIGURE 8–4
THE RELATIONSHIP OF TACTICS TO MISSION

FIGURE 8-5
TACTICS CATEGORIZATION SCHEMA

Tactical Category	Sample Tactics
Off-Campus Programs	1. Regional receptions 2. NACAC college fairs 3. NSSFNS fairs
On-Campus Programs	1. Campus tours 2. Overnight visits 3. Financial aid workshops
Direct Marketing	1. Student search 2. Print publications
Mass Media	1. Newspaper advertising 2. Popular press advertisement 3. Radio/television advertising
School Relations	1. High school visits 2. Counselor receptions 3. Counselor mailings
E-Recruiting	1. Web site 2. Electronic publications 3. Chat rooms 4. Electronic applications
Cost Management	1. Financial aid leveraging 2. Institutional loan programs 3. Financial aid

Comprehensive recruitment programs normally employ the full range of tactics in a coordinated fashion. Employing only one kind of tactical intervention may not achieve the desired result because different kinds of individuals will respond differently to different kinds of approaches. By deploying different kinds of tactics designed to support a strategy within a particular target market, the institution increases the probability of achieving a positive response.

Building and Selecting Tactics

In selecting tactics from the universe of available options, the manager needs to be guided by two basic principles: do the *right things* **AND** *do them right*. In other words, use appropriate tactics that can be effectively executed by those responsible for the task. Sound tactical interventions may not achieve the desired result if they are poorly executed. While mounting a telecounseling program may appear to be an effective tactic for establishing close personal contact with the prospective student, the utilization of such a tactic could have an adverse impact if the nature of the telephone contact is poor.

As with goal setting, the number of tactics selected will also impact the institution's ability to effectively pursue the selected tactics. If too many intervention programs are being pursued, the task of intervention management becomes unmanageable. Given the fact that most enrollment managers operate with limited resources, selecting too many tactics will result in spreading the available resources "a mile wide and an inch deep." This will limit the penetration required to achieve the desired outcome.

In the final analysis, the individuals responsible for designing and selecting tactical interventions must evaluate all of the available options using criteria similar to the following:

- The projected effectiveness of the tactic – the volume of positive response that is anticipated

- The cost of the tactic – the cost per anticipated positive response

- Expertise – the needed expertise to effectively pursue this tactic

- Appropriateness – the tactic's confluence with institutional goals and strategies and relevance to mission and goals

THE DEVELOPMENT
OF TACTICS
AND PLANNING
FOR EXECUTION

110   PART TWO
      CHAPTER 8

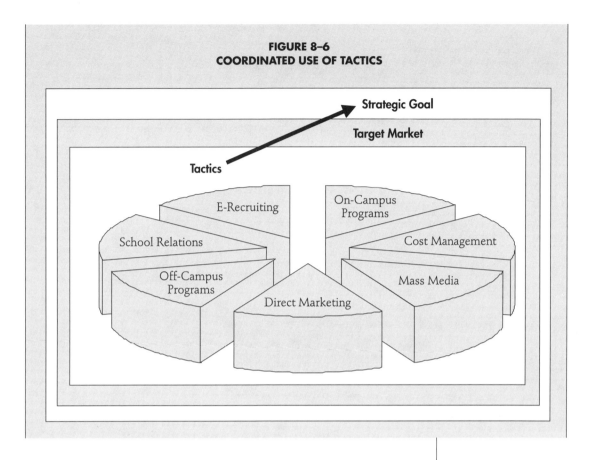

FIGURE 8–6
COORDINATED USE OF TACTICS

Strategic Goal

Target Market

Tactics

E-Recruiting

On-Campus Programs

School Relations

Cost Management

Off-Campus Programs

Direct Marketing

Mass Media

Assessment of Effectiveness

Assessing the effectiveness of individual tactics is tricky business and almost impossible if the assessment measure is not defined as a part of the process used to develop the tactic. In enrollment management there is no "silver bullet" or single tactic that will solve all problems. Instead, it is the cumulative impact of a set of tactics on a goal that ultimately determines if the institution is making progress. The assessment of individual tactics is simply determining whether or not the investment made in that tactic (money, personnel time, political capitol, etc.) is worthwhile. In any given cycle, some tactics are likely to be highly effective while others may contribute only marginally to the outcome. If assessments are made only at the strategy level, a favorable outcome at that level may mask the fact that considerable resources were wasted in the pursuit of a tactic or tactics that contributed little to the successful outcome. When this occurs, the enrollment manager has little information to demonstrate that all of the resources available were used in an optimal fashion.

On the other hand, no single tactic in the marketplace is likely to be the sole cause of success. If assessment occurs only at the tactical level, the manager

STUDENT
MARKETING
FOR COLLEGES
AND UNIVERSITIES

PART TWO
CHAPTER 8   111

may walk away with the impression that all of the tactics worked – even though progress toward the strategic goal was not achieved.

Any thoughtful assessment program must include multiple assessment levels. The effectiveness of each tactic must be assessed. The effectiveness of a set of tactics as a device for pursuing a strategy must be assessed. Based on these assessments, the line manager will continually redesign and refine the type and nature of the tactical interventions employed as devices for advancing the institution.

For most, enrollments – their number and kinds – will be the dependent variable in the effort to market the college or university. The use of bench-mark goals will help us determine the effectiveness of individual tactics and cumulative impact of a set of tactics. Sometimes these goals are expressed in the form of "key performance indicators," or KPI's (Dolence, 1993). These indicators form a type of report card summarizing our performance against key milestones. Figure 8–7 provides a sampling of key performance indicators developed by one institution. While an important aspect of assessment in the global sense, the presence of KPI's does not mean that we have a way of determining the effectiveness of a particular tactic – one among many such

FIGURE 8–7
SAMPLE KEY PERFORMANCE INDICATORS

Key Performance Indicators						
	2004	2005	2006	2007	2008	2009
# of students searched	50,000	55,000	60,000	60,000	60,000	60,000
# of inquiries generated	20,000	22,500	25,000	27,500	30,000	30,000
# of test scores received (ACT or SAT)	4,000	4,200	4,300	4,400	4,500	4,500
# of applications for admission	2,500	3,000	3,100	3,200	3,300	3,400
% of applications accepted	62.5%	52.0%	49.2%	46.9%	44.7%	42.7%
# Accepted	1562	1562	1525	1500	1,475	1,452
Yield of accepted to enrolled	25.6%	28.8%	29.5%	30.0%	30.5%	31.0%
# of students enrolling	400	450	450	450	450	450
SAT Average	1100	1110	1120	1130	1140	1150
% in Top Ten of class	47%	50%	52%	55%	57%	60%
High school GPA average	3.30	3.40	3.45	3.50	3.50	3.50
# of school visits made	100	120	140	160	180	200
% of persons of color	10%	12%	14%	16%	18%	20%
# of campus visitors	1,000	1,250	1,500	1,700	1,700	1,700

tactics – targeted at achieving the benchmark outcome on one of these important indicators.

Each tactic should have its own built-in indicators of success. For example, if an institution decides to run a newspaper advertisement campaign as a device for generating interest in its part-time program offerings, the tactical design should include a mechanism for assessing response to that area of the campaign – a device separate from the measurement of the overall KPI assessment that might be made on the overall enrollment of part-time students. In addition, the institution should also track the timing of the responses to individual tactics.

The pace and flow of response is a critical factor in determining the effectiveness of a tactic. By defining expectations for the rate and timing of response, one can assess whether or not a particular tactic is performing as intended with respect to volume and timing. For example, let us assume that the newspaper campaign previously mentioned is scheduled to take place over a two-week period prior to the start of classes. If the institution establishes only a quantitative measure for the number of responses, it must wait for the entire two-week period to determine if the tactic has yielded the desired response. However, if the institution also specified that it expected to experience 50 responses by the end of the first two days and a cumulative response of 150 by the end of the first week, it is in a position to determine whether or not to continue the strategy into the second week. Should response be considerably lower than expected, the institution might want to pull or modify the campaign and save the funds it would have otherwise invested in a tactic that was performing below expectations in order to improve overall campaign performance.

Managing Tactics

By now it should be apparent that the management of tactics is at least as important as the selection and design of tactics. The sheer number of tactics that an institution utilizes creates a thorny management issue. How does one remain aware of all of the tactics?

The number of tactics to design and implement can easily grow to a number far too large to be managed easily. If there is any validity in the statement that goals drive strategies and that the pursuit of these strategies involves different tactical interventions appropriate for the target market, the number of necessary tactics will grow geometrically. Perhaps this is best illustrated by the formula in Figure 8–8.

Such an explosion in the number of tactics to be managed creates a daunting problem for many enrollment managers. The problem can be somewhat reduced by approaches designed to "leverage" tactical interventions so that a single tactic is useful in more than one target market, a part of more than a single strategy or supportive of more than one goal. Clustering tactics provides an approach for achieving some measure of manageability. For example, an individual tactic may simultaneously address more than one strategic intent or more than one goal. Identifying individual tactics that can achieve multiple purposes helps reduce the overall number of tactical inter-

FIGURE 8–8
DETERMINING THE NUMBER OF TACTICS

Goals x # of Strategies x # of Segments x # Tactics Per Segment = Number of Tactics To be Managed

or

2 Goals x 3 Strategies x 3 Segments x 4 Tactics Per Segment = 72 Tactics To Be Managed

ventions to be designed and managed. Such a clustering can be accomplished using a variety of systems. Figure 8–9 shows one possibility for clustering tactics. In this illustration the goal is to stabilize undergraduate enrollment and the target audience is out-of-state residents. In order to achieve the goal, the institution has identified four separate strategies: 1) increase the size of the freshman class; 2) increase diversity in the freshman class; 3) increase the size of the applicant pool; and 4) increase the yield of accepted to enrolled.

Using the classification system for the grouping of tactics presented previously, the institution can identify individual tactics that are appropriate for more than one cell in the matrix created by the intersection of "strategic intent" and "target group." The realization that one tactic can serve more than one strategic intent makes it possible for the planner to structure the tactic so that it has the maximum chance of achieving the desired effect. In the illustration, the planner has noted that the tactic labeled "Regional Reception" has the potential for impacting all four elements of the strategic intent for the goal of stabilizing the undergraduate enrollment in the out-of-state resident target market. The planner is then in a position to formulate the content, scheduling and promotion of the Regional Reception program in ways that increases its effectiveness in reaching each strategic intent. Given the reality that the number of possible interventions typically exceeds both the planner's available resources and the planner's abilities to manage the many interventions possible even if resources are available, the planner is well advised to place a high priority on the implementation of those tactics that have multiple uses.

The clustering suggested in Figure 8–9 is by no means the only possible approach for clustering goals, strategies, segments and tactics. The approach presented is for illustrative purposes only. The important concept underlying clustering lies in the fact that any clustering system helps the planner to separate those tactics that have the greatest potential impact from those that may have only limited impact. The approach an institution adopts for the purposes of achieving clustering will vary depending upon the number of goals, segments and strategies it identifies. An institution that is pursuing a single target market should not create individual matrices based on market segmentation factors. Likewise, an institution pursuing only one goal need not create matrices for multiple goals.

THE DEVELOPMENT
OF TACTICS
AND PLANNING
FOR EXECUTION

114   PART TWO
CHAPTER 8

FIGURE 8–9
CLUSTERING TACTICAL INTERVENTIONS

Goal: Stabilize Undergraduate Enrollment
Segment: Out-Of-State Residents
Strategic Intent: *Increase size of freshman class*

Tactical Group		Increase size freshman class	Increase diversity in the freshman class	Increase applications for admission	Increase yield of accepted to enrolled
	Off-Campus Programs	Regional receptions Attend NACAC College Fairs Attend regional college fairs	Regional receptions	Regional receptions	Regional receptions
	On-Campus Programs	Overnight hosting	Overnight hosting Paid travel to campus		Paid travel to campus
	Mass Media			TV/Newspaper/ Radio advertising campaign in key cities	
	Cost Management		Offer differential financial aid Offer merit scholarships for target groups Waive application fee for Title IV schools	Waive application fee	Offer merit scholarships for target groups
	School Relations		Visit out-of-state inner city schools		
	Direct Marketing	Increase search purchase			
	E-recruitment	E-mail campaign			

CONSUMER BEHAVIOR OF THE COLLEGE-BOUND STUDENT

PART THREE

COLLEGE CHOICE: A CONSUMER DECISION-MAKING MODEL

DR. PAMELA KIECKER, PH.D.
Head of Research and Issue Analysis, Royall & Company
Professor of Marketing and Executive Director of the Interactive Marketing
Institute in the School of Business at Virginia Commonwealth University

In *Millennials Go to College*, Howe and Strauss (2002) open their chapter titled "Graduation and Beyond" with the (following statement: "For a generation, as for a person, college is preparation for life" (p.133). This contention is supported when looking at college choice from the perspective of consumer decision-making. For most college-bound youth, selecting a specific college or university is the first major *consumer* decision they will make. Among all of their early experiences in the marketplace, it is likely to be the most comprehensive, complex, and consequential. As such, it provides a unique "socialization" opportunity for this burgeoning segment, whereby they learn important lessons in the marketplace. While it may not rival the actual college experience in terms of academic lessons, what teenagers do learn about the marketplace and their role as consumers through the college search process is likely to influence their futures in significant ways.

Consumer decision-making is at the core of our study of consumer behavior, which has been defined as "the study of people and the products that help to shape their identities" (Solomon, 2002, preface). A student's college choice is, perhaps, the best example of how this phenomenon takes place for an increasing number of Americans each year as it is now estimated that 70% of all high school graduates will go on to college. And when a young person selects either a small private college or a large public university, decides to attend college either in her home state or across the country, or accepts a financial aid package that will obligate her to a repayment scheduled for more than a decade, that individual begins a journey that will shape her personal and professional life like no other single "shopping" experience. From their search for information about different colleges and universities to their evaluation of available alternatives and their choice of a specific school to attend, young people experience the marketplace as consumers and begin to define who they are, and who they will become, by the college choices they make.

This chapter describes the decision-making process associated with college choice. Its objective is to provide admission and enrollment professionals with a framework for developing appropriate and effective marketing strate-

STUDENT
MARKETING
FOR COLLEGES
AND UNIVERSITIES

gies for college-bound students. It begins by defining college choice as a complex, high involvement decision-making task. Next, a simple model of consumer decision-making is described. A discussion of key concepts related to the model and its application to college choice is included. Finally, the chapter concludes with a summary of interpersonal influences on student decision-making. While the chapter's focus is on traditional undergraduate student recruitment, issues related to retention and other outcomes of enrollment and matriculation also are discussed.

College Choice: The Nature of the Decision-Making Task

To understand college choice from a consumer decision-making perspective, it helps to consider the nature of the task. While individuals may approach the college choice process somewhat differently, most would agree that the process by which they select a college or university requires *extensive decision-making.* In contrast, deciding how to travel to and from the campus or choosing bed linens and other supplies for student housing would generally be classified as *limited decision making;* selecting a television program to watch or a soda to purchase during a study break would be considered *routine decision-making.*

Generally, consumers are motivated to use extensive decision-making for more expensive products that are infrequently purchased or unfamiliar. The nature of such products (e.g. the purchase price or the risk associated with making a poor choice) engages people and produces what consumer behaviorists call "involvement" with the product and/or the decision-making process. A high level of involvement results from the belief that something is important and relevant. When this is the case, consumers devote more time and energy to the decision process: more information is considered, a greater number of alternatives and characteristics of the alternative products are examined, and multiple sources – personal and commercial – are consulted. They are motivated to make a careful, informed purchase decision and perceive greater risk of making the wrong choice. In short, the higher the involvement, the more difficult the process is.

Extensive decision-making is usually initiated by a motive that is fairly central to the individual's self-concept. In the case of college choice, many students are looking for a school where they will "fit in," "be who they are," or develop toward their "ideal" self. In research into reasons why students do not apply to specific schools, the majority of students indicate that they applied to schools that were a "better fit." A school that resonates with a student's sense of self is viewed as the "perfect place." The campus visit is so critical to student college choice because it offers a good opportunity for them to determine whether or not there is a fit. Parents, too, are interested in the "feel" of the campus and often leave a campus visit with a strong sense of whether or not their child will be happy in the college environment offered by a particular school.

The high-involvement, extended decision-making process related to college choice implies that student prospects (and their parents and other influencers) collect as much information as possible, both from memory and from outside sources. Due to the importance of the decision, each school they consider is

COLLEGE CHOICE:
A CONSUMER
DECISION-MAKING
MODEL

carefully evaluated. The evaluation is made by considering institutional attributes (e.g. reputation, availability of majors, student housing, etc.), one alternative at a time, and seeing how the attributes of each compares to a set of desired characteristics (e.g. a national ranking, strong liberal arts program, co-ed residence halls). Both the choice and the outcome of the decision (e.g. students' satisfaction, academic success, retention, and graduate rates) are based on the performance of specific schools on important matters.

For several reasons, this simple model often provides an imperfect account of actual decision-making processes. One reason is that actual consumer decision-making seldom proceeds in the linear sequence implied by the model. A second reason is that actual decision-making processes involve multiple, continuous interactions among consumers' cognitive processes, their behaviors, and aspects of the socio-cultural environment. A third reason is that most decision-making involves multiple tasks and multiple decisions. For prospective students considering different colleges and universities, the critical decisions include what schools to visit, where to apply and make a deposit, and – finally – where to enroll. And it is more likely than not that prospective students consider a larger set of alternatives in very general terms before they engage in extended decision-making focused on a smaller, more selective set of college options.

There are exceptions to this general model wherein student behaviors are potentially very different. For instance, while most students experience college choice as an initial or first-time purchase decision, there are situations that may make college choice more like a repeat purchase decision. As an example, if a student prospect is the second or third child within the same household, the decision-making process may be streamlined due to previous experiences. In other cases, college choice may be easier because the students always knew they would attend and/or they have a special connection to specific schools (e.g. a college in their hometown, a family member or close friend who is associated with a university, or a strong connection through an alumni network or other special interest such as the school's athletic team). In yet another case, wherein one might expect the decision-making to be more complex, first generation college students and being the first children within households to attend college may reduce the number of schools they consider and the different criteria they use in the evaluation of alternatives in order to simplify the decision-making process.

Decision-Making for High-Involvement Purchases: The Case of College Choice

Consider the simple model of consumer decision-making presented in Figure 9-1.[1] It is designed to tie together many of the ideas that are relevant when considering college choice. As shown, the process can be viewed as three distinct but inter-related phases: the input phase, the process phase, and the output phase. The *input* phase includes external influences on consumer recognition of a product need and includes two different types of informa-

STUDENT
MARKETING
FOR COLLEGES
AND UNIVERSITIES

---

1   Figure 9-1 is adapted from Schiffman, Leon G. and Leslie Lazar Kanuk (2000).

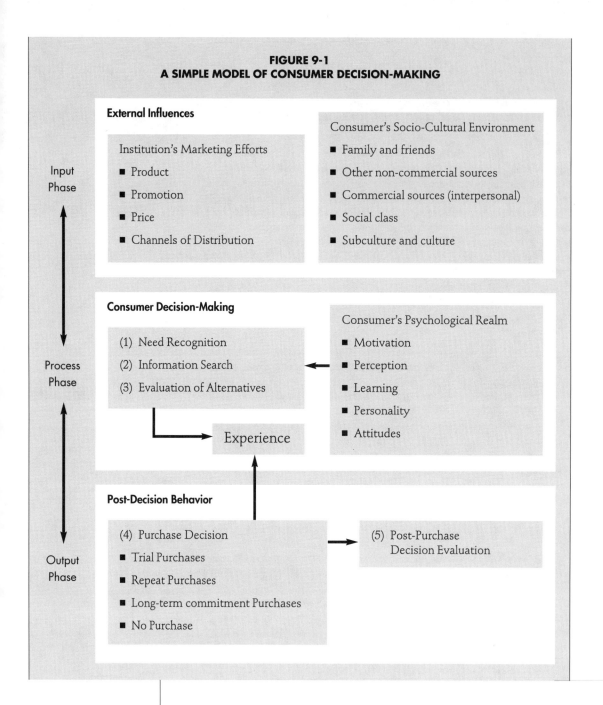

FIGURE 9-1
A SIMPLE MODEL OF CONSUMER DECISION-MAKING

External Influences

Institution's Marketing Efforts
- Product
- Promotion
- Price
- Channels of Distribution

Consumer's Socio-Cultural Environment
- Family and friends
- Other non-commercial sources
- Commercial sources (interpersonal)
- Social class
- Subculture and culture

Input Phase

Consumer Decision-Making

(1) Need Recognition
(2) Information Search
(3) Evaluation of Alternatives

Consumer's Psychological Realm
- Motivation
- Perception
- Learning
- Personality
- Attitudes

Experience

Process Phase

Post-Decision Behavior

(4) Purchase Decision
- Trial Purchases
- Repeat Purchases
- Long-term commitment Purchases
- No Purchase

(5) Post-Purchase Decision Evaluation

Output Phase

tion: those provided by college or university marketing efforts and those provided by external sociological and cultural influences on the consumer.

College and university marketing efforts are a direct attempt to reach, inform, and persuade qualified students to apply and enroll. They include elements of the product (the structure of academic programs, aspects of student life), promotions (advertising, direct mail, publications), pricing (tuition, fees, scholarships, aid), and distribution (the campuses, classrooms and other support facilities, use of technology for distance learning). The potency of a school's marketing efforts is governed by the prospective student's perceptions of these efforts. Consequently, it is important to remain diligently alert to students' perceptions by engaging in systematic research, rather than relying on the *intended* outcome of marketing messages.

The second type of input – the socio-cultural environment – also exerts a major influence on prospective students. The socio-cultural inputs consist of a variety of personal and other noncommercial influences. Comments from a friend, an article in the newspaper, a teacher's recommendation, discussions among peers in online chat rooms, are all sources of information that prospective students may encounter. The influences of social class, subculture, and culture – while less tangible and direct – also are important input factors that affect how students evaluate different schools and ultimately lead to a student's decision whether or not to apply or enroll. Because both types of inputs may be directed to the individual or actively sought by the individual, the model shows a two-headed arrow linking the input and process phases.

The *process* phase focuses on how consumers make decisions. It includes individual psychological factors (motivation, perception, learning, personality, and attitudes) that determine how the external inputs from the input phase affect consumer need recognition, information search, and evaluation of alternatives. In the process phase, the experience gained from evaluating alternatives affects the consumer's psychological realm. As depicted in the model, there are three stages of decision-making that construct consumer experience during the process phase: (1) need recognition, (2) information search, and (3) evaluation of alternatives. Each is described below.

(1) Need Recognition
High school students faced with the prospect of attending college recognize the need to begin the college search process. For most, this is a multi-stage process that includes identifying a specific set of schools where they will visit, apply, and make a deposit, and ultimately – identify the one school where they will enroll. Recognizing the need to begin searching for colleges is the "triggering event" for students and their families that launches the decision-making process. And, because of the high-stakes nature of the decision, for many young people this phase of the decision-making process may last for years – quite literally.

For some students, the decision-making process begins at an early stage in their academic careers—sometimes as early as grade school when their first achievement tests are taken. For both high and low performing test-takers, the need to think in terms of "college preparation" is identified by their teachers, coaches, parents, and older siblings, among others, who then participate in the subsequent phases of the decision-making process to varying degrees. Some high school students report that they always knew they would go to college and never considered the possibility of not doing so.

Others indicate that they only started to think about it when they realized that they would need to do *something* after high school. The majority of college-bound students are somewhere between these two extremes and begin to think seriously about college prospects in their sophomore or junior years of high school. It is important to note that many situational factors influence the nature and timing of need recognition, including student aptitude and interest, parental involvement, household income, ethnicity, and the student's family position (i.e., first or second student to attend college).

(2) Information search

Students recognizing the need to attend college are motivated to gather data and insights to use in their decision-making. Because consumers are instinctively interested in minimizing the effort associated with decision-making, they first assess the information they have already stored in memory, which constitutes their current knowledge base. This process is known as *internal search*. Although it is not often the case for college choice, the recollection of past experiences (drawn from memory) might provide individuals with adequate information to make their decisions.

To fare well in a student's search, a college or university must already occupy some position in their minds. For many institutions, general marketing programs or image campaigns are in place to increase awareness of the school among student prospects and their influencers, and to build the institution "brand" so that the name of the school carries relevant meaning to student prospects and other stakeholders. When the existing level of awareness and knowledge of schools is not strong enough to result in a choice on its own, consumers engage in a search of the outside environment for useful information on which to base their choice. In other words, students will be motivated to conduct an *external search* when their current knowledge and past experiences are deemed inadequate to result in a choice.

The act of "shopping" is an important form of external information search. When shopping for colleges, students are likely to use a variety of external information sources. As examples, prospective students seek recommendations of friends, family members and other personal contacts (classmates, counselors, teachers, coaches, etc.), talk to professionals who represent the institution, read publications such as college guidebooks and schools' viewbooks, attend regional receptions or other activities hosted by colleges and universities, and visit campuses. While it seems unlikely that a student would select a college without engaging in an extensive external search, it is well known that students will enroll in a school sight unseen! In such cases, there is likely to be a strong positive predisposition based on reputation or personal connection and an effective marketing communications program including many of the elements listed above.

As in the case of any extended decision-making task, the timing and intensity of information search depends on level of involvement and perceived risk. Risk is often associated with students' lack of confidence regarding how well they know the schools they are considering and their fear of failure (i.e., the anxiety they feel about not getting in to the school of their choice). Importantly, and only in part due to economic resources, students from more

COLLEGE CHOICE:
A CONSUMER
DECISION-MAKING
MODEL

124   **PART THREE**
CHAPTER 9

affluent households search more. And young women are more inclined to search than are young men. All things being equal, students who enjoy the shopping/fact-finding process tend to conduct a more extensive information search. More and more, college and universities with a strong Web presence are benefiting from student interest in the Internet and their ability to conduct more effective information searches online.

(3) Evaluation of alternatives

The relatively systematic process by which consumers evaluate the options identified in the information search process results in three classifications of alternatives that are of interest to marketers. For the case of college choice, these are displayed in Figure 9-2 in the larger context of all schools known and unknown to the prospective student.

The first classification of alternatives is known as the consideration set or the *evoked set*. It includes the students' top-choice schools. The schools included

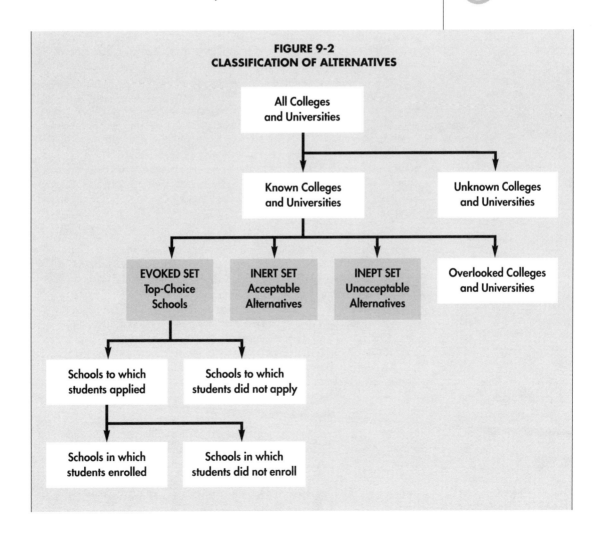

FIGURE 9-2
CLASSIFICATION OF ALTERNATIVES

in the evoked set will be the focus of students' information searches, and they will be the schools that are evaluated during this phase of student decision-making. For many students the evoked set will include different types of college options, including aspirational (or "reach") schools, moderate risk schools, and "safety" schools. In addition, a second set of schools that may be considered "back up" schools is known as the *inert set*. While these schools are considered acceptable, they are not at the top of students' lists of potential institutions. As such, they are not likely to be evaluated in any systematic fashion unless (or until) the options within the evoked set are eliminated for one reason or another. The third set of schools includes those that have been eliminated from consideration. It includes schools that students have identified as unacceptable options and have ruled out of consideration. These schools make up the *inept set*.

The criteria used for evaluating different colleges and universities are usually expressed in terms of important product attributes. Because colleges and universities know that most student prospects will be evaluating a number of different institutions, well-designed marketing communications emphasize criteria that highlight the competitive advantages of their schools. The strongest messages are those that favorably present the school in terms of attributes that are most important to students. Specific criteria include academic options (available majors and minors), academic/instructional facilities (classrooms, labs, library), faculty interactions (class size, student-to-faculty ratio, opportunities to work with faculty on joint research projects), internships and other applied learning experiences, advantages of the school's location, campus safety, and the like. When evaluating alternatives, students employ decision rules (also known as heuristics, decision strategies, or information processing strategies) to assess school performance on these criteria, often weighting performance scores based on their relative importance. The use of decision rules simplifies the decision-making process and thereby facilitates choice.

Behavioral researchers have broadly classified consumer decisions into two major categories: compensatory and non-compensatory. When using a compensatory decision rule, students evaluate school options in terms of each relevant attribute and compute a weighted or summated score for each school across attributes. The computed score reflects the school's relative merit as a potential purchase choice. The assumption is that the student will select the institution that scores the highest among the alternatives being evaluated. Importantly, a compensatory decision rule allows a high score on one attribute to balance out a low score on another attribute. For example, a high academic ranking can compensate for a lower financial aid award. Consumers that use compensatory decision rules tend to be more involved in the purchase and thus are willing to exert the effort to consider the entire picture in a more exacting way.

In contrast, non-compensatory decision rules do not allow positive scores on one attribute to balance out negative scores on another attribute. People simply eliminate options that do not meet some basic standard. How non-compensatory decision rules are specifically applied, however, varies. For instance, according to the *conjunctive decision rule*, the student establishes a

COLLEGE CHOICE:
A CONSUMER
DECISION-MAKING
MODEL

126   PART THREE
CHAPTER 9

separate, minimally acceptable level as a cutoff point for each attribute. If any school falls below the cutoff point on any one attribute, the school is eliminated from further consideration. For example, a school without a strong science program would be eliminated by any student interested in a career in medicine. This process is particularly useful in quickly reducing the number of alternatives to be considered. Once they have reduced the number of options in this manner, students are likely to use another, more refined decision rule to make their final choice.

Alternatively, students may use the minimally acceptable cutoff level for each attribute to accept different alternatives. That is, if the school meets or exceeds the cutoff established for any one attribute, it is included in further consideration. As an example in this case, if a school has the desired major, *or* the desired academic ranking, *or* the desired student housing, etc., it would be retained as an acceptable alternative. Because more than one school may be deemed acceptable according to this rule, the student may accept the first satisfactory school as their final choice or apply another decision rule to derive their final choice (the most affordable or the closest to home, for example). This non-compensatory decision rule is known as *disjunctive*.

A third non-compensatory decision rule, known as *lexicographic*, begins with a ranking of attributes in terms of perceived relevance or importance. Students then compare the different schools in their evoked set in terms of the single attribute that they consider to be most important. If two or more schools "perform" equally well on the most important attribute, the second (or third, or fourth, etc.) most important attribute is considered to determine the final choice. In this case, the highest-ranked attribute may reveal something about the student's basic consumer/shopping orientation. For example, a "select the most affordable school" rule might indicate that the student is value-oriented; a "select the most prestigious school" rule might reveal that the student is status-oriented.

There is evidence that prospective students are now applying to an average of seven different colleges and universities. It is likely that a much larger set of schools is initially considered and then narrowed to a smaller set of schools to which students will apply. Assuming this behavior, non-compensatory rules are most likely to be used to determine the set of schools to which students will apply; compensatory rules are likely to be used to decide enrollment among schools to which students are admitted.

In contrast to both compensatory and non-compensatory decision rules, some students hold in memory overall evaluations of the schools in their evoked set, making evaluation by individual attributes unnecessary. In other words, students can produce an overall rating for the school without distinguishing specific attributes, which allows them to select the school with the highest overall rating. This rule is known as the *affect referral decision rule*. It is a simple and easily applied decision rule, and it may reflect a more emotional (less rational) response to marketing messages and other student recruitment efforts.

STUDENT
MARKETING
FOR COLLEGES
AND UNIVERSITIES

DECISION RULE	MENTAL STATEMENT
Compensatory rule	I picked the best school for me after balancing the pros and cons of each alternative.
Non-compensatory – Conjunctive	I picked the school that had no bad features or characteristics.
Non-compensatory – Disjunctive	I picked the school that scored the highest in one area.
Non-compensatory – Lexicographic	I picked the school that scored the highest on the attribute that was most important to me.
Affect – Referral	The school is the best all around, so that's where I'm going to enroll.

The final phase of consumer decision-making as depicted in this table is the *output* phase. It includes both the purchase decision (the actual choice) and post-purchase decision evaluation. In terms of purchase behavior, consumer behaviorists have identified three types of purchases: trial purchases, repeat purchases, and long-term commitment purchases.

While many college choices result in a long-term commitment purchase, it is possible for students to engage in both trial purchases and repeat purchases. In the case of trial purchases, high school students may "sample" the college experience by enrolling in special programs (summer camps, for example). In this way, the experience is part of the exploratory phase of a student's purchase behavior. By taking classes with the college faculty and living in the residence halls, students attempt to evaluate the college based on direct use. Going back to the same summer program year-after-year, students exhibit *repeat purchase behavior*. Students who take classes at another school during the summer term, transfer from one school to another, or "drop-out" and then re-enroll, also provide examples of trial and repeat purchases. However, considering traditional students who enroll as freshmen upon graduation from high school and complete their college education in four years, consumers usually move directly from their evaluation of alternatives to a long-term commitment through their purchase behavior (enrollment). It is important to note that all decisions do not result in a specific college choice. The process outlined here may lead students to decide to delay college. Some may elect to travel or work after high school and postpone their college education by a year or more.

As suggested above, most decision-making actually involves multiple tasks and multiple decisions. At the most abstract level, students first decide whether or not they will go to college. Next, college-bound students are faced with a "product category decision," such as a public or a private, religious or secular, single sex or co-ed institution. At the most concrete level, students make a "brand" choice, by selecting a specific school. For prospective students, in addition to the choice regarding enrollment, they make several decisions that effectively lead up to their college choice. Specifically, these

COLLEGE CHOICE:
A CONSUMER
DECISION-MAKING
MODEL

128   PART THREE
       CHAPTER 9

include selecting what college-sponsored events to attend, where to apply, what campuses to visit, and where to make a deposit.

Finally, post-purchase decision evaluation is the outcome that focuses students' attention on the degree to which their experiences match their expectations. The three possible outcomes of these evaluations include (1) a neutral reaction due to the fact that experiences match expectations; (2) satisfaction, resulting from experiences that exceed expectations; and (3) dissatisfaction caused by experiences that fall short of expectations. An important part of post-purchase decision evaluation is reassurance that the student made the right choice. Some customary means by which such reassurance occurs include rationalizing the decision as the best one, seeking support for their choice from third-party endorsements, avoiding experiences with schools they "rejected," attempting to persuade others to select the same institution and thus confirm their own choice, and turning to other enrolled and satisfied students for reassurance.

In all of these areas, college marketing efforts targeted to enrolled students can support their decision and thereby increase their satisfaction with their college experience and positively influence student retention rates. In addition, research among enrolled students can help identify potential areas of dissatisfaction and inform the school's retention efforts. Surveying consumers has in itself been shown to increase overall satisfaction by demonstrating a genuine interest in opinions and attitudes and concern for the consumer.

Interpersonal Influences on Student College Choice

It is impossible to talk about decision-making regarding college choice without giving special attention to the role of students' friends and families in the process. For many college-bound students, "fitting in" is simply a matter of doing what their friends do. The behaviors of others who students admire, seek to imitate, or with whom they identify are powerful influences on student choice. In research into reasons why students do not apply to specific colleges and universities, a significant number of them indicate it is because "none of my friends applied." While peer influence is age-old, and few college-bound students make their college choice without gathering information and advice from others, no previous generation of prospective college students has embraced parental involvement in their decision-making as has the so-called Millennial Generation. The Millennials are more likely than any other consumer market segment to "co-purchase" a college and make most of the critical decisions related to college choice jointly with their parents.

(As reported by Howe and Strauss (2003, p. 11), parents of the Millennials have been described as "helicopter parents" due to their tendency to hover over their children through active and structured participation in their decisions and their actions. This generation of college-bound children expects its college choice to be influenced by their parents' preferences, desires, and needs, as much for their socio-cultural support as for their financial support. For example, more and more students are reporting that they will attend a "second-choice" school for one of two reasons related to their family situation: (1) to be closer in proximity to their parents and siblings and/or (2) to

STUDENT
MARKETING
FOR COLLEGES
AND UNIVERSITIES

PART THREE
CHAPTER 9   129

make their college education more affordable for their family. Due to their parents' high level of involvement in their lives, students are more aware of family resources, competing demands on their parents' time and finances, and their parents' wishes for their college placement and professional careers than ever before.

This chapter began with a reference to how students are "socialized" in terms of their roles as consumers in the marketplace through the decision-making process that results in college choice. It is important to note here that both friends and family members play a critical role in this socialization. As depicted in Figure 9-3[2], the socialization of a young person can be extended to family members of all ages. Note that the arrows run both ways between the young person and other family members and between the young person and his or her friends. This bi-directional arrow signifies that consumer socialization is really a two-way street; the young person is both socialized and influences those who are doing the socializing.

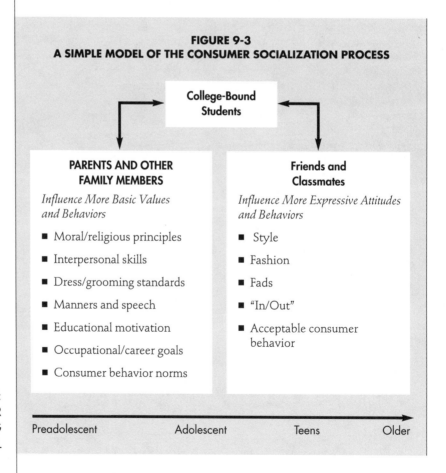

FIGURE 9-3
A SIMPLE MODEL OF THE CONSUMER SOCIALIZATION PROCESS

College-Bound Students

PARENTS AND OTHER FAMILY MEMBERS

Influence More Basic Values and Behaviors

- Moral/religious principles
- Interpersonal skills
- Dress/grooming standards
- Manners and speech
- Educational motivation
- Occupational/career goals
- Consumer behavior norms

Friends and Classmates

Influence More Expressive Attitudes and Behaviors

- Style
- Fashion
- Fads
- "In/Out"
- Acceptable consumer behavior

Preadolescent   Adolescent   Teens   Older

COLLEGE CHOICE:
A CONSUMER
DECISION-MAKING
MODEL

130   **PART THREE**
CHAPTER 9

2. Figure 9-3 is adapted from Schiffman, Leon G. and Leslie Lazar Kanuk (2000).

While the preceding discussion focused on the consumer/student side of the exchange represented by college choice, it is important to acknowledge the academic institution's side of the exchange. The bottom line is that students' choices do not always coincide with college admission decisions. Not unlike other consumer–vendor/supplier relationships in the marketplace, college choice is a matter of getting the right students enrolled at the right schools. Toward this end, it is critically important that college marketing efforts accurately and realistically represent the opportunities presented by the institution and support the underlying counseling function of admission professionals.

Summary

The current segment of college-bound Americans has spent more time and more money in the marketplace than any previous segment. They have more of their own money and more influence over household spending than any previous generation of teenagers. In addition, today's college-bound students have unparalleled access to information. Not only is there more information available, it can be more easily gathered, screened, and evaluated than ever before.

This reality, combined with the co-purchase behavior within college choice, demands high quality marketing communications that specifically speak to the needs of students and their parents. As more and more colleges and universities engage in multi-year, multi-class recruitment efforts, the timing of specific communications becomes more important. Not only do the messages need to be on target, they must also coincide with the appropriate phase of the decision-making task (i.e., need recognition, information search, evaluation of alternatives). The strategic management of information flow is critical to successful recruitment and enrollment programs.

For prospective students and their parents, e-mail messages and Web-based resources, newsletters and other university publications, regional receptions and campus visits, all must reflect the high-involvement nature of the complex decision they are facing. They are engaged in a very serious shopping trip. And like no previous generation, current consumers – students and their parents – are motivated to make the "right" choice and are looking for all the help they can get.

STUDENT
MARKETING
FOR COLLEGES
AND UNIVERSITIES

PART THREE
CHAPTER 9   131

DIRECT MARKETING & DIRECT RESPONSE IN UNDERGRADUATE STUDENT RECRUITMENT

CHAPTER 10

ELIZABETH CLARK
Chief Strategic Officer
Royall & Company

Direct response: *Promotions that permit or request consumers to directly respond to the advertiser, by mail, telephone, e-mail, or some other means of communication. Some practitioners use this as a synonym for Direct Marketing.*[1]

INTRODUCTION: WHY BOTHER?

A few years ago, a book by the title of *Being Direct* was published. For a few fast minutes, it was a national bestseller. It was the professional reminiscence of one of America's unsung, entrepreneurial heroes: Lester Wunderman. Never heard of him? You're not alone. But you're living in his world.

American Express is what it is today because of Wunderman. Columbia Music Club was also his creation. He revolutionized personalized direct response communications. It was his way of seeing, of reinventing, our universe: because he saw as a first-generation American that it was a promise America had made to him, to all of us, to treat each costumer with respect, as an individual.

Like it, hate it, indifferent: it doesn't matter. It is a way of seeing the world, and Lester Wunderman, whether he knew it – I don't think he did – or not, created a legacy for all of us. He was in his way a 'founding father' of America: he's in large part the reason why every single person born later than 1965 considers personal direct communications just "what people do."

In some ways it is strange that direct response is so suited to undergraduate enrollment: Admission is such a personal, intimate business. It is, after all, about families trying to make the right choice about those who will be acting *in loco parentis.* Anyone in the higher education business during the 1960s,

STUDENT MARKETING FOR COLLEGES AND UNIVERSITIES

'70s, and '80s recalls admission as highly personal. We remember when the counseling component was paramount.

Direct response has often and rightly been called "salesmanship in print." For colleges and universities, direct response is counseling in print (or online) – it is a way to extend institutional counseling opportunities. Through good direct response, colleges can virtually sit down in the kitchens, living rooms, and dining rooms of all sorts of families, and have the same kinds of conversations they would have had in person in an earlier day. The medium is different. The sequencing is different. But the message is the same. The reach and scope are magnified, and the power to do good for American families and for the institution is magnified thousands-fold.

Direct response for colleges and universities accomplishes public service goals. Why? Because first, the American college system is uniquely *American* in a way almost nothing else is. It is the tangible, experiential, *bona fide* fulfillment of the American experience to help others achieve the American dream. There is very little so American as direct response. Like jazz, it is a uniquely American art form. These uniquely American endeavors, the pursuit of higher education and direct response, are intertwined. American college recruitment is about three things:

- *Crowd control.* The United States is a big country. It is difficult to sort through the millions of new multivariate statistics each year to find the right matches for a single institution.

- *Potential.* A student can achieve anything in the U.S. if she has the courage, the commitment, and the capability.

- *Individuality.* Part of the uniqueness of being American is the allure of being *The One*: the one who will write the great American novel, the one who will be President or the one who will fulfill, and surpass, her parents' dreams.

These three things are what direct response is all about. Direct response for today's colleges and universities is today's virtual Ellis Island. If one out of five college-bound students has one parent who was not born in the U.S. and if one out of ten college-bound students has *two* parents not born in the U.S., the country's colleges and universities are laying a bright path to the American dream for people who have demonstrated the courage and the commitment to come here. Therefore, colleges owe it to prospective students to use direct response tools ethically, responsibly, and productively.

What is direct response? One business owner is said to have stated, "I know half my advertising dollars are wasted – the problem is, I don't know which half."[2] While this is a commercial analogy, it holds true for colleges as they market to students. Direct response is the half that colleges will always know about because it is in their control. Direct response is:

DIRECT MARKETING
& DIRECT RESPONSE
IN UNDERGRADUATE
ADMISSION

134   PART THREE
       CHAPTER 10

CHAPTER 10

2 This quotation has been attributed to John Wanamaker, and many others.

- *Measurable*. Specific individuals on campuses are responsible for communicating with students and their work can be measured and refined again and again.

- *Intelligent*. The definition of junk mail is a piece of mail sent to someone with no interest in what a college has to offer. True direct response, on the other hand, is *never* junk, because it is targeted with precision and an awareness of one's responsibility in initiating a conversation with a child.

- *Personal*. Direct response treats people as special. It doesn't mean that a personal letter or e-mail was written – but it means that it was personalized for a certain type of individual. Direct response is polite. It treats individuals with respect by recognizing their individual needs.

- *Honest*. Words, as Frank O'Hara (1995) tells us, have meaning. Words are strong as rocks. And when colleges are speaking with children and families, they must at all times remain steadfast in their integrity and remain conscious of the words they use. Practitioners of direct response must act with clear and absolute integrity at every stage – from targeting their lists to designing their programs to writing their copy and selecting their images. Those who fail to act with integrity discredit all of higher education. More emphatically, those who fail in this area are likely to provoke federal legislators to draft new laws that inhibit the entire higher education community in the work we do.

- *Actionable*. Recipients of direct response know what a college wants them to do, because they are asked to do something quite specific. If someone is sent a direct response message, he has been given a clear choice, with a sense of the benefits of both action and inaction.

"DR" is different from other tools because it is a way to reach students who otherwise would not think of a particular college. It encourages them to think they *might* want to learn more about a college, to just say "maybe."

For colleges and universities, no matter how campuses feel about it today, direct response is a necessity, and, this author would argue, an obligation. Direct response is never junk mail or spam. The selection of a college is for many families the most significant and high-risk purchase they have ever made. While colleges are asking for the trust and money of families, they make no promises in return.

Well-practiced direct response is not about climbing the rankings (though it can have that effect) or social engineering (though it can do that, too); it is a way to extend counseling opportunities. Used with honesty, expertise, and intelligence, direct response is an essential tool from which colleges and families benefit.

So, if one accepts that direct response is something he or she must do well to succeed, the next questions become how and when is it used, and what are its financial costs?

Good direct response recruitment must succeed in three functional areas. Those three areas are: Lead Generation, Qualification, and Cultivation.

STUDENT
MARKETING
FOR COLLEGES
AND UNIVERSITIES

PART THREE
CHAPTER 10   135

Area One: Lead Generation

Lead generation, in the commercial world, is the first step in a multi-step, high ticket sales process. A college choice is an extremely high ticket, high-risk purchase. In pro bono counseling with families on college choice and admission, this author has found common needs — with a range of families that runs from the heirs to major fortunes with parents with terminal degrees from Ivy League institutions, to families well below the poverty line whose parents speak little or no English and have extremely limited formal education. Regardless of a family's background, college choice is viewed as a high-risk decision. The college choice process is imbued with anxiety and uncertainty. That is so because all parents in America want their children to be happy and successful as a result of their college decision. Lead generation programs allow students and their parents to "just say maybe."

For colleges and universities, "Search" has been the lead generation tool. It is still an incredibly potent tool, when it is well planned, well executed, and well measured. Search can be regarded in terms of sequential and consequential events.

Step One: Goal Identification.

First identify the goals of a Search campaign. Identifying what the institution should do differently or better before embarking on a search campaign is vital to assessing success or failure at the outcome.

There are two levels of goals that Search can help institutions accomplish. The first is about the program, and its immediately measurable impact. The second has to do with institutional goals, and the role that Search – usually the largest or second largest first source of inquiries – can play in achieving those goals.

When considering the first level, or program, think about it in a number of ways. An experienced Search practitioner will likely think in terms of response rates: "I want to achieve a 15% response to Search, instead of a 5% response." A very experienced Search practitioner may think in terms of conversion: "I want my Search inquiries to convert at a rate of 4% instead of 2%," or "I want my Search to be better targeted." If the Search is new, or if the institution has not yet begun using online and e-based tools, it may be regarded in terms of media or implementation: "I want to have a good eSearch," or "I want my Search program to be performed effectively and without adding unreasonable work to my team." The good news, of course, is that all of this is achievable without compromise.

The second tier to Search goals has to do with institutional goals – the mandates for change or improvement. Often, these goals are beyond the

PARTNERS IN *SEARCH*

Any good partner in a Search program will want to know the institution's goals and have or build a plan for how they can help achieve them. A good Search partner should be able to guarantee that they can help you achieve your goals. They should understand that you are placing your professional future, at least to some degree, in their hands, and that there is an ethical consequence of that choice on their part. They should have sufficient expertise and information to be able to make such a guarantee, and back it up not with just a refund but with the results you deserve, even if those results must be achieved at the partner's expense. But of course, you cannot hold anyone to a guarantee without a set of measurements – your goals for Search.

control of the senior enrollment professional at an institution, so buy-in from multiple constituencies should be sought.

There are a number of common institutional goals that must be supported by Search:

- *Gender Balance.* The odds, and the demography, are against most institutions in this. Unless the institution is a technological or business institution, or has colleges within the institution that are "male-heavy," it is likely to experience a slant toward over-enrollment by females. It is essential that any corrective or preventative needs in this area be addressed responsibly. There are multiple tactics, which should be used in conjunction, to ensure that the college does not have to "dig deeper" to get either men or women.

- *Ethnic, Cultural, and Socio-economic Diversity.* In general, colleges and universities seek to "look like America" on campus. And they must comply with the law, with institutional policies and with the consciences of their administrators. Search is a tool by which institutions can reach these talented students – again, through a combination of tactics, which are all too often invisible in the letters, e-mail messages, or applications of even the most successful peer institutions.

- *Academic Quality.* Search can support any goals in this area, however far-reaching, provided the institution has a strong base of market intelligence, a "secret playbook" about what works for others and can be adapted to the college's needs, and an absolute assurance of the "heavy lifting" Search can and cannot do.

- *Geographic Diversity.* If a campus President wishes to have the college become "national," how can one go about it? Search can do it, without breaking budgets, but it requires a keen and judicious eye.

- *Affluence.* Most institutions are tuition revenue-driven. That requires many administrators to seek out a certain percentage of students with the ability to pay something close to "sticker price." Search can support your goals in this area without "red-lining" the most deserving and talented students, whom you most want.

Step Two: Targeting

Lead generation in the commercial world relies on a fairly simple equation: an opportunity for success based on four items, and targeting – ensuring that the right people receive a message at the right time – is tied for first in importance in Lead Generation.

Effective and informed targeted communications, combined with the right timing, is an enormous part of what separates a Search program from junk mail.

What is effective and intelligent targeting? A few things:

PLAN, PLAN, PLAN

Search can meet virtually any goal – or combination thereof – that an institution strives to achieve. But the exercise of identifying goals and expectations is essential, even if Searching with in-house resources, but especially if Searching using an external partner. "The plan may be useless, but the planning process is invaluable."

Dwight D. Eisenhower said of planning, "It's valuable because one articulates what victory means – and what failure would look like."

- Accomplish saturation in the primary market. All national data indicate that the vast majority of students will ultimately enroll at a college within 150 miles of their homes. That means that for most institutions, the primary market is the area of greatest importance and opportunity.

- "Rifle shot" in secondary and outreach areas. Very few colleges can afford to blanket the country, yet most are asked by campus leaders to achieve a more aggressive or expansive regional or national profile. How does the enrollment manager balance this mandate against a budget that is fixed?

- Craft a list recipe. Most institutions today can effectively use a mixture of list sources – combining survey-based sources and test-based sources. No one source provides blanket coverage. If an institution uses only one list, it is missing at least half of its best prospects. The numbers support this fact.

- Build around proven academics parameters. Institutions should be cautious in refining based on desired majors, since most students will change their major choices while in secondary school and even through the first two years of college. As important, Searching to "social climb" – to cover only the highest ability students — is usually ineffective, as it places an institution firmly within the competitive set in which it is at greatest disadvantage. Most institutions find Search effective in their "bread and butter" academic range.

- Be judicious with segmentation, ensuring appropriate inclusion. Colleges should strive to reasonably and ethically convert targeting to ensure that it covers all markets, and reaches all groups. Institutions risk leaving strong students out of their programs, or overreaching for prospects that will never enroll there.

- Achieve perfect timing. This is an essential part of targeting. If the Search message is not reaching the best prospects on time, they are no longer your best prospects, they are now someone else's! This does not mean that campuses should simply get mail out early – it means a good deliverable eSearch, it means sophomores, it means getting "names-to-mail" in five days. If a window is missed in any of those areas, the college risks being viewed as a junk mailer or spammer.

Step Three: Message & Design

The purpose of message and design – or copy and art – is to provide a strong "call to action" for the student that strongly embodies the voice of the institution. While copy and art are important, in traditional lead generation, they contribute only about 20% to the opportunity for success. Why? Because if the targeting, timing, and medium is wrong, outstanding creative work will *never have*

TEST NEW CREATIVE APPROACHES

New creative approaches have an immense ability to jeopardize enrollment outcomes. Institutions should test new approaches in the smallest statistically significant segments, and build systems which allow them to account for the meaningful impact of competitive, programmatic, and situational variations. There is no such thing, in direct response, as a "great idea that didn't work." Testing will inform your creative development – oftentimes in surprising ways. Even experienced marketing, branding, or advertising professionals find that their "tried and true" methods go awry within the higher education market, when they have not accounted for the immense complications of the business.

the opportunity to be seen by students. Another blunt fact is that untested creative work has limited ability to improve direct response results.

Step Four: Offer

Offers are the promises made to prospective students: they are a way of opening doors for them. If a student chooses to respond to a Search solicitation, he will receive this "offer" – typically a publication of some kind. The "offer" is the *quid pro quo*, what a student can expect to receive as a result of responding to Search. Offers are an early first opportunity to indicate what kind of experience a student will have at an institution. He or she can be treated as an anonymous face – "You'll be placed on our mailing list" – as a possibly interesting student in a sea of interesting students – "You'll receive our viewbook" – or as a student whose life is understood and whose time is valued – "You'll receive this helpful tool."

In a basic way, offers are essential in Search. If good offers are not developed, Search will not perform well.

If a school is performing well in Search, it has opened a door for the optimal group of students – students who are likely to be interested in what the college provides, likely to be admissible, and likely to enroll if admitted. And, of course, this pool of students is also in line with institutional goals.

If sound offers have been developed and a successful Search program is in place, a college has built a good pool, and is practicing direct response in a way that is both ethical and pragmatic. You are, as Dick Whiteside says, doing the right things, and doing them right. There are only two more areas to conquer.

Area Two: Cultivation

In a recent issue of *The Weekly Standard*, David Gelernter (2003) noted that he had been e-mailing since the early 1970s. Such "new media" is more than 30 years old. E-mail is *not* new. Around about the time David Gelernter sent his first e-mail, another important thing was happening in America: the world of mass marketing was coming to a final, and well-deserved, death...except in the market of higher education.

E-mail and online technologies are the lifetime realities for most of the prospective students colleges contact, and are the work essentials of their parents. However, e-mail requires some extremely careful and diligent stewardship – just as all college communications do – if it is to convert the right prospects into applicants.

Mass marketing is still alive, if not well, in higher education undergraduate recruitment. Too many campuses still build a "publications array" based on our own traditional schedule, and not on students' and parents' needs. Institutions all too often try to force-feed families information on *college* timelines; for instance, viewbooks are often printed once a year, if that frequently, and mailed out only to rising seniors. Families do not want to wait, and will not do so. If institutions cannot deliver, they are likely to miss out and be the second college to reach out to prospective students—"second" is often too late.

One institution that this author has been working with for the past decade has been climbing the rankings at an incredible pace. They have done it by being first: first to talk to students, first to respond to them, first to send them critical information, first to admit them when they apply, first to award them financial aid. This institution – not an Ivy – has been winning time and time again against some of the top institutions in the world. Because it is there *first* and it is there at the *right time for the family*, the family and student know they are *special* to that college. Good cultivation of inquiries is, quite simply, good stewardship. It is simply good manners to be responsive. It is direct response in action.

National research has shown for quite a few years that most students build their short list – and identify a first choice – before the mid-point in their junior year of secondary school. Institutions should consider whether their critical argument is made before that point, or whether it is, for instance, passively waiting for viewbooks to get back from the printers. Institutions should refer not to a calendar for production and mailing, but to the student's calendar of need in order to be proactive. The critical moment will pass otherwise.

The cultivation of inquiries is perhaps best considered as a communications stream in a sequential, and a consequential, way. A cultivation plan must be crafted from the perspective of a student, not an institution, in order to be sensitive to the needs, interests and experiences of students as they consider the major decision of college choice.

In cultivation, there are several critical factors, or genres of information, that are essential to parents and children in ensuring that they have what they need to say "yes" or "no":

■ *Academics*. Time and time again, national research shows that giving students information about the major they desire early is essential. This may seem fundamentally counterintuitive since somewhere between seven and nine out of every ten students is actually undecided about major. And yet students choose based upon this information. Colleges must use what they know of commercial direct response, and impart to students the critical information they desire and require in the slender window of opportunity.

■ *Affordability*. This is such a struggle. How can colleges impart messages of affordability without

RE-EXPERIENCE THE COLLEGE CHOICE DECISION

A long-dead Scottish poet wrote, "O wad some Power the giftie gie us/ To see oursels as ithers see us!"[3] As enrollment managers cultivate potential students, they must strive to recollect the college choice experience as though it was once again their own. And they must strive to hold themselves and their partners accountable for *making and measuring* success by *seeing themselves as others see them*. Failing to measure success means that schools will never know if they are doing the right things, and doing them right. Institutional partners should have a plan and a system that will allow for measuring success.

3   Robert Burns, *The Poetical Works of Robert Burns*, New York, 1904, p. 133

either making the institution sound "cheap" or presenting a message to an audience that shall never encounter that reality? The simple balance is to tell the truth to everyone, but send the right people (which means different targets for appropriate messages) the information they need, at the right time.

- *Campus – Student Life.* This is vital. Students think: "Will I fit in?" This is foremost in students' minds. It is such an overwhelmingly influential factor in students' happiness during college that it is a large part of what their families care about as well.

- *"What Happens Next?"* Students want to know how their lives will be *different* if they attend a particular school. This is one of the most profound – and often unacknowledged – questions students ask as they choose a college. Only Harvard, perhaps, need not consider this question. But almost any other college must, and it is a real puzzler since it is impossible to guarantee results for students, four years' time and study into the future. Nonetheless, a promise and commitment can be made to the student in exchange for the student's right fit and commitment. Colleges must articulate to potential students what is possible if they choose to enroll.

The difficulty with cultivation is not that these arguments must be made. It is not even how to make them. It is that they *must be made on the student's and her family's own timeline, and made preferably before the mid-point of the junior year.* Also, no one is more interested in the details of a high-ticket purchase than within the first 30 – 90 days of when they first inquire. When so many colleges are not able to invite prospects to their campuses – and so many do not have the "second best" option of inviting them to a regional event – it is difficult to communicate to potential students before that critical decision point or even before the proven point of short-listing in the junior year. And yet, it can and must be done. Colleges that fail to do so will have to struggle feverishly in the future to maintain their identities.

Of course, there *is* a silver lining, which is that it can be done in time with the resources at hand. But it demands a *plan* that is guaranteed to get the institution closer to its goals.

Direct response is *not* rocket science. It is highly complex, as numerous perspectives and processes need to work together. The higher education business demands a high degree of information, integrity, and accountability, used in balance and with intelligence. All too often, it demands a partner from outside the institution – someone who knows how to do this with limited resources. There are superstar teams out there in admission offices all over the country, who are doing this on their own successfully. Many colleges can replicate their success. But to do so requires working as hard as they do or much harder while making profoundly intelligent choices.

Area Three: Qualification

"How has it come to this?" ask colleges and universities. "It never used to be this way!" they say. Also: "I never got this much mail when *I* was looking at colleges!"

But look at it this way: This is the consequence of the world's best techniques powered by a college's best intentions. This is a world in which the children of migrant workers can go to MIT, to Agnes Scott, to Champlain, to UVA. It is an American world, a world that exists in *actuality and potentiality* – of *infinite choice*, in which choice is combined with information, capability, and ... saying no when no is the right answer for *you*.

This is the world of the individual – individual students and individual families. No one knows what is right for another person or family.

But direct response tools empower choice. They provide choices and make the crooked path plain, comparable and decisive. **Therefore,** colleges must empower students to say no when they mean no. Students can say no at any point after they have received the critical information outlined previously. There are many ways to give them that information; it requires knowledge of how students and families process information. It is completely doable, it just is not often *done*.

If colleges qualify students – by which I mean, give students a chance to say *yes* or *no* when they have sufficient information to make the right and mean-ingful choice for them – schools can save a great deal of money downstream. Qualifying students in recruitment is not new. There is a long history of *tele-phone* qualification, particularly. However, in today's world – with Americans clamoring to sign up for the National "Do Not Call" list, with students busier than ever with extracurricular activities, etc. – tele-qualifying is far less prac-tical than it once was. Difficulties in implementing tele-qualifying programs lead to delays, which in turn produce increased cost and limit the ability to apply what the program has taught. That means net benefit from this type of qualification program is in fact quite limited.

However, qualification is a program that is profoundly adaptable to online and e-based media. At Royall & Company, such programs can be achieved with great speed, with virtually no risk to the institution (either in terms of public relations or in alienating students), and at very low cost. Knowing how easily achievable this can be, it is surprising that more colleges choose not to use these tools.

Conclusion

Direct response in undergraduate recruitment is no easy task despite the fact that colleges know what must be done. In the movie *The American President*, Michael Douglas says, "America is not easy. America is advanced citizen-ship." That is what direct response is, in this worthwhile, frustrating, complex and difficult professional world in which we live: advanced citizen-ship, in order to be more ethical, honest, and fundamentally in tune with families' needs.

DIRECT MARKETING
& DIRECT RESPONSE
IN UNDERGRADUATE
ADMISSION

142 PART THREE
CHAPTER 10

TECHNOLOGY & STUDENT MARKETING

PHIL CIFARELLI
Chief Financial Officer

&

MARK CULLEN
Managing Director
Exeter Group, Inc.

O ver the course of the past fifteen years, technology has played an increasingly important role as a strategic tool of the effective enrollment manager. Understanding how technology can support and augment enrollment and marketing goals, brand initiatives and tactical plans is critical to the success of the enrollment management plan and the overall success of the institution.

In addition to remaining expert in the ever-changing thinking on marketing, branding, and the host of other topics covered in this monograph, today's enrollment professionals must also be well informed about the selection, implementation, and use of technology. Today's enrollment information systems are more varied and complex, prospective and enrolled students are more technologically demanding, and the rate of technological change continues to increase every year. In the past ten years alone, technology has fundamentally changed the recruitment, admissions, and retention strategies of almost every institution.

While most enrollment managers have gained the requisite strategic enrollment expertise through the traditional tutelage model, familiarity with highly complex information systems is frequently outside their training and experience. Further, as technology has continued to permeate every administrative and academic area of higher education, information technology (IT) support has been stretched thinner; in many cases in today's environment, enrollment managers receive proportionally *less* support than they did ten years ago.

Properly implemented, today's systems can add tremendous value to the marketing function, but following the path to state-of-the-art technology is frequently an arduous, risky, and expensive journey. Current systems are as complex as they are powerful, and require careful thought and planning when being considered and implemented. Most importantly, technology should be evaluated as a tool to help enrollment managers execute a well thought-out marketing strategy; technology should not be regarded as a strategy in itself.

STUDENT
MARKETING
FOR COLLEGES
AND UNIVERSITIES

This chapter will explore the changing role technology has played in the enrollment management process. It will track the history and evolution of enrollment management systems; explore systems' roles in defining and executing an enrollment management strategy; and lay out a framework for the evaluation and implementation of the new innovations that will inevitably arise.

A Brief Overview of the Evolution of Administrative Systems

Mainframe Systems

The stalwart of administrative systems from the early 1970s through the 1980s was the mainframe or minicomputer batch-based system. Engineered to handle large numbers of transactions and provide detailed reporting on the data, these systems allow for automation of many tasks and consolidation of information. Mainframe systems are considered "workhorses," and are still in widespread use today for many applications. Data are entered into these systems through "dumb terminals"; the data are batched; and processes (programs) periodically run against the data to transfer information, print reports and letters, or perform calculations. While the user interface (UI) is not particularly friendly (character-based and menu-driven) by current standards, it is very efficient for data entry. Most mainframe systems are monolithic in design, with information stored centrally and enrollment management functions supported mainly as a front-end to the registration and records systems. The record-keeping focus of these systems makes them well suited to storing and reporting on static data, but very inefficient at processing *ad hoc* requests and poorly designed to handle the flexible requirements of today's proactive recruiting environment.

Client–Server Systems

In the early to mid 1990s, the increasing power of desktop computers with graphical user interfaces (GUI) and improved campus networking infrastructures paved the way for client–server based systems. This shift in technology allowed admission offices to transfer computing power, which traditionally was available only on the mainframe host and meted out by IT administrators, directly to end users. The result was the introduction of personal computer (PC) based marketing and enrollment systems designed to allow enrollment managers to manage and execute an enrollment management strategy directly from their desktops. Recruiting and enrollment management solutions took advantage of GUI front-ends, distributed computing, and integration with commercial word processing and reporting software to allow schools to interact with prospects and students in a much more flexible manner. Until that point higher education administrative systems had been designed and built almost exclusively by vertical niche companies focused on higher education. The adoption of PC-based systems allowed schools to begin to take advantage of best practices and functions formerly reserved for private sector corporate sales and marketing organizations.

The explosion of function associated with client–server systems allowed schools to deliver their message to students in new and exciting ways. Correspondence became highly customizable, and schools could dynamically add and remove students from series of letters and e-mail campaigns based on changing interests, demographic information, or any other piece of collected information. Contact management data, until that point maintained on paper-based media, became integrated with the basic record-keeping functions of the system. Ad hoc reporting became available to admission and retention counselors, and some system functions were made available to admission officers while out on the road recruiting. In essence, as admissions and retention had become more competitive, the record-keeping mainframe systems had lost pace with the goals of their users. This new technology allowed enrollment managers to use software as active, supportive tools rather than as tangential and at times totally disconnected data repositories.

While these systems provided big advances in function for enrollment management users, the flexibility introduced by these systems came at a price. Highly network-intensive, early client–server systems taxed early campus network bandwidth, and distributed applications proved costly to maintain for IT organizations. Also, first generation PC-based databases were not nearly as robust or scalable as their mainframe counterparts. Integration with common productivity tools like Microsoft Office(tm) allowed admissions offices to leverage existing skill-sets, but IT support for these decentralized systems proved difficult and costly. Many offices that implemented these systems were left to technologically fend for themselves, and the integration of these "shadow systems" with the rest of campus was often ignored or performed in the most rudimentary way.

Finally, the decision to implement these specialized solutions was often made at the departmental level, leaving their implementation and integration to the enrollment management administrators. Rich in function, many recruiting and enrollment offices struggled with the implementation and rollout of the functions supported by these applications. The result was often under-optimized and poorly configured solutions introducing process change for technology's sake. The lack of integration with the institutions' marketing plans and strategies weakened their strategies' effectiveness and limited the potential impact of their systems.

Integrated ERP Systems

In the mid 1990s, domestic and international software vendors began to develop and sell comprehensive Enterprise Resource Planning (ERP) solutions to the higher education market. These systems integrate financial, human resource, and student systems into one centrally managed database. They are designed to combine the best of the mainframe and client–server architecture, offering universities centrally managed integrated systems with rich client interfaces.

A significant benefit of ERP systems is the high level of integration they provide between the various functional areas on campus. The data model and architecture of the applications allow for flexibility in accommodating a variety of underlying business processes and the distribution of those processes across campus. The flexibility of these systems is generally marketed as "rules-based," referring to their ability to be highly configured to meet the specific needs of any client requirement or practice. The hope was that institutions would no longer have to modify their business processes to

STUDENT
MARKETING
FOR COLLEGES
AND UNIVERSITIES

PART THREE
CHAPTER 11   145

fit the design of the software. The rules engines would be easily modified to accommodate all of the requirements on campus.

Rather than act as a panacea to the stresses imposed by inflexible mainframe solutions, flexibility of ERP systems often leads to many unanticipated and at times animated implementation discussions concerning boundaries between offices. Traditional silos of functionality are not honored by these new applications, which were designed to share information and eliminate duplicate processes wherever possible. The result is often some discomfort for departments as they try to determine where their "turf" begins and ends. If handled properly, these exercises can be a very healthy means to evaluate the efficacy of existing business process on campus; if not handled properly, they can result in organizational stress and costly time and resource overruns.

The flexibility of ERP rules engines can also result in expensive implementations. While these engines are generally designed to upgrade smoothly, setting up and maintaining a rule often requires advanced technical capability. Similar to programming a customization, the effort and cost of a configuration in most ERP applications can be significant. The skills required to manage configurations are not typically resident in an enrollment office, creating a dependence on IT staff or external consultants for modifications and adjustments. Finally, because the focus of ERP systems is on the breadth of function provided to the university as a whole, individual modules are often less capable than their best-of-breed counterparts. The tradeoff between ideal departmental function and institution-wide integration should be considered carefully.

Internet and Web Systems

The next major technological shift that affected the enrollment management process was the introduction of Internet-based applications and services. To use a cliché, it really did "change everything." Rather than access systems through a program that is run and maintained on a PC, Internet-based applications are accessed via a standard Web browser. This shift allows for access to systems from anywhere in the world thereby allowing institutions to extend functions directly to prospective students. Extending the new functions and ease-of-use introduced in the client–server model, the Internet provided a host of new applications designed to allow schools to communicate their marketing messages to prospects and students. By enabling this direct interaction with prospects, students, and others involved in the recruiting process, the Web computing architecture brought students and enrollment managers closer together.

The Internet also provided new opportunities for active marketing to prospects and students. While traditional mail and e-mail campaigns are reactive to initial student interest and passive in nature (in that they are dependent on active interest and ongoing solicitation of information to be effective), the Internet provided students an opportunity to seek out and enter information for schools. Online college search engines, Web portals, online application processors, Internet-based guidance and tours, and Web site personalization provided schools with services and capabilities not imagined just five years earlier. No longer can institutions rely on a carefully crafted and timed brochure mailing to students to control their image development. With the Internet, students can browse, formulate impressions, and make decisions with no formal interaction with the school.

In stark contrast to the highly controlled and managed mainframe world, the Internet empowered the student in favor of the institution, reduced a school's control of its message, and created a completely new environment in which to compete for qualified candidates. Institutions find themselves in an intense race to adopt this technology to keep up with students' demands, struggling with the challenges of consolidating and integrating the data, and under pressure not to fall further and further behind the technology curve.

Conclusion

This high-level overview of the development of technology as it relates to student marketing demonstrates a series of tradeoffs to be weighed as one evaluates and adopts new systems. Mainframe systems provide efficient data entry and centralization of data at the expense of flexibility and end user empowerment. Client–server and best-of-breed systems provide rich user interfaces and flexibility at the expense of integration and cost-effective maintenance. ERP systems allow schools to integrate their administrative data and work with a single vendor, but can be costly and less functional than specialized products. And, while Web solutions provide exciting new ways to reach out to students, if not managed properly they can erode the control a school has over its image, message, and relationship with students.

Ultimately, technology should be measured as a tool that allows schools to protect and extend their competitive advantages. Understanding, managing and resolving technology tradeoffs are among the most important challenges facing today's enrollment manager, as there is no right or wrong set of solutions. The remainder of this chapter will explore how technology fits into a student marketing campaign and provide a framework for evaluating and implementing new technologies that come along.

Student Marketing Functionality – *The State-of-the-Art*

To help understand the role systems play in the formulation and execution of a marketing strategy, one must first understand the types of applications and functions available to today's enrollment professional. The pages that follow will explore the different categories and types of tools available, and establish a context in which new tools can be evaluated, selected, and implemented.

Recruiting Functions

Despite the wide differences between schools' branding strategies, the underlying recruiting and admission processes are rather similar. Although there are clear differences between rolling and fixed date admission processes; highly selective and open enrollment programs; for-profit and not-for-profit institutions; public and private institutions; and certificate and degree programs, for the most part schools employ similar communication and evaluation processes to identify, recruit, and enroll students. In order to actively recruit their classes, most institutions purchase voluminous lists of names from testing services; conduct direct mail campaigns aimed at generating prospective interest; visit feeder institutions; advertise; hold informational events for prospective students; and develop and nurture relationships with guidance counselors. Most schools have supported these efforts to some degree with one or more technology solutions/offerings, but rarely are the possibilities and limitations of these systems taken into consideration when formulating the recruiting strategy.

In addition to the traditional admission and recruiting ERP module in use at most institutions, over the last five years or so several new modules have emerged in the recruiting system arena. One of the most well known of these is a group of applications referred to as customer relationship management (CRM) solutions. CRM products are end-to-end marketing and sales support systems designed specifically to allow schools to establish and develop complex relationships with prospects, advisors, recruiters and all other individuals and institutions associated with the recruiting process. While initially developed for corporate sales and marketing organizations, the relevance of such tools to the tactical goals of higher education recruiting has resulted in the inclusion and integration of these modules into many student system ERP suites.

CRM tools allow schools to more easily set up, execute, and manage multiple marketing campaigns, and to do so in a way that fits into the context of a broader lifelong relationship management program. Once campaigns are defined and associated with target audiences and objectives, communication tracks (supporting e-mail, Web, and written correspondence) can be attached to an individual based on the candidate's interests or responses. In other words, series of contacts can be tailored to individual students within a given cohort, creating a dynamic one-to-one marketing model.

Contact management features allow detailed notes to be stored for every contact with the individual – a valuable feature both for ensuring each additional contact is personalized as well as enabling schools to measure the effectiveness of any given type of contact or campaign. Further, CRM call center management functions allow schools to execute and manage telephone campaigns, including script prompting, auto-dialing, full interaction history tracking, and integration with other contact management functions of the system. Automatic collateral fulfillment and event invitations can be integrated within communication tracks, and event management (scheduling, logistics, RSVP tracking, etc.) is also a feature of this class of software.

Finally, by integrating the data from each of these different marketing and recruiting campaigns, the CRM-based recruiting modules allow users to easily track and report on critical performance metrics. This reporting capability allows users of CRM systems to track the effectiveness of any given recruiting campaign or initiative, allowing enrollment managers to effectively test new, imaginative contact and communication strategies against sample groups to continually refine their strategies and effectiveness, and adjust efforts accordingly to better shape the applicant pool.

CRM type functions are integrated into today's systems in many ways, making it difficult at times to compare one solution with another. Some specialized admission and marketing systems incorporate these features directly into the base function of the admission system, while other vendors take advantage of existing private sector-based CRM modules as branded add-ons to the admission or recruiting module. Either way, it is important to make sure that the contact and communication functions are integrated with the other aspects of the admission and recruiting modules and the feature set offered with the product is easy to use and can support your contact management and communication requirements. At a minimum, the contact and communication engine should provide the ability to dynamically add individual and series of letters, contacts, and follow-ups to students based on customizable key events in the admission process. It should also provide for the easy integration of all recruiting and admission data easily with letters, e-mails and telemarketing scripts.

Augmenting traditional contact and communication strategies, intelligent portals are beginning to serve as front-ends for prospects and applicants to institutions' administrative systems. Far more than a static admission Web site with online prospect and application forms, an intelligent portal utilizes technology similar to that used by advanced online retailers to track customer habits, buying patterns, and tastes. With an intelligent portal, once a prospect registers on the institution's Web site, the profile information they provide (combined with purchased and previously gathered information) is employed to establish an automated, customized Web page for future visits. A potential music major might receive notices of performances or streaming audio of those performances, while athletic recruits might see updates on athletic programs, up to the minute scores, or video from the latest game. The possibilities are limited only by the imagination, and because the systems continually "learn" during each interaction, institutions continuously hone the image presented to each. When used to complement the traditional recruiting process, this information can be utilized to further personalize e-mails, correspondence, and other contacts by the institutions.

Back Office Functions

The enrollment management concept of "one-stop-shopping" became popular on many campuses in the 1990s. While all institutions continually work to improve their services to students, some institutions went so far as to build student service centers to house all related departments under one roof to make it more convenient for students to shuttle between offices. While the principles behind such an approach proved sound to good student service, the expectations of students today have surpassed that model in favor of "no-stop shopping." Specifically, students are increasingly expecting to be able to conduct all interactions with their institution online, at any time during the day or night. The move to consolidate and strategically locate departments is being replaced by an expectation that there are no departments per se, only transactions. Today's students obtain goods and services in the world at-large with a mouse click, and are drawing less distinction between these services and their interactions with educational institutions. Students are increasingly expecting that they be able to apply for admission and financial aid, register for room and board, register for classes, drop and add courses; initiate petitions for special permissions and waivers, clear holds, request transcripts, receive and pay bills, take classes, and perform any other transaction online at their convenience from anywhere in the world.

Today's software is capable of accommodating student expectations through the use of enterprise portals combined with robust self-service functions and integrated workflow. However, while this model brings with it much efficiency, it is often difficult to implement in a way consistent with the culture, personnel, organization, and controls on many campuses. The challenge for institutions that embrace this technology is striking a balance between the virtual and human interactions. While this might at first seem daunting, most institutions find that by moving routine business transactions to the Web, staff is able to focus on more meaningful, higher-value interactions with students. This, of course, is the trick – employing technology to simultaneously decrease the transactional workload of staff while enhancing the students' experiences.

Integration with Financial Aid

The use of financial aid as a recruiting tool to increase academic quality and/or net revenue has become more important in the admissions process at many institutions. In order to effectively leverage financial aid during the admissions process, institutions need to be able to integrate financial aid packaging information with admission data for purposes of communications and data modeling. More specifically, the contact and communication engine must be capable of integrating information from both the Admissions and Financial Aid Office into a single communication strategy, and the appropriate data must be available and accessible to integrate with institutional leveraging models. ERP systems usually have an advantage over best-of-breed solutions because of their inherent centralization of data, but even within ERP applications, cross-departmental information can be segregated, requiring that the systems be carefully configured to allow both departments adequate access to the other's data.

Evaluative Feedback Mechanisms, Data Mining & Business Intelligence Functionality

A key driver in employing technology in the recruiting process is to reduce the cost of routine transactions to allow greater focus on high value activities. The return on investment associated with the collection of prospect and applicant data can be measured by increased contact personalization, the ability to conduct advanced decision support, and ultimately, achievement of institutional goals. If captured information is stored but not sufficiently accessible, organizations end up being data rich but information poor. The most effective administrative systems provide useful information gathered from across the organization to facilitate timely and sound decision-making. To be truly effective, this reporting capability must enable each office and department in an institution the ability to monitor and measure their particular processes and objectives as well as provide support to senior administrators to allow for a holistic view of the institution.

Most institutions rely on a number of different technologies to help them answer questions about their prospects' demographic makeup and behavior, the effectiveness of marketing campaigns, and their performance compared to prior periods. Performance and demographic related questions are best handled by querying an institution's data warehouse, while new, Internet-based survey tools provide innovative options for answering more difficult questions concerning prospective students' attitudes, beliefs, and behaviors over time. With careful thought given to the questions asked and the data collected, Web-based surveys aimed at specific audiences can be extremely successful. They can be executed quickly and cost-effectively, and generally yield a significantly higher response rate than traditional paper-based surveys.

Data warehouses are employed to make data easier to find, format, and distribute. They are typically designed separately from the administrative transaction systems that supply them with data to ensure the transaction systems remain fast and that the reporting systems remain flexible and easy to access. Transaction-oriented systems are traditionally engineered to store data in a very compartmentalized manner (highly normalized) to optimize transaction speed, while data warehouses store data in a way that makes comparative and *ad hoc* reporting easy for individual office administrators. Typically, only data relevant to reporting are stored in a data warehouse, and the data are fundamentally organized in a manner that makes it easy to conduct longitudinal analysis, simulations, and modeling. Reporting tools typically front-end the data warehouse for the design, distribution, and display of reports to end users. Collectively, the products that allow users to organize, query, extract, format, and distribute information are known as business intelligence tools. More than a typical reporting tool, these products provide advanced analysis engines, sophisticated paper, Web, and e-mail report distribution, and support for data mining – the screening and filtering of large volumes of data to unearth relevant trends hidden in the data.

Once a data warehouse is established, advanced tools such as executive dash-boards can be developed. Executive dashboards provide Web-based summary views of the data created to keep administrators apprised of key performance indicators in their areas and across the institution on a near real-time basis. For example, an enrollment manager could log in and immediately see how recruiting campaigns are progressing; how specific events are shaping up; where applications stand; etc.

Data warehouse projects are typically undertaken at the institutional level. While the process is technical and most of the work is handled by an institu-tion's IT department, it is critical that the recruiting and enrollment teams have input at the design and implementation stages. The majority of the value of a well-constructed data warehouse is contained in the design of the database architecture. By communicating to the technical design team the kinds of reports and information that are needed, chances of getting that information in the end are increased. The more thorough and imaginative the enrollment team can be in collaboration with design team about the informa-tion ideally needed to run recruiting, admissions, and enrollment processes, the more flexible and capable the end solution will be.

STUDENT
MARKETING
FOR COLLEGES
AND UNIVERSITIES

Issues to Consider When Making Technology Choices

Technology Is Expensive – Choose Wisely & Understand What It Costs

It is doubtful that any single institution is currently employing all of the technological capabilities described above. In fact, it would be risky to do so. Institutions need to decide where they want to be on the technology adoption continuum – bleeding edge (explorers), cutting edge (pioneers), or mainstream adopters (settlers). The answer depends on the severity of the need and individual circumstances, but most institutions conclude they are better off waiting until the technology is proven and cost-effective.

The question of what technology to implement should be considered in terms of two primary factors – 1) the ability of the prospective tools to help the institution protect or improve its competitive advantages and achieve recruiting objectives; and 2) the availability of human and financial capital. It is easy to get caught up in the whirlwind of options available, but the number of systems that can be safely implemented in any given year is low. Even over time, schools are typically better off focusing on using a few tools well as opposed to supporting a host of different tools that are used less effectively.

With respect to cost, it is surprising how many organizations commit themselves to significant technology projects without fully understanding the initial and ongoing cost dimensions. A careful due diligence process is essential to obtaining an understanding of the true cost of ownership of a technology decision. When considering new technology solutions, consider benchmarking against other institutions that have done similar projects; utilizing the services of independent research organizations (such as Gartner Inc., Eduventures, etc.); and/or employing external consultants to assist in the assessment. Investing in a detailed "total cost of ownership" analysis is always worth the effort since "going back to the well" mid-way through a project for more funds undermines credibility of both the project in question and future initiatives.

It's Your Technology – Be Involved in the Decision

Enrollment managers are responsible for the life-blood of an institution – enrolling the right number of qualified students. Accordingly, enrollment managers should be heavily involved in the selection of the tools they use to reach their objectives. While it is essential that significant technology choices be made carefully and thoughtfully in the context of a broader institutional-wide plan, the plan should not be so rigid that institutional technology choices are made at the expense of critical enrollment management practices.

Implemented and used effectively, technology enables flexible and agile decision-making, but it is not possible to change technologies quickly or easily. Recovering from a bad choice can be financially and politically expensive, just as one bad recruiting year can impact an institution for many years thereafter. IT organizations must by definition and necessity play a critical role in the process of developing a technology plan and the selection of products to meet the goals of that plan, but it is essential that all senior administrators play an equal and active role in the process. Technology has become too pervasive and strategically important to be left to any one area of the institution to drive, and while the interoperability and support of the

TECHNOLOGY EVALUATION & SELECTION – PRACTICAL SUGGESTIONS

The most effective technology evaluation and selection techniques vary depending on the specific application under consideration, but there are some common questions and practices to keep in mind when considering any major technology commitment. Assuming that an institution-wide IT plan is in place and all stakeholders agree that the direction makes tactical and strategic sense, a good first step is to gather as much information as possible to make as informed a procurement decision as possible. Research the particular segment of the market thoroughly; determine which vendors are likely to be stable partners; and if they are public companies, research their financial position. Learn about their respective product lines, including technical specifications, and where the products fall within their given life cycle. While a class of applications might be mature, a specific product from a specific vendor within that class might be in the early stages of its life cycle. This is not necessarily a negative, as the underlying technology is likely to be more current, but it raises other issues. No institution likes becoming an "accidental beta site." Institutions should assess their appetite for the risk that accompanies each choice, and make an informed decision.

Once all of the information has been analyzed, make a preliminary assessment of total cost of ownership for each possible alternative to determine which options make sense from a budgetary perspective. With a little digging, much of the information is freely available on the Web or the broader public domain (e.g. from colleagues at other institutions; professional associations; etc.). It might also be wise to subscribe to analyst reports from independent research organizations.

Once the procurement process has begun, take deliberate action to create a competitive environment among interested vendors. Many institutions hire independent consultants to guide the vendor evaluation and selection process. They can be very helpful in maintaining a fair, balanced and informed process, and often understand how to pressure vendors for the best deal. Listen carefully to what software salespeople say about their product, and how they say it. Today's products are complex. Carefully worded responses can be technically correct, but might cover up a gap between the product and an institutional requirement. Also, reflect on what salespeople do not say. All products have gaps, but sales representatives will not necessarily point them out.

Finally, look at the products in detail. Demonstrations are a critical part of the buying process. When evaluating product demonstrations, be a skeptic. Do not allow a vendor to rely on a "canned demo." Make them show how the software will meet your institutional specific needs. If possible, send the vendor institution specific scenarios prior to the demo, but make sure to get "off the script" several times during the demonstration. Pick random areas of the software to dig deeper. Ask to see detail screens or functions. If told something cannot be demonstrated

STUDENT
MARKETING
FOR COLLEGES
AND UNIVERSITIES

but that the software can be easily configured to meet the need, ask to see *how* it would be configured right then. In general, responses such as "I don't have access to that particular function on my laptop" or "My demonstration version is not configured to show that feature" are often used to hide a product gap. The vendor knows institutions might not follow up on the request, and even if they do, it gives the vendor time to piece together a non-optimal solution. Vendors almost never do demonstrations on partially functioned demo systems. If the presenter cannot show you what you want to see at the presentation, chances are that the software does not support the request or a costly modification is necessary to achieve your requirement.

The procurement process is a constant intelligence gathering exercise. To get independent validation of your choices, try to do at least one site visit at a customer institution without the vendor. During the visit, inquire about their experience with the implementation, the product functionality, ease of reporting, community satisfaction levels, ease of upgrade, quality of support, etc. Don't expect all positive news – implementing solutions is a difficult process and always has positives and negatives – but do expect to hear that the vendor was easy to work with during the highs as well as the lows. Consider attending a user group meeting, and monitor user listserve discussion forums if available.

If possible, put off buying decisions to the end of a vendor's fiscal quarter or year-end. While this can often result in a larger discount, make sure you can execute a contract by the date in question as the discounts usually go away at the start of the next fiscal period. Finally, keep expectations reasonable. No matter how much due diligence is undertaken, there will be surprises along the way.

underlying technology is important, so too are the business processes that technology supports.

There is also a tactical dimension to this debate: who should lead large IT projects? For many years the default for project leadership was the IT organization, but in recent years leadership from the functional ranks has become much more common. There is no one correct answer, as it depends most upon the individual talents among the leadership candidates, but it is certainly an issue that should be discussed during the assessment and selection stages of new technology. All else being equal, functional leadership with the strong support of and collaboration with the IT group is usually a better solution because, in the end, function is much more important than the underlying technology.

Use Consultants Wisely

Consulting is another critical dimension to technology implementations. It is common knowledge that many of the high profile, failed technology implementations of the past ten years have left the IT consulting industry with a black eye. It is easy to understand why. As a rule of thumb, for every dollar spent on licensing software, one to seven dollars is spent on implementation.

A significant portion of those funds typically is spent on consulting assistance, so it makes consultants an easy target when projects fail to meet expectations. That said, when utilized properly consultants can cost-effectively add domain expertise and play an integral role in the successful implementation of a product. IT implementations are exercises that institutions and departments engage in only on rare occasions. Maintaining one-time expertise and implementation capacity in-house can be very expensive. IT consultants offer an alternative solution by enabling schools to ramp-up and draw-on specific domain expertise for a limited time, relieving themselves of the long-term obligations of supporting that staff.

To understand the optimal way to employ external consultants, it is critical that institutional executive sponsors and project managers first understand the dynamics between the three essential components of any project – 1) scope; 2) schedule; and 3) resources. By understanding exactly what needs to be accomplished at each stage of a project, they can determine how many and what type of resources (i.e., people) will be needed to do the job. The tradeoffs between these three dynamics drive project economics.

Institutions typically staff projects from three channels – existing employees, new hires (regular or temporary), and consultants. The former two options will be almost always nominally less expensive compared to the latter; if the institution has adequate existing technical skills, project management experience, and personnel/supervisory capacity, existing employees and new hires are the preferred choices. However, due to all the varied skills needed to make a major technology project successful in a limited timeframe, this course of action is often not feasible. Most projects rely on a blend of resources from each of these channels, with a heavy reliance on consultants for specific areas of expertise (e.g. technical or project management) and/or one-time only tasks.

The ideal consulting firm should have experienced resources available that understand the technology, the product, higher education business practices, and project management – people that have done similar projects before successfully. Like any professional services relationship it is first and foremost about the quality of the people and the organization the firm represents. Accordingly, insist on meeting senior members of the firm, the proposed project manager, and key members of the team, and carefully check references.

Contracting with a consulting firm requires careful definition of the three project dynamics described above and a detailed understanding of the agreed-upon pricing structure. With respect to pricing, most consulting projects follow one of two common models – time and materials (T&M) or fixed price. Both models have merit depending on the circumstances of a given project, but generally fixed price contracts are in an institution's best interest as they force a careful listing of tasks to be performed, tie those tasks to a timeline, and mitigate the risk of cost overruns. While most firms build a risk-premium into the fixed price offered to account for the transfer of "cost overrun risk" onto the firm, in the long run it is generally a worthwhile investment.

Regardless of the structure selected, failure to adequately document what the firm is obligated to deliver greatly increases the odds of a less than satisfac-

CHAPTER 11

STUDENT
MARKETING
FOR COLLEGES
AND UNIVERSITIES

tory experience. On a T&M contract, less specificity generally correlates to more billable hours and revenue to the firm. With fixed price contracts, while an institution's initial costs are capped, the firm is only obligated to perform tasks specifically identified in the contract. Omission of a critical piece of the project will not be covered under the pricing cap, and failure of the client to meet its obligations (which can be significant) can cancel a fixed price project mid-way through and automatically convert it to T&M. Because the project is underway and the client is dependent on the consulting firm at that point, it can turn into a costly engagement.

To control costs and optimize the use of consultants once the engagement is underway, pay careful attention to the project plan and make sure the institution's team is organized and empowered in a way that they can make decisions quickly and decisively. Not unexpectedly, this is an area where higher education's predisposition to deliberate decision-making and consulting industry economics clash. As alluded to above, most fixed price consulting contracts will include a clause requiring the institution to provide certain deliverables with a commitment to stay on schedule. Next to conflicts over scope definition, this is probably the most common cause for client/consultant disagreement. Institutions should realistically assess their ability to stay on schedule and be cautious about the commitments they make before the contracts are executed.

Lastly, leverage the consulting resources as much as possible to maximize value. One- time tasks (e.g. data conversion) are typically best suited to consultants. For areas where consultants take a lead role that will be relevant beyond the initial implementation, plan for knowledge transfer from the consulting team to the institutional team. Relying too heavily on consultants or choosing to stay removed from the process increases the risk that all of the know-how will walk out the door at the end of the project. Always demand excellence, but keep expectations reasonable and lines of communication open. Consulting firms want their clients to be successful, and depend on them for good references for future projects. Both parties share the desire for a successful project, and with the right incentives in place, they can work together as a single, motivated team.

Developing Technical Skills

It appears certain that institutions will become even more dependent on technology in the future. In order to optimize the value of the systems used to support the marketing and enrollment processes, departments must make a commitment to developing and maintaining the appropriate technical skills within their offices. Reducing dependency on external organizations for system support (including internal IT) will ultimately give enrollment managers more control over their processes, data, and results.

To this end, a new class of power users has emerged. Not quite as technically proficient as programmers but far more trained and comfortable with the operation of software systems than a typical end user, these functional information specialists combine in-depth business process knowledge with a detailed understanding of how to configure software solutions and extract data for reporting and management purposes. These users effectively manage the ongoing configuration and tuning of the office's systems and serve as local extensions of the IT staff. They know how and when to roll out features of new systems, and can do so in a way that maximizes impact to the marketing and enrollment processes with a minimum of disruption.

Contemporary skill sets are necessary to effectively manage and leverage these systems. This represents a difficult fiscal challenge because systems are funded from capital dollars, while people represent an ongoing commitment to operating budgets. While debating the tradeoffs between adding or developing staff with these skills versus other institutional needs can be contentious, the potential enrollment benefits of these technical resources make them strategically important positions. An institutional commitment to appropriately skilled staff and their continual retraining and professional development can more than pay for itself by giving the institution competitive enrollment advantages and allowing for realization of the value of the systems in which the institution has invested.

Creating a Framework for Evaluating New Technology

Implementation and maintenance of new technologies are very large undertakings and represent a substantial ongoing commitment to be effective. Such projects often take on a life of their own, and their impact is pervasive throughout an organization. The evolution of technology and host of new products being offered suggest that systems selection and integration will be an ongoing dimension of enrollment management offices. In fact, an argument can be made that the process of selecting and implementing new systems in and of itself is critical to retaining competitive advantages. To illustrate this point, one needs to look no further than online applications. While initially thought of as novel, these services are quickly becoming the preferred means for students to apply to school. Institutions unable to select or integrate these types of services risk being disadvantaged in the competitive recruiting process. Institutions that are able to effectively analyze, choose, and integrate technology on an ongoing basis stand to gain ground on their competition.

With the factors that contribute to a successful selection and implementation of technology having been addressed, the remainder of the chapter will construct rules for a framework to evaluate the new technologies that will threaten to change the way prospects apply to schools.

Technology is a Tool

Institutions that use technology most successfully are constantly mindful that it is merely a means to an end, not an end in and of itself. No technology can recruit, enroll, and retain students automatically. It is merely a tool that can help staff fulfill these critical functions when used properly, and enrollment professionals are wise to evaluate new technology with this backdrop in mind. While it is easy to get caught up in the marketing hype offered by vendors, most technology decisions can be reduced to simple questions. Such as...will the technology enable the staff to spend more quality time with applicants during the recruitment process? Will it assist staff in answering prospects' questions or concerns more effectively? How will it help us reach strategic objectives more efficiently? Not surprisingly, these are, in essence, not technology questions at

STUDENT
MARKETING
FOR COLLEGES
AND UNIVERSITIES

PART THREE
CHAPTER 11   157

all. Rather, their foci are on how to provide staff with tools to do their jobs better by focusing on human activities that technology can never replace.

Focus on Function

The benefits of client–server systems make a compelling argument to mainframe users and Web-based systems present a formidable challenge to the client–server model. In reality, there is no one right answer. While there are certainly advantages to many of the new systems on the market, many schools continue to operate quite effectively with mainframe technology that has been enhanced and customized to fit existing processes. The reason this is the case is that ultimately the benefit of new systems is dependent on function, not technology. A marketing staff armed with a tailored, customized, efficient mainframe system can be just as competitive as their neighbor armed with the latest Web-based system.

When evaluating technology or products, look for solutions that fit current processes best and provide flexibility to meet future needs. Good technologies should seem intuitive and feel as if they were designed to support current processes out of the box to as great a degree possible. Giving up function for a given technology, integration, cost, or any other reason presents risks that should be carefully assessed. In the end, the ability of the system to support institutional processes to reach strategic goals and grow with the organization is the most critical aspect of the solution.

Dream of Running, but Walk First

When implementing new systems, start slowly. Make sure all of your current processes are supported, and then add new features and process changes in a measured way to find out what works best for your organization. Watch how the staff uses the system, and how prospects respond to new contact methods and services. Rolling out new capabilities in a deliberate manner allows organizations to measure results more accurately and manage change more carefully. Adding multitudes of new correspondence tracks, initiating active Web pages, and beginning a telemarketing campaign all at once can be overwhelming and risky if all are new undertakings. Not only is it unlikely that these new features will be configured optimally, the institution runs the risk of losing control of its message and existing advantages.

Technology is in many ways a metaphor for change, and introducing and managing change is difficult, takes time, and should be done carefully. Fortunately, despite the stress inherent in adopting new technologies, most users want new system implementations to succeed. Remember that it is the *people* who will use the systems that will ultimately be responsible for the system's success or failure. Make everyone in the organization partly responsible for the new system. Leverage their experience, perspective, and ideas. If the time is taken to get their "buy-in" along the way, the process of adopting new software can be very rewarding – even fun. As discussed, innovation and application of new technology in the student marketing process provides exciting opportunities for organizations. System innovations challenge staff to think creatively and imagine new possibilities, which can result in valuable new student marketing techniques and initiatives. Take advantage of it, and enjoy it.

INTEGRATED MARKETING AND THE STUDENT MARKETING PLAN

PART FOUR

INTEGRATED COLLEGE AND UNIVERSITY MARKETING

JIM BLACK
Associate Provost for Enrollment Services
University of North Carolina Greensboro

The notion of integrated marketing in colleges and universities is more myth than reality. In truth, very few higher education institutions have mastered the art of integration. This chapter will explore the market forces that compel us to strive for integration along with the barriers that retard or derail our progress.

Kurt Lewin (1947) described competing forces like these using a force field analysis metaphor. Diametrically opposed forces often yield organizational inertia or maintenance of the status quo. Such is the case with integrated marketing. In this chapter, models of integrated marketing will be compared looking specifically at their orientation and strategic nature. And, approaches to overcoming the inertia that grips us in order to truly integrate marketing will be explored.

Defining Integrated Marketing

The term, "integrated marketing," often is confused with "integrated marketing communications," when in fact, the latter is a subset of the former. Integrated marketing communications focuses exclusively on the communications and promotional aspects of marketing. For example, consistency of message and design, segmented communications, and the marketing mix are typically integrated marketing communication issues. While integrated marketing includes communications and promotion, it extends to the strategic matters of product, place, price/cost, convenience, and the customer.

Sevier (1999) identified six elements of integrated marketing in colleges and universities:

1. Integrated marketing must have an outward focus. This often consists of efforts to understand the needs of the marketplace, cultivate relationships with customers and suppliers, and develop strategic partnerships that support marketing objectives.

2. Integrated marketing must address strategic problems strategically, rather than tactically. This requires a commitment to addressing problems and opportunities in academic programs, methods of delivering instruction, pricing, and the like.

STUDENT
MARKETING
FOR COLLEGES
AND UNIVERSITIES

3. Integrated marketing must occur at three levels: strategic, organizational, and message. The strategic level requires the alignment of institutional mission, resources, and marketing priorities. At the organizational level, the focus is on coordinating resources and marketing efforts. Sometimes, this coordination is formalized by the reshaping of the organizational structure, creating cross-functional teams or marketing committees. The third level, message integration, refers to having "a common look, sound, and feel across various mediums and over time" (Sevier, 1999, p. 5).

4. Integrated marketing involves active listening to the customer.

5. Integrated marketing is most effective when databases are used to provide empirical data for decision-making. Marketing expenses can be an endless black hole, and no institution has an infinite supply of resources. So, we must know what works, what marketing strategies resulted in the obtainment of their stated objectives, and most importantly, what strategies provided the best return on investment.

6. The final element of integrated marketing is message coordination. Message coordination is different from message integration in that it refers to a focus on the timing, synergy, and logical linkages between messages, rather than a focus on consistency among messages.

Black (2001 & 2003) extends the definition of integrated marketing to include an institution's culture. According to Black, integrated marketing implies that every marketing enterprise on campus should pull together with a common purpose. And, beyond those formally charged with marketing some aspect of the college or university, every faculty and staff member should know and reflect its brand promise. The institution's brand promise and related marketing messages should become part of the organization's genetic constitution – integrated into the institution's belief system and reflected in organizational behavior. No amount of external marketing will alter an institution's image without the internal belief in and daily practice of the brand promise.

Historical Context

Tangential elements of marketing in college and universities originated with the opening of America's first institution of higher learning, Harvard College. According to Brubacher and Rudy (1976), Colonial college presidents performed related functions along with their other duties by default. For example, there was no one beneath them in the administration to ensure that students met entrance requirements. Requirements were usually evaluated through in-person interviews and, in the case of Harvard, with an essay written in Latin. At Yale, applicants also had to submit evidence of high moral character and the father or guardian of the student had to post a bond sufficient to cover the bill. While higher education during the Colonial Period was primarily for the elite, some college presidents did award scholarships to "poor boys." They also managed loans when colleges were paid with promissory notes and payment in kind – usually in the form of grain, cotton, sheep, pewter, and the like. Among their other responsibilities, college presidents registered students in courses, managed student records, served as librarians, and awarded degrees.

Much like today, Colonial college budgets were largely funded through tuition and fees (Brubacher & Rudy, 1976). The need to produce tuition and fee revenue combined with pressures from England to educate "learned clergy and a lettered people" (Rudolph, 1962, p. 6) led college presidents to feel enrollment pressures not entirely unlike those of today's presidents and enrollment managers. Brubacher and Rudy (1976) indicated that Yale began in 1710 with only 36 students, and in that same year, Harvard enrolled only 123. Throughout the entire seventeenth century, Harvard enrolled less than 600 students. Of those, only 465 ever graduated – far from Harvard's current graduation rate. Even though the disciplines of student marketing and retention were nonexistent at the time, concerns over institutional image and attrition were ubiquitous.

The next major shift in the college student market occurred following World War II when the number and diversity of students pursuing a college education increased dramatically (Rudolph, 1962). Correspondingly, the number and kinds of colleges and universities expanded. "Supported by unprecedented public investments in their facilities, research efforts, and instructional programs, institutions did build – and students did come, paying whatever price they were quoted in an effort to increase their own chances for personal as well as economic success" (Zemsky, Shaman, & Iannozzi, 1997, p. 23). Then, the baby boomers, representing some 76 million people in the United States (Merritt, 1999; Howe & Strauss, 2000), flooded college campuses in the 1960s and early 70s. College and university enrollments reached unparalleled highs. Demand far exceeded supply, and hence, marketing was not a priority.

In the late 1970s, however, administrators began to worry that expanded capacity had outpaced a shrinking demand for postsecondary education (Zemsky, Shaman, & Iannozzi, 1997). Marketing, as we know it today, emerged as a potential solution to this supply and demand problem. The renowned author, Philip Kotler (1975 & 1976), began to link established marketing principles and practices to non-profit organizations and specifically to college and university admissions operations.

In the early eighties Huddleston (1980), Blackburn (1980), Lay and Maguire (1980), Kemerer, Baldridge, and Green (1982), Hossler (1984), and others brought a marketing research focus to determining the needs of internal and external student constituents. In particular, they studied factors that influence student choice and identified marketing approaches such as differentiating, institutional positioning, prospect segmentation, target marketing, and pricing as means to influence choice. As with most significant change, theory and some level of practice preceded wholesale adoption. Into the mid-1980s the term "marketing" was rarely used on college and university campuses (Lauer, 2000). Many thought that responding to the needs of the market by treating students as customers would inevitably lead to commercialism of the academe and pandering of students (Swenson, 1998). Common sentiment among many administrators and faculty was largely that the academe should not resort to slick gimmicks and tricks (Sevier, 1998). After all, higher education is not a business. Of course, that attitude only prevailed until market pressures forced institutions to think otherwise (Zemsky, Shaman, & Iannozzi, 1997). This market shift left some college and university leaders scrambling to respond to 1) unprecedented levels of competition, 2) a need to diversify student enrollments (specifically to increase the number of females, minorities, and adult students), 3) increasingly savvy consumers, and 4) an exploding cottage industry of companies providing a plethora of marketing tools.

Like most change of this magnitude, there emerged winners and losers. Few, however, were insulated enough from market pressures that they could ignore the phenomena (Sevier, 1998). Marketing efforts, often sporadic and knee-jerk in nature, swept over the nation's institutions. While the nomenclature is readily accepted, even embraced, on most campuses today and the tools of the trade are much more sophisticated than in the 1980s, few institutions have developed and implemented integrated marketing plans (Percy, 1997). Though some give lip service to the value of a unified, consistently articulated marketing message and design, the number of institutions that has achieved this status is relatively small.

Today's Market Forces

"Peter Drucker warns that the failure of traditional colleges and universities to respond to market forces will result in their demise. He sees little likelihood of their overcoming the structural inertia that grips them" (Swenson, 1998, p. 35). These bastions of academic knowledge, once seemingly invincible, have been shaken to their very foundation by the emergence of a borderless, educational economy (Black, 1999). The barriers of time, space, and place no longer exist. Consequently, many of today's learners are seeking convenience and customization – benefits for which they or their employers are willing to pay a premium.

David Siegel, a leading Internet strategist, predicts that e-customers will pay to build their own products and services (Siegel, 1999). We are already beginning to see evidence of this in higher education. Students are increasingly earning their degrees through multiple educational providers and modes of instruction. Educational services are becoming unbundled, with different providers supplying various components: curricular development, delivery of instructional modules, provision of student services, student evaluation, and even awarding of credentials (Wallhaus, 2000).

Market forces such as these have compelled institutional leaders to consider, even embrace, marketing principles. Demographic shifts, increased competition, a rise in consumer sophistication, demands of society, political pressures, changes in the economy, globalization, advances in technology, and poor institutional image are among the market forces that can lead to declines in enrollment or fundraising. Since most colleges and universities are dependent upon enrollment and external funding to thrive or, in many cases, to survive, a decline in either creates a sense of urgency powerful enough to result in real institutional change.

Demographic Shifts

Unlike the American colleges and universities of the 18th and 19th centuries, the academe is no longer educating just the genteel elites (Swenson, 1998). The U.S. Census Bureau estimates that by the year 2005, fifty percent or more of the U.S. population under the age of eighteen will be people of color. By 2010, a third of all youth in the U.S. are expected to reside in four states: California, Texas, Florida, and New York (U.S. Census Bureau, 2000). Over the next decade, the two fastest growing populations by age range are predicted to be 15–24 and 45–54 year-olds (U.S. Census Bureau, 2000). And the population growth of women will continue to significantly outpace that of men for the foreseeable future (U.S. Census Bureau, 2000).

Consequently, the student market and the alumni base are becoming increasingly diverse. An institution's ability to segment and differentiate by population without sacrificing its cohesive identity or blurring its image is one of the great challenges facing higher education marketers (Topor, 1998). In fact, contemporary marketers believe in the power of one-to-one marketing – tailoring each communication to the individual (Peppers & Rogers, 1996). The seemingly contradictory goals of segmentation of the audience into discrete groups or individuals and consistency of the message find common ground in the threads that run throughout all institutional communications: the primary marketing message, design elements, and navigation. Differentiation is achieved through secondary marketing messages and relevant content, accompanied by testimonials and visuals with which the recipient can personally identify.

Increased Competition

"The essence of marketing strategy is to attract and keep customers while keeping competitors at bay" (Schnaars, 1998, p. 10). As previously inferred, when the supply is high and the demand is not, competition is more intense. Today's parents of prospective students can hardly fathom the level of interest colleges and universities are demonstrating in their sons and daughters. This was certainly not the case when they were considering higher education options. The barrage of glitzy brochures, videos, CD–ROMs, phone calls, e-mails, and advertisements has had a numbing effect on their recipients. Jockeying for position, each institution is attempting to win the hearts and minds of these prospective students. Saturation of the student market with messages and images is a symptom of a highly competitive environment.

A proliferation of competitors combined with pressures to compete on price has forced higher education institutions into an upward spiral of aggressive marketing (Aaker, 1991). However, so much focus has been placed on promotion that most higher education institutions have neglected the other elements of marketing: product, price, and place (Hayes, 1991). Robert Sevier (1999) rightfully classified promotion as tactical and product, price and place as strategic. While tactical strategies may provide an institution with a competitive advantage, such strategies can easily be replicated and therefore are not sustainable. Enduring competitive advantage is only possible through strategic solutions, but of course, strategic matters of product, price, and place are the most difficult to affect.

STUDENT
MARKETING
FOR COLLEGES
AND UNIVERSITIES

For example, few institutions have used their curriculum to differentiate themselves from the competition (Sevier, 1998). Formal mechanisms for providing information about market demand, potential market niches, demographic trends, competitor analyses, data-driven enrollment projections, price elasticity, and the like are virtually nonexistent on most campuses (Black, 2000). Hence, the product mix is typically not market-driven. Instead, it tends to be driven by what faculty wants to teach.

"One of the biggest mistakes colleges and universities make is to continually expanding their mission. However, smart institutions strive to focus their mission and thereby develop even higher levels of relevance" (Sevier, 2000, p. 7). The degree of relevance an institution has to a student or donor determines his or her affinity to the school. By trying to be "all things to all people," institutions risk diluting quality to the point of offering very little of relevance to anyone. Market responsiveness should not be confused with mission drift. Responses to the market should occur within the context of the institution's mission. Clarity of mission can position an institution uniquely among its competitor set.

Consumer Orientation

Students and parents are sophisticated consumers, comparing financial aid packages, campus visits, orientation experiences, and every encounter they have with colleges and universities (Lauer, 2000). Institutions that ignore the consumer do so at their peril. "Not unlike customers in the private sector, our students often voice their dissatisfaction with their feet or, in the era of distance learning, with their mouse. They simply leave" (Black, 1999, p. 24).

If internally as well as externally colleges and universities embrace the notion of service to students, they will dramatically influence marketing, enrollment, and management outcomes (Dimun, 1998). Institutions adopting a service model are more likely to be consumer-focused. Organizations that are in tune to meeting or exceeding customer needs generally have strong customer loyalty. "Higher education is beginning to understand that people don't change doctors, lawyers, dentists, where they shop for groceries, what airline they use for frequent flying, or tax accountants at the drop of the hat or by whim" (Topor, 1998, p. 2). Such organizations typically have intentional strategies designed to cultivate customer relationships. As learning providers, colleges should be about the business of establishing lifelong relationships with students and alumni. Those who have enrolled in or contributed to institutions in the past, unless they have been disenfranchised, are the most likely to continue their involvement in the future.

For some time now, enrollment managers and institutional advancement officers have given lip service to a "cradle to endowment" model of operating (Kvavik, 2000). But the truth is that few actually have implemented a model that begins to cultivate an institutional relationship with an individual from the first contact as a prospective student, through his or her enrollment, into life as an alumnus. And, the models that do exist are disjointed. The admissions office courts prospective students and encourages them to enroll. Various individuals and departments, often in an uncoordinated fashion, establish relationships with students in and outside the classroom. The alumni and development offices connect with graduates and solicit donations of their time and money. But, almost never are these efforts integrated into a seamless continuum of the student's lifelong relationship with the institution. Where is the integrated, campus-wide plan to cultivate a "cradle to endowment" relationship? Even in the most visible aspects of campus interactions with customers, integration is blatantly absent (e.g. a common portal, consistent message and design, shared events).

Technology and Globalization

Philip Kotler, a marketing icon, calls the two most powerful forces in today's economic landscape – technology and globalization. He views technology as a driver for globalization and as "the ultimate shaper not only of the material structures of society but also of human thought patterns" (Kotler, 1999, p. 4). Certainly, technological advances have enabled the information explosion that characterizes the Information Age. The paradigm shift from a manufacturing to an information economy has resulted in a profound social transformation that requires institutions of higher education to adapt (Swenson, 1998).

Furthermore, the Internet and the World Wide Web are fundamentally changing the way companies promote brands, sell products, communicate with customers, and manage suppliers (Oblinger & Katz, 2000). Higher education is not immune to this paradigm shift. Though at a slower pace perhaps, technology has influenced how universities and colleges are promoted, sell their programs, and communicate with students, alumni, and other key constituents. In higher education, the Internet and Web also are changing instruction, research, administration, public service, and student services (Oblinger & Katz, 2000).

A myriad of new educational products, services, and providers are entering the e-learning marketplace. Ranging from university spin-offs such as On-lineLearning.net and NYU Online to educational management organizations like the University of Phoenix and Jones University, the array of providers is expanding exponentially (Oblinger & Katz, 2000). Many traditional campuses are developing their own electronic-based courses or contracting with software firms (e.g. Lotus, Convene, WebCT, Blackboard, and Eduprise.com).

With instruction available whenever and wherever a learner wants it, students have virtually unlimited options. More learner-centered choices result in greater competition and specialization across a wider range of educational providers, and simultaneously a greater need for providers to cooperate and share resources (Wallhaus, 2000).

The emergence of e-learning, e-books, e-recruiting, e-care, e-mail, and e-commerce on college campuses has markedly impacted the marketing paradigm with our internal and external constituents. For instance, the back-to-college buying experience was decidedly different for students enrolling in the fall of 1999 than prior years. Small but significant numbers of these students ordered textbooks, computers, dorm furnishings, and other products from the rising tide of "dot com" companies focusing exclusively on the college market (Green, 2000). Web portal products, like Campus Pipeline, that deliver customized information and student services captured substantial

STUDENT
MARKETING
FOR COLLEGES
AND UNIVERSITIES

portions of the higher education market in 2000. The development of new technologies such as these creates opportunities for some organizations while closing off opportunities for others (Schnaars, 1998). Only those organizations that are strategic in their thinking and have speed itself as a strategic thrust will be successful in this rapidly changing information economy (Schnaars, 1998).

Societal Demand and the Economy

In today's economy, "knowledge" workers must be both technically skilled and broadly educated. "For some in traditional higher education, however, preparing students for careers in this new economy seems inevitably a less worthy undertaking than the pursuit of knowledge for its own sake. They divide the world of learning into 'education' and 'training' and speak condescendingly of the latter" (Swenson, 1998, p. 34). If traditional higher education providers fail to seize the expanding "training" market, others will. In fact, they already have (Dolence, 1999).

People in our society have changed dramatically over the past decade or so. According to Kotler (1999), they:

- Have grown more sophisticated and price sensitive;

- Are short of time and consequently, want more convenience;

- Are less brand sensitive and more accepting of lesser known and generic brands;

- Have high service expectations; and

- Have decreasing levels of supplier loyalty.

Kotler (1999) goes on to say that the difference between competing products is becoming indistinguishable to the consumer; companies are giving away costly discounts and add-ons (akin to tuition discounting in higher education); price is readily met by competitors; advertising is becoming more expensive and less effective; and organizations are spending exorbitant amounts on promotion and their sales force. Sound familiar? Indeed, the academy is a mirror reflection of most things that occur in society.

Depending on one's perspective, higher education has been a victim or a beneficiary of many of the trends in society and specifically the business world. Whether it has been an emphasis on cutting costs to remain competitive, ruthless restructuring in an attempt to get "lean and mean," increased international competition, or the total quality movement of the '80s and '90s, ivory towers have not served as a refuge from these market forces (Schnaars, 1998). Nor have colleges and universities been protected from changes in the economy such as deregulation or privatization (Kotler, 1999).

The ability of higher education institutions to anticipate and respond to these inescapable forces will determine their positions in the higher education marketplace. Product, price, promotion, and place are each important dimensions of the marketing response to the changing needs of society.

Political Pressures

Pressures from federal, state, and local entities have been escalating during the decade of the '90s. Federal legislation such as the Student Right to Know and Campus Security Act, the Taxpayer Relief Act, the Higher Education Reauthorization, and the American Disability Act or court rulings like those on Affirmative Action often impact our students and thus, are a part of their college experience. Whether colleges agree with a piece of legislation or court ruling or not, their ability to administer or explain it is connected to a student's image of the institution.

At the state level, mandates like the one in Virginia that impose market discipline on public colleges and universities are becoming more common (Archibald & BeVier, 1998). Similarly, public colleges and universities in Texas recently have been mandated to produce enrollment management plans. A number of states have adopted performance-based funding models (e.g. South Carolina, Texas, and Florida) which typically have criteria related to student satisfaction, retention, and graduation rates. Decisions about preferential admission, state scholarship and financial aid programs, tuition planning programs, reporting requirements, and the like all influence priorities within the walls of our campuses. Some bring clarity and focus to the marketing enterprise while others detract from marketing priorities.

Local political pressures typically take the form of Board mandates, president or chancellor priorities, faculty resistance or support, or community interests. Regardless of the source, local pressures have the most immediate and emphatic affect on marketing priorities. If institutional image is not a priority from the top to the bottom of the organizational chart, integration will be impossible. Integrated marketing is more about organizational behavior and culture than it is about promotional consistency.

Poor Institutional Image

According to Fred Gehrung, president of Gehrung and Associates, a media-relations company in Keene, New Hampshire, "In today's uncertain economy and intensely competitive environment, there is one thing a college or university cannot economize on – its reputation. Prospective students and families need to be even more certain about the institution they select, about the quality of the education it offers, and about the outcome, meaning the return on the investment of effort and money. Reputation now is more important than ever" (Sevier, 1998, p. 68). In a thirty-five-year longitudinal study of college freshmen, the California Institutional Research Project, conducted by Alexander Astin and his colleagues, "reputation" has consistently ranked among the top reasons for selecting a college (Dey, Astin, & Korn, 1991). Colleges live and die on their reputations.

Image-oriented institutions recognize that the marketplace is dynamic, competitive, fluctuating, and forgetful (Sevier, 1998). According to Robert Sevier, such colleges and universities possess one or more of the following characteristics:

1. Embracing a comprehensive definition of marketing

2. Recognizing marketplace dynamics

STUDENT
MARKETING
FOR COLLEGES
AND UNIVERSITIES

PART FOUR
CHAPTER 12   169

3. A belief in the constancy of change

4. Transforming vision

5. Primacy of the customer

6. Clarification of stakeholder roles

7. Redefinition of quality and success

8. A culture of "now!"

9. Data-based decision-making

10. Variation of product, price, place, and promotion

11. Clear criteria for evaluating progress

A school attempting to overcome a negative or "plain vanilla" image should begin by defining its audience. Then, it should assess its current image among key customer and stakeholder groups. Once benchmark data has been collected and analyzed, the institution should identify image gaps, clarify goals, and develop marketing strategies to address the gaps. A realistic budget should be established to support the marketing strategies. It is important to execute well. And finally, it should measure effectiveness and use findings to continue improving upon marketing efforts. In short, strong images do not just happen. They must be managed.

Implementation Barriers

To understand the barriers to implementing an integrated approach to marketing, one must first understand the higher education culture. Not every collection of people necessarily forms one distinct, overarching culture (Schein, 1992). If culture formation is "a striving toward patterning and integration" (Schein, 1992, p. 11), why then is the notion of "patterning and integration" so counter to the culture of higher education?

According to Black (2001), independent thought and individuality are highly valued in the academy. Burton Clark describes the distinct subcultures common among academics: the culture of the discipline, the culture of the profession (i.e., the professorate), the culture of the organization (i.e., a college or university), and the culture of the system (i.e., higher education). Two additional subcultures are described in the work of George Kuh and Elizabeth Whitt: student cultures and administrative cultures (Seymour, 1993). "For each of these subcultures, multiple segments exist – each with their own lexicon, rituals, customs, social structures, power struggles, and accepted norms" (Black, 2001, p. 24).

Such diversity adds to the richness of the higher education experience but it also causes fragmentation. The academic department, the athletic program, the advancement office, the continual learning division, the graduate school, and the admissions office each have their own subculture and marketing objectives. One could also argue that they have very distinct audiences and hence, a degree of fragmentation may be acceptable. This argument assumes marketing efforts, once disseminated, remain isolated to the intended audience. Of course, marketers have minimal control over who views their television public service announcement, newspaper advertisement, airport kiosk, billboard, Web banner, and other forms of broadcast marketing. Whether intended or not, these images shape the institutional image in the mind of the consumer. If institutional marketing efforts are fragmented they create indiscernible static resulting in a blurred institutional image. Instead of speaking with one voice, the higher education community sounds more like the Tower of Babel (Black, 2001).

Historical Paradigms

Sevier suggests that one of the barriers to marketing colleges and universities is a fixation on historical paradigms. He claims that institutions paralyzed by traditions, antiquated self-perceptions, and historical patterns will find themselves out of date, ill-suited for today's marketplace, or overly costly (Sevier, 1998). Similarly, Daniel Seymour describes these historical paradigms as "deep grooves that permeate organizations" (Seymour, 1995, p. 100). These "deep grooves" take the form of ingrained habits – ways of doing things that evolved over time. Often, their origin is unknown and the assumptions on which they are based go unchallenged.

"Thinking patterns crystallize, stabilize, and then calcify. Regardless of the situation or changes in circumstances, old programming begins to dictate everything" (Seymour, 1995, p. 100). "New insights fail to get put into practice because they conflict with deeply held internal images of how the world works, images that limit us to familiar ways of thinking and acting" (Senge, 1990, p. 174). Peter Senge, founder and director of the Center for Organizational Learning at MIT's Sloan School of Management, calls these phenomena "mental models." Mental models are learned ways in which we view the world (Senge, 1990). For instance, many faculty members teach the way they were taught, lecture-style, even though research clearly shows that today's students, particularly Millennial students, are visual, hands-on learners (Merritt, 1999). Usually, mental models are deeply entrenched and seemingly immutable but in fact, can be changed (Black, 2001).

Academic Culture

"For many years, academics resisted marketing because they believed that it was not consistent with the goals or image of institutions of higher education" (Clark & Hossler, 1990, p. 68). Even though the idea of marketing programs and services is more accepted today, the notion of treating the student as a customer still raises the hairs on the neck of many academics. A customer orientation is viewed condescendingly from ivy-covered towers yet it may be the very focus that will ensure success in today's competitive environment (Swenson, 1998). Not unlike any other competitive industry, college and university customers have options (Seymour, 1993).

"The differences between academic organizations and other institutions are often overstated by academicians. On the other side, they are all too often unrecognized or ignored by marketers" (Litten, Sullivan, & Brodigan, 1983, p. 19). Like most organizations, colleges and universities value collaboration and consensus building. However, in an academic culture, institutions are so determined to be collegial that endless discussions often yield little in the way of action. Colleges become terminally collegial (Black, 1999). The very

STUDENT
MARKETING
FOR COLLEGES
AND UNIVERSITIES

nature of decision-making in higher education is largely incremental and reactive rather than proactive (Hayes, 1991). The inability to shift rapidly in response to the ever-changing needs of the market is one of higher education's greatest flaws.

Admittedly, there often exists a huge disconnect between marketing priorities and academic priorities. This chasm will exist until faculty, who already are overburdened with teaching, research, and service activities, understand and appreciate, from their own perspective, the value of marketing to their school, their department, and themselves (Sevier, 1998). Unquestionably, academic priorities should drive marketing decisions, and conversely, marketing-related information should inform academic decisions (Black, 2001).

Harmony and appropriate balance between the academic and marketing enterprises is essential to perpetuating the institution's image in an integrated fashion. While many academic deans, department heads, and faculty aspire to elevate the stature of their program or bolster enrollments and see promotional marketing as a means to that end, they must be persuaded to understand the importance of a unified corporate image as well. In their honorable attempts to convey the distinctiveness of their program, they often further dilute the institution's image by failing to incorporate the institution's word mark, approved design, primary marketing message, or Web navigation and architecture. The English Department, for instance, must be seen by the customer as an integral part of a larger whole.

Resource Constraints and Competing Priorities for Funding

In "The Survey of College Marketing Programs," 52 percent of the respondents had a budget dedicated to marketing activities (The Survey of College Marketing Programs, 1998). According to the "National Enrollment Management Survey," compared to the prior year, 1999–2000 budgets for student recruitment and marketing increased for 50 percent of the respondents, remained the same for 40 percent, and decreased for the remaining 10 percent. Including personnel costs, the mean expenditures for student recruitment and marketing at participating institutions was $1,050,699 (National Enrollment Management Survey, 2000).

Influencing student choice, donor decisions, and public perception are expensive propositions. Because no institution has unlimited resources, marketing priorities must compete with all other institutional priorities (Black, 2001). "Unfortunately, many administrators consider marketing dollars spent rather than invested" (Sevier, 1998, p. 174). "To affect institutional image, sufficient resources must be committed over an extended period of time" (Black, 2001, p. 26). Patience is not part of the constitution of most senior administrators, and consequently, pressure to produce short-term results and to invest in other priorities can derail a long-term marketing strategy (Sevier, 1999).

Lack of Ownership, Organizational Structure, and Turf Issues

"Marketing functions at the vast majority of colleges and universities are scattered throughout the organization – possibly haphazardly, certainly with little or no thought to integration" (Black, 2001, p. 26). "In most institutions, undergraduate student recruiting, graduate student recruiting, adult student recruiting, public relations, and fund-raising all take place in different offices supervised by different executives" (Lauer, 2000, p. 102). Simply put, postsecondary institutions have not come to grips with the reality that they are not organized to integrate marketing (Lauer, 2000).

Inherent in these silo-oriented marketing structures are turf issues that inhibit and often derail integration efforts. Communication and coordination among a loose federation of marketing units is seldom adequate to ensure pervasive integration. When each unit is doing its own thing, the result is hundreds, even thousands, of conflicting messages, a proliferation of logos as well as other design elements, and a confused audience (Ohio State University, 2000). Most institutions lack the will to address turf issues (Sevier, 1999). But, unless a common marketing vision is established and supported at all levels within the organization, there will never be consistency or clarity of image (Black, 2000). There must be a campus-wide willingness to focus on marketing strategically and comprehensively (Black, 2001).

Marketing must be everyone's business (Lauer, 2000). If everyone is on the same page, the message will be clear and amplified. Conversely, if marketing is the responsibility of everyone, it may not belong to anyone. Therefore, along with a formal or informal structure to overcome turf issues and facilitate integration, it is imperative to have a marketing champion (Sevier, 1998; Lauer, 2000). This individual builds consensus, overcomes barriers, sets the marketing agenda, and keeps others focused and moving forward. In essence, the marketing champion is the caretaker of the institution's image and as such, is responsible for helping others to view image as one of the institution's most precious assets.

Speaking with a single institutional voice requires buy-in and acceptance of marketing messages and themes. Generally, people will not believe in the message unless they believe the messenger (Black, 1999). The marketing champion should be someone who has the respect of all constituents (Ferrari & Lauer, 2000). Through aggressive internal marketing, the marketing champion can begin to gain widespread support of the marketing effort.

Leadership Commitment

The president must visibly support the integrated marketing efforts. He or she should be involved with key decisions such as the commitment of initial and continuing dollars, the selection of a marketing champion and team, the formation of marketing goals, the selection of target audiences, and the establishment of an action plan (Sevier, 1998). In addition to the president, "The entire executive staff should 'walk the talk' in supporting the marketing concept and reinforcing its themes" (Lauer, 2000, p. 379). Without strong leadership, particularly at the top, effective marketing may occur in pockets of the campus but is unlikely to be fully integrated.

STUDENT
MARKETING
FOR COLLEGES
AND UNIVERSITIES

Traditional vs. Integrated Marketing

Sevier (1999) recognizes two fundamental differences between traditional thinking about marketing and emerging views of integrated marketing:

- Orientation and

- Strategic thinking.

He uses a comparison between the "4 P's" (promotion, product, price, and place) of marketing and what he calls "the 4 C's of integrated marketing" (communication, customer, cost, and convenience) to differentiate between the traditional and integrated approaches to marketing (Sevier, 1999, p. 5).

The

While there are obvious similarities between the 4 P's and 4 C's, a primary difference is one of orientation. The orientation of the 4 P's tends to be inward – examining the institution's academic programs on the basis of faculty and departmental strengths, setting price based on anticipated expenses and projected enrollments, promoting the institution's strengths without regard to customer demand, or delivering courses from locations and through mediums based on faculty desires or to address institutional capacity issues rather than customer preferences.

Contrary to what the aforementioned characterization of the 4 P's might suggest, there is value in an internal orientation. In fact, integrated marketing cannot be effective without an understanding of institutional strengths and weaknesses. When internal marketing intelligence is used to design promotion, pricing, academic product, and instructional delivery strategies, the result is typically markedly better than those institutions that launch strategies void of any such information (Kotler, 1999; Strauss & Frost, 2001). With marketing intelligence, institutional marketers can understand and influence buyer decisions (Kotler & Armstrong, 2001) as well as effectively position the institution among its competitors (Buell, 1986; Topor, 1997; Schnaars, 1998; Kotler & Armstrong, 2001; Strauss & Frost, 2001).

As previously stated, product, price, and place certainly have strategic elements. Lauer (2000), for example, believes strategic thinking about the product is guided by an analysis to determine how academic programs are differentiated from programs offered by competitors. The product strategy will vary depending on institutional factors such as mission, resources, and aspirations. Consideration of these institutional factors in the context of marketing requires a degree of strategic thinking.

Likewise, pricing becomes strategic when positioning price in relation to competitors. Pricing also requires strategic thinking when considering institutional expenses, student affordability, and net revenue. Financial aid becomes a part of the pricing strategy when it is used to influence enrollment behavior – either initial decisions to enroll or decisions to persist (Hossler, 2000; St. John, 2000; & Kimrey, 2002). For instance, tuition discounting is a commonly practiced pricing/aid strategy, particularly among private colleges and universities. By discounting the sticker price, many institutions hope to attract and retain an increasing number of students while bolstering net revenues.

Of course, tuition discounting is not the only pricing/aid strategy that influences enrollment behavior. By tracking yield and persistence rates for students who are assigned to a group based on their "ability to pay" (usually determined by their documented financial need) and their "willingness to pay" (estimated using some academic criteria such a standardized test scores, high school grade point average, or college grade point average), aid administrators can theoretically ascertain the "optimal" amount and mix of aid necessary to influence enrollment decisions (Hossler, 2000). Commonly referred to as financial aid leveraging, this strategy is designed to make strategic use of limited institutional resources to achieve specific enrollment and frequently, net revenue objectives.

Another such strategic approach is preferential packaging that is targeted towards students the institution highly values (Chin, 2003). Value is assigned to students based on institutional goals such as increasing the academic profile, enhancing racial and ethnic diversity, expanding geographic diversity, or optimizing existing capacity by driving enrollments toward academic programs with empty seats in the classroom.

Place becomes strategic when the method of distributing the academic product is examined within the context of space management, facility planning, faculty workload, profit/loss margins comparing class enrollments with the cost of delivery, and the like. Note, however, that none of these examples addresses the issue of student convenience seen in the 4 C's. Instead, the emphasis is on managing institutional resources. Given the dwindling state support for higher education, the poor performance as of late in the stock market, and spiraling tuition increases resulting in the public's growing discontent with the cost of higher education, it is vitally important that institutions be strategic about managing their resources.

The Four C's of Integrated Marketing

In contrast to the 4 P's, orientation of the 4 C's is outward – viewing the marketing enterprise through the lens of the customer, instead of the institution (Sevier, 1999). Through the 4 C's lens, the academic product is largely influenced by the needs of the student and employer markets; price elasticity, meaning the perceived worth of the educational offering from the consumer's perspective, drives cost; course and service delivery are designed around the preferences of the student to provide convenience and access; and one-way, generic promotion is replaced by two-way communication directed towards a specific target audience.

The benefits of a customer-oriented approach to integrated marketing can extend far beyond the direct impact on the marketing enterprise as cited above. Swenson (1998) suggests that a customer-orientated approach to marketing can foster an environment where student learning supplants teaching as an institutional instructional model. In a learner-centered model, students are encouraged to actively engage in the learning process even to the point of helping to establish their own learning objectives. Swenson believes that another byproduct of student-centered integrated marketing is improvements in customer service. The notion of seamless student services available anytime, anywhere aligns with the mantra of convenience of the 4 C's.

STUDENT
MARKETING
FOR COLLEGES
AND UNIVERSITIES

PART FOUR
CHAPTER 12   175

Lastly, Swenson sees value in a customer-orientation that includes constituents other than students. In particular, he emphasizes listening to the corporate customer as the academic product is designed or evaluated.

As for strategic thinking, any organization that plans its future without a focus on the needs of its customers is destined to fail. Indeed, the voice of the customer should drive strategic planning. This concept, however, is alien to most college campuses primarily because academicians and to a lesser degree, administrators tend to reject the notion that they have customers (Seymour, 1993). To overcome some of the disdain associated with the term "customer," it is better to use phrases like "those we serve" or "constituent groups." It is not the nomenclature that matters. It is the act of listening to the voice of the customer as strategic opportunities are explored that positions an institution to become a thriving, highly competitive organization. Colleges and universities that adopt a customer-oriented approach to integrated marketing and strategic planning will enhance their market position as an institution of first choice while building brand loyalty among students and alumni.

The four P's and C's both have merit and actually work best in combination. Similar to the SWOT analysis described in Chapter 6, a view of internal strengths and weaknesses blended with an understanding of external opportunities and threats provides marketing intelligence that is chocked full of rich insights. Such invaluable information about the institution and the customer can be used to determine strategic directions as well as influence marketing efforts.

Concluding Thoughts: Integrating the Institution's Marketing Effort

Lewin's (1947) constraining forces as well as those specific to integrated marketing (see Figure 12-1) can be overcome, but not without radical organizational change. Following Lewin's model, the first step would be to unfreeze

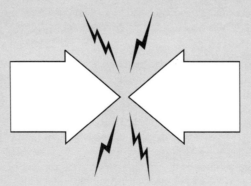

FIGURE 12-1
FORCE FIELD ANALYSIS OF COLLEGE AND UNIVERSITY INTEGRATED MARKETING

Market Forces	Implementation Barriers
Competition	Historical paradigms
Demographics changes	Academic culture
Consumer orientation	Resource constraints
Societal demands	Competing priorities
Political pressures	Lack of ownership
The economy	Organizational structure
Technology	Turf issues
Poor institutional image	Leadership commitment

the organization – specifically the deeply ingrained patterns of behavior described earlier in this chapter. Secondly, implement the change. Third, sustain the change by refreezing behavior reflecting the changes within the organization.

From a theoretical perspective, Lewin's model sounds relatively simple. However, as a practical matter, changing the culture within the academy is difficult under any circumstances but is particularly problematic when the change is centered on a foreign concept such as integrated marketing.

Dimun (1998), Topor (1998), Sevier (1999), and others have developed neatly packaged steps to achieving integration in a higher education setting. The formula is not surprising. What is surprising is how much consistency there is between the various models and even the key concepts within this very book. Most of the models begin with defining the mission and vision (see Chapter 2) followed by the kind of situational analysis depicted in Chapter 5. Next is the identification of target audiences as seen in Chapter 7. While Topor's model differentiates between external and internal audiences, the process is consistent between models. Logically, target audience identification is followed by segmentation and then differentiation by segment (see Chapter 9). Dimun's model calls for the infusion of market research to inform action plans for each segment while Sevier's model requires that market research be used to assess target audience needs before segmentation occurs (see Chapter 7). Then, Sevier's model moves from segmentation directly to the creation of a marketing mix (Chapters 6 and 8). He incorporates the four C's (customer, cost, convenience, and communication) and advocates for the ongoing evaluation of each. All three models include evaluation that is used to continuously improve the process.

So, if the steps to integration are intuitive, why is integrated marketing more myth than reality? To paraphrase a recent U. S. president, "It's the culture stupid." The conceptual framework depicted in Figure 12-2 represents one approach to changing the culture and incorporates the four frames identified by Bolman and Deal (1991) as a lens through which an organization can be viewed.

According to Bolman and Deal (1991), the *structural frame* refers to structures or systems. Often, elements of the structural frame consist of organizational structure, policies, procedures, or processes. In the conceptual model illustrated in Figure 12-2, the structural frame specifically relates to the architecture that will influence the academic culture.

The design begins with *understanding the culture*. What are the organizational artifacts, espoused values, and underlying assumptions that govern current behavior (Schein, 1992)? What is the institution's readiness for change? What are the forces (e.g. attitudes, beliefs, structural barriers, resource constraints) that are likely to produce resistance to change? How can identified impediments to change be overcome?

These questions should be answered by means of triangulation – collecting information and perspectives from a variety of sources and then synthesizing the findings to identify patterns from three or more sources. Research

STUDENT
MARKETING
FOR COLLEGES
AND UNIVERSITIES

PART FOUR
CHAPTER 12   177

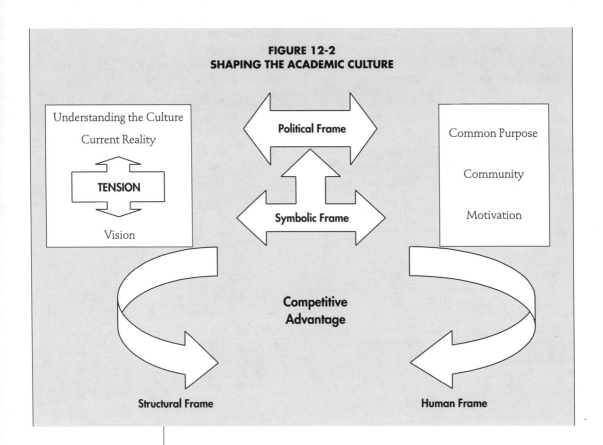

FIGURE 12-2
SHAPING THE ACADEMIC CULTURE

Understanding the Culture

Current Reality

TENSION

Vision

Political Frame

Symbolic Frame

Common Purpose

Community

Motivation

Competitive Advantage

Structural Frame

Human Frame

methods appropriate to this situation include observation, interviews, focus groups, historical research, and perhaps, survey research.

In the course of this analysis, the marketing champion should be constructing a picture of the *current reality*. A situational analysis, like the one described in Chapter 5, could be used to complement information gathered using the aforementioned research methods. Once a description of the current reality is constructed, it should be presented to various groups on campus. The purpose of these presentations is threefold. First, findings need to be tested for accuracy considering the experiences and perceptions of others. Second, the presentation should be used to create discomfort and a sense of urgency – the *unfreezing* described in Kurt Lewin's change model (1947). By pointing out discrepancies between desired behaviors and outcomes and those that currently exist, people can be motivated to engage in change activities (Cummings & Worley, 2001). Finally, the presentation of findings should lay the groundwork for future discussions about the marketing vision.

Armed with a clear understanding of the current reality and a newly crafted shared vision, the marketing champion can begin to ratchet up tension related to the gap between the two. Asking penetrating questions will stimulate discussion and cause some level of dissonance: What will it take to move from where we are to where we want to be? How should we be organized to achieve our vision? How should resources be redistributed? What academic programs need to be added, strengthened, or eliminated? What new faculty talents are needed? Questioning should be followed by structural redesign that corresponds with the new vision and the discourse emanating from questions posed. Structural redesign might include strategic planning, a revamping of the criteria for budget allocations, systems of accountability and reporting, retooling of the faculty, changes to the promotion and tenure process, a redirection in hiring practices, policy revisions, and the like. Collectively, these actions will generate a sense of urgency and redirect school, departmental, and individual priorities.

Periodically, the current reality will need to be reassessed – each time comparing it against the vision. As warranted, identified gaps should be used to direct tension points but also to praise efforts where progress has been made. Continual improvements to structural issues should become a matter of course. In the interim between assessments of the current reality and improvements to the structural architecture, the marketing champion should keep the vision in front of the faculty and staff. Every publication, media event, speech, or meeting is an opportunity to reiterate the marketing vision and reinforce the importance of staying the course.

In the *human frame*, the focus is on the needs, values, roles, skills, and interactions of people. The presence of the human frame in Figure 12-2 clearly suggests that no single person can change the academic culture. It requires the active involvement and commitment of others.

Vision, in the structural frame, and *common purpose*, in the human frame, are tightly coupled yet not identical concepts. While creating a vision involves people, it is primarily a utilitarian, largely intellectual activity with a tangible deliverable. Cultivating a common sense of purpose, however, is more emotional and personal in nature. It requires individual adoption rather than corporate endorsement. It emerges from individual values and beliefs and is reflected in daily behavior. Marketers can affect behavior without changing underlying values and beliefs, but such changes evaporate all too quickly. Influencing underlying values and beliefs is a long-term, time-intensive endeavor. Successful marketers accomplish this daunting feat through a balance of education, persuasion, and relationships based on mutual trust.

The *political frame* intersects both the structural and human frames. Academic institutions are highly political organizations. Failure to recognize and work within the political dynamics of an institution will significantly diminish the marketing champion's effectiveness. Knowing who the "power brokers" are on campus, and how they can best be influenced; recognizing political "land-mines"; understanding the political machinery that makes the institution work; and knowing how to identify and exploit points of leverage are all skills a savvy marketer possesses.

Indeed, the marketing champion must be politically savvy to confront people about the current reality without alienating or demoralizing them. Likewise, he/she must use political skills to get others to embrace the marketing vision as their own. However, the most challenging political feat in the structural frame is that of continuously creating tension. Many institutional marketers

STUDENT
MARKETING
FOR COLLEGES
AND UNIVERSITIES

have met their untimely demise while pursuing the worthy goal of excellence at the expense of relationships and even staff positions.

Keen political wits also are needed while operating in the human frame. For example, marketers who do not "walk the talk" are unlikely to succeed. Faculty and staff observe what administrators do much more than they listen to their rhetoric. A marketing professional who quietly demonstrates caring for others or recognizes individual contributions privately is much more revered than the charismatic leader who says much but does little.

Studying the operational style and motives of others enables an intuitive marketer to adapt his/her approach accordingly. As Covey (1989) found, one should seek first to understand, then to be understood. By doing so, the probability of achieving one's objective is increased dramatically. Overcoming resistance to change is not just about being an empathetic listener but is also about taking action. Kotter and Schlesinger (1979) have identified several methods for dealing with resistance. Methods consist of education and communication, participation and involvement of those who may resist change, the facilitation and support of people who are struggling to adjust, negotiation towards a modest compromise, and manipulation or coercion when speed is essential. All of these methods have inherent advantages and disadvantages, so the politically astute marketer must decide which approach is best given the situation.

Finally, the *symbolic frame* typically assumes the form of stories, rituals, images, or myths. It also can be manifested in actions or inactions. It is highly volatile and can occur without warning in the structural, human, or political frames. It is powerful enough to jeopardize a large-scale change effort and even a marketer's career. Of course, symbols can be positive or negative. Hence, an insightful marketing professional plans for the worst while inventing or perpetuating positive symbolic events. Orchestrated events might include celebrations, informal gatherings with the marketing champion, sponsored service projects, collaborative activities with other units or institutions, reward programs, or public recognition of faculty and staff contributions.

Assuming the marketing champion successfully navigates the four organizational frames, it is possible to shape the institution's culture. By shaping the culture in response to constituent needs and in the context of the institution's competitors, a unique market position can be captured. Sustaining this position, however, can be an elusive goal. Only institutions that are continuously reshaping their culture in response to market changes and do so more rapidly than their competitors will sustain competitive advantage. Only these institutions can successfully integrate marketing and create a "cradle to endowment" model of relationship management.

DEVELOPING THE MARKETING PLAN

RICHARD WHITESIDE
Vive President for Enrollment Management
Tulane University

The determination of the marketing direction for a college or university is a complex task involving the delineation of goals, identification of target segments, formulation of strategies, allocation of resources and selection of tactics. Institutions that move through the process to define a marketing strategy have engaged in an important exercise intended to somehow improve institutional performance in the area of recruiting and enrolling the kinds and numbers of students it desires. The value of the exercise is lost, however, if the institution fails to act on its findings. In this regard, effective marketing must be an action-oriented activity.

Moving from the realm of planning into the reality of execution is often a difficult step for colleges to take. All too often, institutions lose their way in the execution phase – a phase where all of the planning plays out in a series of activities involving relationships and interdependencies that may not be entirely clear to all those involved in the execution. Preparing a written marketing plan designed to document the key components of the planning process and to delineate the essential action elements can significantly reduce the likelihood of losing one's way. This document is the institution's "strategic marketing plan."

Institution-wide strategic or marketing plans tend to be overly generalized and address many facets regarding what the institution stands for and how the institution desires to position itself in the marketplace. Such plans may also articulate some key high-level strategies for achieving those goals. Institution-wide plans are designed to influence the thinking of all of the institution's constituencies: prospective students, alumni, political leaders, community leaders and other important stakeholder groups. The institution-wide strategic marketing plan is the foundational document that guides all activity related to positioning the institution. However, because of its multi-purpose mission, the institution-wide plan will often lack the specificity required by individual offices or functions within the institution. These units require more detailed marketing plans to effectively pursue their objectives.

Because of the need for detailed marketing guidance at the functional unit level, institutions will often develop individual marketing plans targeted at different stakeholder groups. It is in the development of these functional level plans that institutions will often experience difficulty. In order to be effective, such sub-unit plans must be fully consistent with the institution-wide plan and they must be developed in the appropriate sequence.

STUDENT
MARKETING
FOR COLLEGES
AND UNIVERSITIES

Since learning is typically a key element in institutional mission, the development of strategic plans or marketing positions for the academic units must occur before the development of marketing plans for the service units that provide support for the academic units. With respect to enrollment marketing plans, these must occur after the academic units have determined what they want to do. If the compilation of the marketing for enrollment plan occurs before the creation of the academic objectives, the marketing plan for enrollment plan may well be seen as a case of "the tail wagging the dog." If this perception occurs, it will be difficult for those charged with executing this plan to gain the support of academic leadership and the faculty.

A marketing plan for enrollment may itself generate individual plans focused on one or more kinds of enrollments. For example, in a university with graduate and professional schools the responsibility for student marketing may be decentralized with one office responsible for recruiting undergraduate students but another office responsible for recruiting law students. Figure 13-1 shows the relationship between the various levels of marketing plans that might be found in a complex institution.

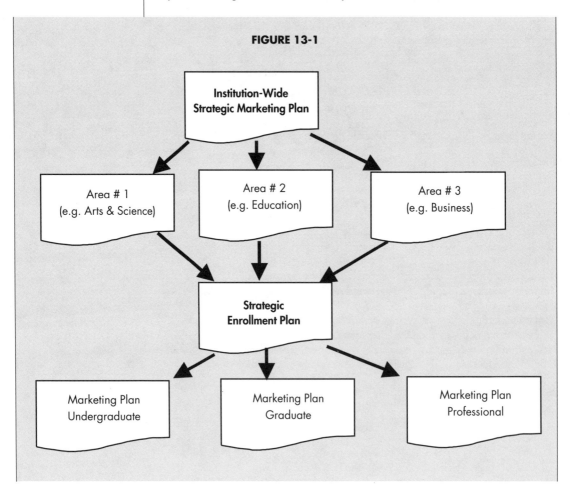

FIGURE 13-1

Institution-Wide
Strategic Marketing Plan

Area # 1
(e.g. Arts & Science)

Area # 2
(e.g. Education)

Area # 3
(e.g. Business)

Strategic
Enrollment Plan

Marketing Plan
Undergraduate

Marketing Plan
Graduate

Marketing Plan
Professional

The overriding consideration in the compilation of plans at the various levels is that the individual plans must be totally consistent with all preceding plans in the planning hierarchy. Such consistency enhances the probability that the institution will achieve its strategic goals and intents. Each successive plan is derived from the preceding plan's goals and strategies. If unit-level plans are truly derived from other plans higher in the hierarchical sequence, the institution will have an internally consistent position and its strategies will be tightly linked, across all units, with the institution's goal and objectives. Inconsistency leads to confusion in the institution and in the marketplace.

Higher Education Marketing Plans – A Special Case

The use of marketing techniques and marketing language is pervasive in the for-profit sector of the American economy. The folks at General Motors embrace marketing as a fundamental element of the corporation's operations. American for-profit companies typically have business units dedicated to marketing and market research. Titles like Vice President for Marketing are common titles on the organization charts of American corporations.

College and university organization charts do not normally include a "box" for marketing. The absence of such a defined function is not accidental. It is the result of institutional culture – a culture that frequently denies that education is a "business." On many campuses an effort to make the institution function like a business would be staunchly resisted. Those who would seek to apply business techniques are branded as outsiders, individuals who "just don't understand at all what we do." On the other hand, it is clear that the nature of the undertaking requires some of the elements and rigor of business operations for there to be an orderly pursuit of research and delivery of instruction and its associated educational support services. If no business principles are brought to the table, colleges and universities would be in utter managerial chaos.

The challenge for those charged with the task of "marketing the institution" is to pursue their assigned responsibility without creating a situation in which the use of marketing techniques itself becomes the focus of criticism. The practitioner must balance the prevailing attitudes of university culture against the need to use sophisticated marketing techniques designed to achieve the institution's enrollment goals.

In large measure, this balance can be achieved by employing nomenclature that is familiar to those in the educational setting and which does not carry a highly negative emotional impact. To illustrate the point, in classic marketing terminology those whose behavior we seek to influence are normally called "customers" – individuals or organizations in a position to purchase the goods and services we offer. On many campuses however, the concept of the student as customer or client will be rejected out of hand. It raises too many obligations and implies too high a level of consumerism to be accepted by college and university faculties. The use of "socially acceptable" terminology is a key for keeping a student marketing plan on target. Figure 13-2 provides a summary of the educational equivalents for some classic marketing terms. These equivalents can be used in most institutions without undue criticism. The use of these equivalents may not describe the activity or entity with the

STUDENT
MARKETING
FOR COLLEGES
AND UNIVERSITIES

PART FOUR
CHAPTER 13   183

FIGURE 13-2

The For-Profit Nomenclature	The Higher Education Nomenclature
Market	As a noun – Prospective students As a verb – Promote, recruit, etc.
Marketing	Recruiting, promoting, positioning
Product	Academic programs & services Learning, research, scholarship
Market segments	Prospective student groups
Marketing research	Research, intelligence
Market competition	Student choices Other like institutions Colleague institutions
Brand	Academic reputation
Customer/Consumer	Student
Cash discount	Financial aid Scholarships
Profit	Net revenues
Sales	As a noun – enrollments As a verb – recruiting
Internal marketing Consensus	Collegial discussion
Loyalty	Retention
Advertising	Public relations
Strategic business unit Function	Office

same level of precision as the terminology used in the for-profit arena. This lack of exactness is, however, more than worth the gains achieved through the avoidance of nomenclature that is likely to raise criticism.

As marketing plans are being prepared, those involved in the preparation should be attentive to the task of inclusion of non-threatening language. More than one fine plan has been scuttled when the discussion devolved into a philosophical debate on whether or not a student was a customer or if the institution really should be engaged in assessing market competition.

Developing the Marketing Plan for Enrollment

Before pen is put to paper in an effort to develop an enrollment marketing plan, those charged with the preparation of the plan must review existing plans, particularly those prepared by the entire institution and those prepared by the academic divisions of the institution. During this review the authors of the marketing plan for enrollment must extract important information related to strategic intent, goals and priorities. These elements become the central core of the marketing plan for enrollment. Using the key elements contained in the institutional and academic division plans insures a high degree of consistency between various levels of plans. Such consistency is essential. Without it no plan will reach the success level necessary to satisfy stakeholders.

Colleges and universities operate differently than corporations. Perhaps such differences are no more apparent than in the area of decision-making. In a strictly hierarchical setting (e.g. General Motors) all decisions flow from the top down. Ultimately, the CEO of General Motors has legitimate authority for everything that happens in the company. Manufacturing, of its own choice, cannot decide what it will produce. Manufacturing produces what it is told to make, not what it decides to make. Imagine the fate of a GM Vice President for Manufacturing who suddenly decided it would be better to build sailboats on the assembly line than automobiles! In all likelihood, a promotion would not be her reward.

In higher education the decision to "make sailboats" occurs quite often, and in many cases, nobody gets reprimanded. Faculties decide to revise the curriculum. New courses are created, existing courses are deleted and areas of learning are continued even if there is no viable market of consumers! While college presidents can exert some influence over such changes, they do not control these changes. The president cannot tell the Philosophy Department to teach a course on Socrates or not to teach one on Kant. Presidential desires shape the outcome through a process of collegial discussion. This is not to say that presidents do not have other, less direct, ways to make their desires come to pass. But these alternative approaches are less direct and often less effective than engaging in the anticipated process of collegial discussion and negotiation.

It is therefore not surprising that those responsible for creating and executing the marketing program designed to improve the enrollment situation cannot do so in isolation from their colleagues in other administrative units or from the faculty. Any marketing plan birthed in isolation will come under heavy criticism and will fail to garner the broad-based institutional support required for it to be successful. While an individual or a small group of persons may take on the primary responsibility for authorship, the draft plan needs to be vetted through key institutional areas like the academic divisions, the senior administration and other student services offices. Not only must the plan be shared, it must also be organic – the comments, suggestions and criticisms of all need to be addressed and accommodated to the degree possible.

Initial versions of the marketing plan should be clearly marked "DRAFT" and be circulated to those within the organization. The author must take appro-

STUDENT
MARKETING
FOR COLLEGES
AND UNIVERSITIES

PART FOUR
CHAPTER 13   185

priate steps to gather comments and concerns and use this feedback as a device for improving the plan and building consensus. This may require that the author provide interested parties with several versions of the plan – each version annotated to show how the suggestions and comments from previous reviews were used to improve the final product. Draft plans should be shared with campus governance groups and key institutional leaders drawn from faculty, administrative and staff groups. This sharing accomplishes two key goals: it insulates the authors from unwarranted criticism and it educates the community about how the institution goes about achieving its enrollment objectives.

Who is the Audience?

It is natural to assume that the prospective student is the target of the marketing effort in enrollment management. While this is a natural assumption it is also an erroneous one. Every marketing plan serves two distinct audiences: the groups whose behavior we desire to change by the strategies and tactics as they are implemented and those who will be key players in the implementation and evaluation of the selected strategies and tactics.

As a result, the authors of the enrollment marketing plan must be attentive to both audiences during the plan preparation phase. The actual written plan will serve as the guide for the actions taken by those responsible for implementing the plan – those actions intended to change the enrollment behavior of the prospective student. This relationship is shown in Figure 13-3. If either audience is ignored or if the weight given to one over the other is very considerable, the plan will be less effective than intended. In enrollment management and enrollment marketing, two rules govern action: do the right things and do them right! The part of the planning directed toward internal audiences improves the probability that things will be done right. The carefully selected strategies and tactics directed at the external audience will be the right things if the plan is consistent with institution-wide plans and if it has been carefully vetted through all governance groups.

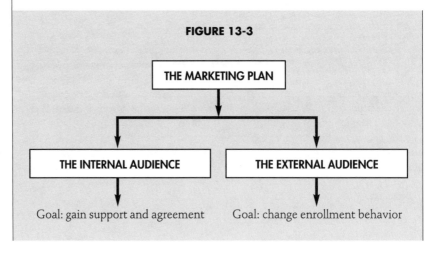

FIGURE 13-3

THE MARKETING PLAN

THE INTERNAL AUDIENCE

THE EXTERNAL AUDIENCE

Goal: gain support and agreement

Goal: change enrollment behavior

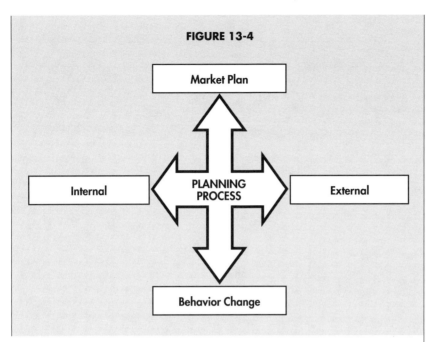

FIGURE 13-4

Market Plan

Internal

PLANNING PROCESS

External

Behavior Change

By being attentive to both audiences, the overall probability of a successful implementation, defined as reaching the goals specified, will be significantly enhanced.

Although there are two separate audiences, the intent of the plan is the same for both: creating a behavior change in both audiences. The market planning process is the mechanism for fostering these changes. Institutions seek to change student enrollment behavior (the external audience) and to modify the performance levels of those responsible for executing the strategies and tactics (the internal audience.)

What are the Purposes of the Plan?

Given that the plan has multiple audiences and contains a compilation of the institution's thinking in a given area, it follows that such a plan serves multiple purposes. Some of the more obvious uses of the plan follow.

Guides Action

Since the strategies and tactics are clearly identified, enrollment personnel have a clear understanding of what needs to be done. In a sense, individuals are following a script carefully built to ensure success. In today's age of limited resources and increasing workloads, it is easy to become distracted and to devote time and resources to activities for which there is no beneficial result. The plan tends to focus energies on the important things to be accomplished and reduces thrashing.

STUDENT
MARKETING
FOR COLLEGES
AND UNIVERSITIES

Facilitates Training

Many admission offices experience considerable turnover. For many it seems that they are always breaking in the new guy. The carefully written marketing plan makes it possible to expedite this training and make sure that everyone is reading from the same page. A written plan also reduces the impact of hearsay – the tendency to draw understanding from the interpretation others have made from important events. In this regard, the marketing plan serves as the primary source of information about goals, objectives, strategies and tactics.

Defines Responsibilities and Assigns Accountability

A well-prepared marketing plan defines what will be done and who will do it. In other words, it establishes responsibility and accountability for the outcome of certain activities and actions. Anyone reading the plan can tell who is supposed to carry the ball on a particular activity.

Establishes Priorities

The areas identified for attention in the marketing plan represent the important dimensions of what needs to be done. Such a list of activities is in a sense a delineation of institutional priorities with regard to enrollment. Activities not included in the plan are not likely to be high priority activities. By having an unequivocal listing of priorities, it is easier to focus energy and resources on important matters.

Provides a Framework for Resource Allocation

A defined set of strategies and tactics provides a framework for determining how to allocate scarce resources. Since resources are limited and need sometimes appears infinite, the manager requires some form of guidance on "where to place her bets." The marketing plan provides such a framework. It provides a listing of activities to be resourced. Managers are then in a position to budget what they have against the activities for which they will be held accountable.

Documents Consensus and Builds Support

If the marketing plan was created through a collegial process, the final document represents a consensus instrument for marketing. Of course, some may still challenge the tactics employed but such challenges will be fewer in number and less likely to be damaging to the marketing program.

One should never forget that many of the most effective recruitment tactics require the immediate involvement of individuals over whom the person responsible for the outcome has little direct control. These individuals choose whether or not to be involved. If they have played an active role in defining the marketing strategy, they are more likely to become directly involved in its implementation simply because they intuitively assume some level of responsibility for the success of the ideas they created.

What is Included in the Marketing Plan?

There are many versions of what a marketing plan contains. None of them is totally right. None of them is inappropriate for our needs. Pride and Ferrell (1995) provide the following outline for a strategic marketing plan.

1. Executive summary

2. Environmental analysis
   a. Marketing environment
   b. Target markets
   c. Current marketing objectives & performance

3. Strengths & weaknesses
   a. Strengths
   b. Weaknesses

4. Opportunities & Threats
   a. Opportunities
   b. Threats

5. Marketing objectives

6. Marketing strategies
   a. Target markets
   b. Marketing mix

7. Marketing implementation
   a. Marketing organization
   b. Activities, responsibilities, & timetables

8. Evaluation & control
   a. Performance standards
   b. Monitoring procedures

This outline can be modified to meet the particular needs of any institution. While the outline suggests categories of information as well as their sequence, these need to be adapted for the higher education environment in which the internal selling is just as important as the externally focused strategies and tactics.

Appendix A contains a sample marketing plan prepared for a fictitious university – Jefferson University – and is provided as an example of what a marketing plan for enrollment might look like. The Jefferson Plan is for undergraduate student enrollments and should be considered in the context that other marketing plans exist for other areas of enrollment as well as other non-enrollment related areas like Alumni Relations and Governmental Affairs. Consequently, the example restricts itself to only one portion of the institution's overall marketing effort. The sample Jefferson plan is a combination of the two types of plans Dave Crockett discussed in Chapter 6: the long-range enrollment plan and the annual enrollment plan. The combination is not accidental. The unique nature of decision-making in the collegiate environment necessitates an approach in which individual actions and activities are plotted against institutional goals and objectives across years.

Closing Comments

The preparation of the marketing plan document is in itself a complex task, one that requires creativity and attention to process. The following represents some guidance for the preparation of the plan:

- Develop the plan with others.

- Share several versions of the plan with key institutional leaders and governance groups before going live with the plan.

- Revise the plan as necessary to accommodate the suggestions made by reviewers.

- Avoid marketing jargon likely to engender a negative reaction from faculty colleagues.

- Remember, the plan has two distinct audiences: those inside the institution and those you seek to enroll.

- Use clear, concise language.

- Make sure that the goals, strategies, and tactics included with the plan are consistent with the goals, strategies, and tactics being employed by those units you seek to serve.

- Include a discussion of the techniques that will be employed to assess the effectiveness of the effort.

- Gain a consensus from those to whom you report that the benchmarks for success are indeed acceptable as indicators of success.

- Include multiple-year goals where appropriate.

- Promise no "silver bullet" interventions in the plan or in the discussions undertaken to create the plan.

- Work for an understanding among key personnel that significant enrollment changes require several years to realize.

- Include some areas in which success can be demonstrated in the short-term (e.g. one year or less).

The marketing plan for enrollment must be one that is under constant review and revision. Not every tactic will achieve its desired result. Periodic review will make it possible to refine marketing efforts to achieve greater success. Ineffective tactics need to be dropped and replaced by new tactical interventions.

SAMPLE MARKETING PLAN

STUDENT
MARKETING
FOR COLLEGES
AND UNIVERSITIES

Jefferson University

OFFICE OF ADMISSION

ADMISSION MARKETING PLAN

November 2003

TABLE OF CONTENTS

APPENDIX A

STUDENT
MARKETING
FOR COLLEGES
AND UNIVERSITIES

Jefferson University

Admission Marketing Plan
Undergraduate Students
Fall 2004

Mission Statement

The mission of the Jefferson University Office of Admission is to take the leadership role in the institution-wide effort to recruit and enroll the number and kinds of full- and part-time undergraduate and part-time graduate students necessary for Jefferson University to realize its scholarly and educational objectives.

Executive Summary

Jefferson University seeks to increase the quantity and quality of undergraduate student enrollments. The five-year performance goals (2004–2008) were designed to achieve the desired growth in increments. The achievement of these enrollment objectives requires that Jefferson utilize an aggressive marketing program involving seven sets of strategies designed to reach the target markets. The strategic intervention groups include: on-campus programming, off-campus programming, e-recruitment, school relations, direct mail marketing, mass media and cost management.

Three target markets have been identified: first-time, full-time freshmen (freshmen), full-time students with prior college or university experience (transfer students) and part-time students seeking professional development or career advancement. These target markets are further segmented by geography (Kennedy Metropolitan Area, in-state, non-metropolitan, out-of-state and international). In addition to the utilization of student type and geographic segmentation strategies, these markets are further refined by student academic ability (high ability, above average ability and average ability.) The mix of strategies and tactics differs by target market, segment and ability level.

The Admission Office assumes primary responsibility for the execution of the strategies and tactics (except for the cost management strategies) designed to achieve Jefferson's goals. The implementation of cost management strategies is the responsibility of the Vice President for Financial Affairs and the Office of Student Financial Assistance.

Resources have been allocated for the various strategic intervention sets and target market combinations. Approximately 75% of Jefferson's resources dedicated toward marketing efforts to attract and enroll undergraduate students have been allocated for the recruitment of full-time students. The remainder has been reserved for the recruitment of part-time students.

As an independent university, Jefferson operates in a highly competitive environment. Major competitors include most of the selective and highly selective institutions in the southeast United States. In distinguishing itself from its competitors, Jefferson relies on its favorable location in Kennedy, its commitment to undergraduate learning, outstanding student support services and favorable reputation of the Jefferson faculty.

Jefferson University Undergraduate Enrollment Goals & Strategic Directions

In its strategic plan Jefferson has established the following goals and strategic directions related to undergraduate enrollment.

- Increase the size of the full and part-time undergraduate student body

- Improve the overall quality of the full-time freshmen enrolling students as measured by standardized test scores and rank-in-class

- Improve ethnic diversity in the freshman class

- Decrease the overall Tuition discount rate

- Achieve a better balance between men and women in the freshman class

- Increase the size and academic quality of the graduate student population

- Improve freshman to sophomore year retention rates

- Improve five-year graduation rates

The *"Admission Marketing Plan – Undergraduate Students"* has been prepared as a guide for achieving Jefferson's strategic enrollment goals relating to undergraduate recruitment and enrollment.

Similar plans have been prepared for achieving the desired increases in graduate student enrollment and for the increases in institutional effectiveness as measured by increased retention and graduation rates.

Market Statement

Jefferson University is a highly competitive, comprehensive university dedicated to the advancement of learning and the discovery of knowledge. Jefferson identifies itself as a direct competitor with other comprehensive universities in the southeastern United States.

The academic programs of Jefferson University are second to none. They are the primary focus of our marketing and recruitment effort. These programs provide a rigorous and innovative educational experience designed to prepare students for the 21st Century. Jefferson's undergraduate programs are designed to ground students in the arts and humanities, social sciences, mathematics, natural sciences, computing, and the emerging technologies. In addition, Jefferson students have the opportunity to engage in a content rich

STUDENT
MARKETING
FOR COLLEGES
AND UNIVERSITIES

area of study (the major) and to experience a cross-disciplinary learning environment by participating in one of Jefferson's areas of interdisciplinary focus – Urban Citizenship, The Environment and International Affairs.

The faculty is drawn from among the world's leading scholars and teachers. Full-time tenured or tenure-track faculty members teach approximately 85% of all classes. The remaining courses are taught by leading specialists in specific areas of applied knowledge or by advanced graduate teaching assistants. In keeping with Jefferson's philosophy that learning is facilitated by close contact between students and faculty, Jefferson's average class size is smaller than is typically the case at comprehensive universities. Faculty members are rewarded for their excellence in teaching and the quality of their scholarly research. As a university with a commitment to undergraduate education, Jefferson provides undergraduates with opportunities for meaningful participation in faculty-supervised research.

As an institution dedicated to the advancement of learning, Jefferson is keenly aware of the importance of state-of-the-art learning facilities. State of the art classrooms, laboratories, world-class information services, and leading instructional equipment are integral components of the Jefferson experience. The revitalization of the learning infrastructure accomplished through the capital construction program is a key element in demonstrating Jefferson's continued commitment to the undergraduate educational excellence.

Jefferson University provides a curriculum that encourages participants to develop and hone excellent communicative and analytic skills. Jefferson students encounter a demanding and intellectually stimulating curriculum designed to challenge the best students drawn from the United States and abroad. The university functions in a national and international educational context and encourages its students to experience other cultures as part of its study abroad programs. Jefferson understands that the pursuit of a productive professional career requires a global perspective on public policy issues and a well-developed understanding and appreciation of diverse cultures. Jefferson seeks to provide its students with the opportunity to develop this perspective.

Jefferson is also dedicated to and supportive of the City of Kennedy. Jefferson understands that the success of the region and the viability of this academy depend upon the continued development of a strong Kennedy economy leading to an enhanced quality of life in all neighborhoods in the metropolitan area. This objective can be realized through the development of a skilled and highly educated work force representative of the city and region's population.

While the quality of the academic experience is the primary reason why students should and will consider Jefferson, the university also offers the rare and exciting opportunity of living in Kennedy while pursuing a college education. In this context, we emphasize the unique cultural, architectural, musical, and historical characteristics of the city, state, and region as they relate to enhancing both the academic and social experience.

Jefferson is committed to student diversity and access. In support of these objectives, Jefferson maintains an aggressive program of cost management and an outstanding program of student financial assistance. The financial aid strategy includes both need-based and merit-based components. These are designed to bring to Jefferson academically superior students from around the world. In its admission process, Jefferson maintains a need-blind posture choosing to admit academically qualified students without regard to financial need or ability to pay. The goal of the Jefferson student financial assistance program is to make it financially feasible and financially attractive for every admitted student to enroll. Jefferson leverages its financial aid resources to bring to the institution the number and kinds of students necessary to effectively pursue its mission objectives.

Jefferson is and will continue to be an exemplary university. Above all, a Jefferson University education represents a "wise family investment." Jefferson continually demonstrates the value of its educational experience by taking the action necessary to ensure that its undergraduate programs maintain (and improve) its national ranking as judged by *US News and World Report*. Jefferson currently ranks in the top quartile of regional universities and a Jefferson education ranks in the top thirty in terms of educational value.[1]

Distinguishing Features

The following represents a summary of the key messages, in order of importance and dominance in our marketing efforts, stressed in the marketing and recruitment activities of the Jefferson University Admission Office.

- *Jefferson University maintains the highest standards of intellectual rigor*
  The Jefferson curriculum is demanding and rewarding. The student body is drawn from the very best the region has to offer and the interplay of the students, the faculty, and the curriculum results in a learning environment characterized by intellectual rigor. Students enrolling at Jefferson are challenged to perform at the highest level. Admission is competitive.

- *Jefferson University is committed to undergraduate learning*
  At Jefferson University, learning is our primary task. While all colleges and universities engage in teaching and research, these are meaningless exercises from the prospective undergraduate and graduate student's perspective unless they advance the quality of student learning. At Jefferson, activities are structured to maximize the student's opportunities for learning. Class sizes are small, learning support services are plentiful (e.g. Center for Educational Resources and Counseling), and instructional technologies are state-of-the-art. We gauge our success by the success of our students and alumni.

- *Jefferson University provides excellent academic advising and career development services*
  Each college of the university has devised an advising system to meet the particular needs of its students. The academic advisor is responsible for knowing what the student needs and for helping the student locate the appropriate university resources to meet those needs. Advisors understand the critical importance of the freshmen year experience and they are prepared to help the student through the freshman adjustment

---

1 *US News & World Report*, 2000 edition

period. Jefferson advisors are proactive; they seek out their advisees and they anticipate problems before they occur.

- *Jefferson offers an outstanding Honors Program*
Jefferson offers talented students the opportunity to participate in an Honors Program featuring honors courses and sections, specialized advising for extramural scholarships, and extracurricular activities. Honors students may also choose to live in the honors residence facility.

- *Jefferson offers a unique first year program*
First year students may participate in the *Freshman Seminar Program* and a variety of activities designed to provide the first-year student with a unique opportunity to interact, in an academic context, with students from all disciplines and with the greater Kennedy community. First year students may also opt to participate in Jefferson's "discipline based" writing courses as a way of demonstrating competency in the writing area.

- *First year students are taught by full-time faculty, including our "star" faculty*
Although many universities employ significant numbers of "adjunct faculty" as teaching faculty for first and second year students, this is not common practice at Jefferson University. Members of our regular, full-time, faculty teach the majority of all freshmen and sophomore year classes. Members of our faculty are selected because of their superior teaching skills.

- *Jefferson University is an ideal size*
With a full-time undergraduate student enrollment of just over 5,000 (3,500 full-time and 1,500 part-time) and a graduate enrollment of 1,500, Jefferson is ideally sized to offer its students a wide array of majors, academic support programs, social life options, and athletic activities. Yet, it can also maintain an "intimate" feel. Students find it easy to develop a sense of community and to come to "know" Jefferson University.

- *Jefferson University is a personal place*
The University treats each student as an individual with different learning needs and learning styles. We stand prepared to work with each student individually to maximize the student's chances for success. The University maintains an active faculty-driven advising system, a large and highly trained residential life staff, and an academic support staff dedicated to meeting the needs of all Jefferson students.

- *Jefferson University is a diverse university*
The University offers more than sixty academic programs in its four undergraduate colleges and graduate divisions. Our 6,500 students are drawn from 50 states and several dozen foreign countries. The student body is multi-national and reflective of the country's ethnic and racial composition.

- *Jefferson University is an urban institution located in a prime residential neighborhood*
  Jefferson University is located in the Mid City area of Kennedy. It enjoys the benefits of a 110 acre green campus bordered by residential neighborhoods. Located approximately two miles from the commercial center of Kennedy, the campus enjoys the advantages of proximity to a major commercial district and the seclusion of a "suburban" campus. The heart of the campus includes superior recreational space and an open design that allows for easy movement between and among facilities. Downtown is easily accessible from campus by using the Kennedy Area Rapid Transit system, which runs 24 hours a day, seven days a week. The campus and surrounding neighborhood is regarded as the safest areas of Kennedy.

- *Jefferson University is located in Kennedy, a leading banking, financial and cultural center in the southeast.*
  The City of Kennedy is the cultural and financial center of the southeast. Long known as the birthplace of southern art, Kennedy also features unique architectural styles and a blend of the Spanish and African cultures. Kennedy has an important place in American history and it serves as the financial center for commerce in the southeastern United States.

Institutional Competitive Advantages

- A comprehensive array of more than 60 major fields of study

- Attractive class sizes (average 25, with 12:1 student-faculty ratio)

- Immediate and close contact with senior faculty

- Opportunities for undergraduate involvement in faculty research

- An attractive and modern campus located in Kennedy's most desirable residential neighborhood

- New academic and residential facilities

- Superior recreational facilities

- Availability of a variety of modern residential accommodations and "living/learning options" (e.g. special interest floors.)

- Strong program of academic and student support services (Deans' Offices, Center for Educational Resources and Counseling)

- Wide array of student activities (100+ organizations for 6,500 students)

- Forward thinking, creative, and committed institutional leadership

- Growing focus on international, urban, and environmental issues

- State-of-the-art library and information services

- Over $25 million in institutionally sponsored financial assistance

- Independent control of the University

- Reasonably high name recognition in the marketplace

- Outstanding marketing materials (national award-winning)

- A unique first year program

Institutional Challenges

- Recent improvements in our freshmen class profile have positioned us in direct competition with the region's most well known and most well respected universities

- Kennedy is geographically isolated from other major population centers

- Jefferson's cost of attendance is among the highest in the region

- Limitations in the pace of growth of the financial aid budget

- Increased competition from regional and national independent universities

- Although Jefferson has reasonably good name recognition, the university has not developed a favorable "brand" position when compared to its competitors

- High ratings in the college selection literature on characteristics like "alcohol consumption," "fraternity/sorority influence," and "party atmosphere." (e.g. *Princeton Review*.)

- Low ratings by prospective students for important academic characteristics like "academic reputation," "intellectual," and "quality of academic facilities." (Source: *Admitted Student Questionnaire*)

- Growth in the number of state funded "Tuition free" programs for high ability students (e.g. Georgia's *Hope Scholarship*, Florida's *Bright Futures*, Louisiana's *TOPS*, etc.)

Current Jefferson Prospective Student Markets

Jefferson University currently seeks to enroll high ability, full- and part-time undergraduates and part-time graduate students with interests in studying the liberal arts and sciences, business, education and health sciences.

Although Jefferson University enrolls a variety of students at different levels and in different time status categories, the Admission Office is currently responsible only for a select portion of the University's overall recruitment program as depicted following.

Admission Market Segment

	Freshman		Transfer		Graduate
	Full-Time	Part-Time	Full-Time	Part-Time	
Business	X	X	X	X	Graduate Admission
Liberal Arts & Sciences	X	X	X	X	Graduate Admission
Education	X	X	X	X	Graduate Admission
Health Sciences	X	X	X	N/A	Graduate Admission

As a highly competitive institution, Jefferson seeks to enroll students whose SAT scores (combined verbal plus math) are in excess of 1150 or who have a composite ACT score of 25 or higher. Preference is given to students with high school grade point averages that place them in the top 25% of their high school graduating classes. Jefferson also seeks candidates whose secondary school record includes a minimum of four years of English, three years of college preparatory mathematics, and two years each of laboratory sciences, social sciences, and foreign language. Operating in unison as a qualitative screen, these factors define a market consisting of approximately the top 25% of all college bound students in the United States.

Geographically, Jefferson's primary undergraduate markets are segmented as follows. The percentages reflect the percent of the Fall 2003 class originating from the identified area.

- Northeast states (CT,DE,DC,ME,MD,MA,NH,NJ,NY,PA,RI,VT)   10%
- Mid-West (IL,IN,IO,KS,MI,MO,NE,ND,OH,SD,WV,WI)   8%
- West (AZ,CA,HI,ID,MT,NV,NM,OR,UT,WA,WY)   7%
- Southeast (AL,FL,GA,MI,NC,SC,VA)   62%
- Mid-South (AR,KY,LA,OK,TN,TX)   10%
- Other (Possessions, International)   3%

Jefferson's historically strong position in some of these regions is under stress. Several states (e.g. Florida, Georgia, Texas, etc.) have implemented "Tuition free" scholarship programs for the strongest students in their high school graduating classes. As a result, increasing numbers of high performing students from these states are opting to attend in-state publicly supported colleges and universities.

When the interactive effect of our highly selective admission standard, limited program offerings, and high cost are analyzed together, the resulting

STUDENT
MARKETING
FOR COLLEGES
AND UNIVERSITIES

market picture is revealing. Out of nearly 1,300,000 college-bound students approximately 150,000 students:

- Meet Jefferson's admission standard,

- Desire a program that we offer, and

- Have sufficient resources to fund a Jefferson education without Jefferson financial aid

Competitive Analysis

Jefferson University competes with the best colleges and universities in the southeast United States for its students. The admission standards utilized by Jefferson define the target population as follows (the group most likely to receive favorable consideration in the admission process):

- Students with combined SAT scores > 1150, or

- Students with a Comprehensive ACT > 25

- Students who rank in the top 25%, preferably in the top 10%, of their graduating class.

- Students who have achieved a B (or higher) high school average

- Students who have some experience with honors, advanced, accelerated, or advanced placement courses as a part of their secondary school experience.

- Students who have completed at least three years of college preparatory mathematics, two years of a foreign language and three years of laboratory science as part of their secondary school curriculum.

- Students who have demonstrated the ability and willingness to become involved in the life of their community.

- Students who have not been suspended or expelled

- Students desiring collegiate programs in the liberal arts and sciences, business, education or health sciences

Taken in combination, these factors eliminate approximately 75% of the college bound high school population. As a result, Jefferson finds itself in direct competition with those institutions seeking to enroll students who have similar characteristics.

Jefferson's direct competitors are listed in the table labeled "Jefferson University – Competitor Analysis." This table shows that Jefferson's direct competitors include many of the top universities in the south.

These analyses reveal that Jefferson must design and execute an aggressive recruitment and admission program in order to realize success in the pursuit of its enrollment objectives.

SAMPLE
MARKETING PLAN

Jefferson University – Competitor Analysis

Institution	Number of Cross Applications	Cross Admits	Enrolled at Jefferson	Enrolled at Named Institution	Ratio of "Wins"	Enrolled Elsewhere
Kinkaid University	1046	588	82	134	37.96%	372
Long University	965	643	127	153	45.36%	363
Forest University	849	629	108	143	43.03%	378
Charles University	760	255	21	91	18.75%	143
Levy University	638	596	161	48	77.03%	387
New University	610	337	50	86	36.76%	201
University of Large State	547	301	24	86	21.82%	191
University of Otto	542	503	135	110	55.10%	258
Georgia University	541	150	21	53	28.38%	76
University of Southern Virginia	510	262	37	96	27.82%	129
President University	509	421	82	76	51.90%	263
Bean College	482	273	34	72	32.08%	167
University of Harrison	477	115	5	43	10.42%	67
University of Southern Utah	453	355	63	143	30.58%	149
Ivy University	453	62	0	38	0.00%	24
Kelly University	452	62	0	38	0.00%	24
University of Young	433	413	127	72	63.82%	214
U. North Hill	425	194	26	48	35.14%	120
North University	416	228	13	81	13.83%	134
Carmel University	401	192	11	57	16.18%	124
University of Lolley	390	365	98	119	45.16%	148
Otter University	390	198	21	57	26.92%	120
James University	375	154	11	48	18.64%	95
University of Mary	375	206	29	72	28.71%	105
Cool University	373	72	0	33	0.00%	39
Vincent University	357	89	8	53	13.11%	28
Hardesty University	343	44	5	10	33.33%	29
Madison University	340	303	69	43	61.61%	191

STUDENT
MARKETING
FOR COLLEGES
AND UNIVERSITIES

Existing Market Performance

At present, Jefferson University's admission and recruitment performance has been adequate but insufficient to increase the size and quality of the undergraduate student body as mandated by Jefferson's strategic plan. Following is a profile of our performance for the last five years.

	1999	2000	2001	2002	2003
Applications, full-time, UG	5,100	5,325	5,210	5,300	5,415
Accept rate, full-time UG	61%	63%	59%	62%	57%
Yield, full-time accept to enroll	28%	27%	26.5%	27%	27%
Full-time freshmen enrolled	875	910	880	920	915
Financial aid discount rate	42%	40%	41%	38%	37%
New part-time UG enrolled	186	200	195	190	220
Full-time UG transfer apps	305	296	410	325	375
Full-time UG transfer enrolled	98	110	140	109	120
Full-time UG enrollments	3,320	3,175	3,300	3,325	3,500
Part-time undergraduate	1,325	1,300	1,390	1,400	1,475
% Full-time men	48%	48%	46%	45%	44%
% Minority	14%	13.7%	14%	14.2%	14%
Average SAT	1165	1168	1172	1177	1185
Top 25% of class	72%	71%	71%	73%	69%
% Full-time from Metro Kennedy	44%	42%	45%	44%	39%
% Full-time, in-state	54%	56%	55%	57%	56%

Current Marketing Efforts

At the present time, Jefferson University relies primarily on newspaper advertising and a program of secondary school relations (school visits and mailings) to recruit its undergraduate student body. These efforts have succeeded in stabilizing student enrollment. They have not, however, created the desired enrollment increases.

Strategic Intent of the Undergraduate Student Marketing Program 2004 – 2008

Marketing efforts for the next five years will employ a diversified effort employing the full range of recruitment strategies as shown in the following illustration.

Jefferson University
Recruitment Strategy

Strategic Category	Sample Tactics
Off-Campus Programs	Regional receptions NACAC college fairs NSSFNS fairs
On-Campus Programs	Campus tours Overnight visits Financial aid workshops
Direct Marketing	Student search Print publications
Mass Media	Newspaper advertising Popular press advertisement Radio/television advertising
School Relations	High school visits Counselor receptions Counselor mailings
E-Recruiting	Web site Electronic publications Chat rooms Electronic applications
Cost Management	Financial aid leveraging Institutional loan programs Financial aid

STUDENT
MARKETING
FOR COLLEGES
AND UNIVERSITIES

Jefferson University
Enrollment Goals 2004–2008

	2004	2005	2006	2007	2008
Applications full-time, UG	6,000	6,200	6,400	6,500	6,500
Accept rate, full-time UG	54%	53%	52%	51%	49%
Yield, full-time accept to enroll	30%	315	32%	32%	32%
Full-time freshmen enrolled	950	975	1000	1025	1025
Financial aid discount rate	37%	36%	35%	34%	33%
New part-time UG enrolled	300	300	300	325	350
Full-time UG transfer apps	450	450	450	450	450
Full-time UG transfer enrolled	125	125	135	135	140
Full-time UG enrollments	3,500	3,550	3,575	3,600	3,650
Part-time undergraduate	1,500	1,525	1,575	1,600	1,600
% Full-time men	45%	45%	46%	47%	48%
% Minority	15%	17%	18%	18%	19%
Average SAT	1185	1190	1995	1200	1200
Top 25% of class	70%	71%	72%	74%	78%
% Full-time from Metro Kennedy	40%	40%	40%	40%	30%
% Full-time, in-state	55%	55%	55%	55%	55%

Target Audiences

The target audiences for this market plan are as follows:

A. First-time, full-time freshmen of high academic ability evidenced by one or more of the following:

   - SAT score > 1150

   - ACT composite score > 25

   - High school grade point average > 3.00

   - Rank-in-class = top 25%

   - High school record containing AP, Honors, & Advanced Courses

B. High achieving transfer students evidenced by:

   - College GPA > 3.00, and

   - Minimum of one year (24 credits earned) collegiate experience

C. Part-time undergraduate students who are:

   - High school graduates

   - Have worked full-time for five or more years

   - Seeking to earn a bachelor's degree or to improve their career opportunities by completing course work in specific subject areas, or

   - Transfers from other institutions

For marketing & recruitment purposes, these target audiences are further segmented by geography and academic ability.

Jefferson University
Geographic and Ability Segmentation Variables

	High Ability	Above Average Ability	Average Ability
Kennedy Metro	A,B,C	A,B,C	A,B,C
In-state, non-Kennedy Metro	A,B,C	A,B,C	A
Out-of-state	A,B	A,B	
International	A,B	A,B	

STUDENT
MARKETING
FOR COLLEGES
AND UNIVERSITIES

Marketing Resource Allocations, 2003–04

The marketing resources of the Admission Office have been allocated as follows. The non-personnel and non-office operating appropriations for FY04 amount to $2,250,000. Each cell shows the amount allocated by target market segment and recruit/marketing strategy. These allocations are subject to adjustment as the marketing program moves through the year.

	Full-time Undergraduate		Part-time Undergraduate		Total Allocation By Strategy
	Freshman	Transfer	No prior college experience	Transfer	
Off-Campus Programs	15% $337,500	0%	0%	0%	15% $337,500
On-Campus Programs	10% $225,000	5% $112,500	0%	5% $112,500	20%
Direct Marketing	20% $450,000	0%	0%	0%	20% $450,000
Mass Media	0%	5% $112,500	15% $337,500	5% $112,500	25% $562,500
School Relations	5% $112,500	5% $112,500	0%	0%	10% $225,000
E-Recruiting	5% $112,500	5% $112,500	0%	0%	10% $225,000
Cost Management *	N/A	N/A	N/A	N/A	N/A
Total Allocation By Segment	55% $1,237,500	20% $450,000	15% $337,500	10% $225,000	100% $2,250,000
	75% $1,687,500		25% $562,500		

* Cost Management strategies do not involve the expenditure of Admission Office marketing dollars. Cost Management tactics are a part of the operational efforts of the Division of Financial Affairs (maintaining a competitive sticker price) and the Office of Student Financial Assistance (leveraging available resources to meet net revenue targets and enrollment goals.) The Cost Management strategies employed by the Office of Student Financial Assistance are described in the section labeled "Cost Management Strategy."

SAMPLE
MARKETING PLAN

Cost Management Strategy

Jefferson pursues an aggressive cost management strategy as part of its enrollment management program. Simply defined, cost management involves everything the institution does to make its offerings affordable to the students it desires to enroll. This strategy is designed to make Jefferson more affordable to a wider range of students than would otherwise be the case.

In 1997–98 Jefferson ranked fourth in cost of attendance among the top 25 institutions against which it competed for new students. This was the result of several years of above average increases in Tuition, fees, room, and board. During the same time, Jefferson's discount rate (total Jefferson funded financial aid divided by the total income from full-time undergraduates accruing from Tuition, fees, room, and board) was escalating. The discount rate reached a high of 42% for the 1999–2000 academic year.

Jefferson University Discount Rate
1999–2003

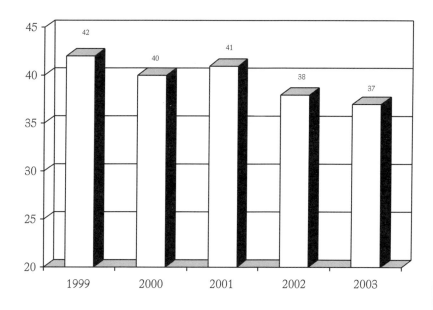

STUDENT
MARKETING
FOR COLLEGES
AND UNIVERSITIES

In the fall of 1998 (for the fall of 1999) Jefferson adopted a net revenue approach to financial aid. The goals of this strategy were to:

- Reduce the discount rate

- Increase net revenues

- Increase new student enrollment, and

- Keep Tuition and fee increases to a minimum.

The results of this effort can be seen in the illustrations labeled "Discount Rate" and "Net Revenue."

The basic strategy employed in the net revenue enhancement program was "financial aid leveraging" – an analytical effort to determine the optimal investment necessary in terms of financial assistance in order to enroll the class desired.

Freshman Class Net Revenues – In Millions
1997–2003
As of 7-28-03

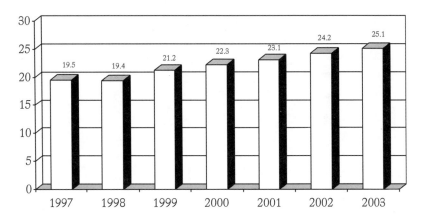

Starting with the freshmen class entering in Fall 1999, Jefferson has leveraged both its "need-based" and "merit-based" aid toward enrolling academically superior students. The use of merit-based scholarships makes it possible to enroll a larger number of strong students who have low or no need. The inclusion of increased numbers of these students in the enrollment mix generates the marginal net revenues required to maintain a strong need-based financial aid program targeted toward needy, strong students. Jefferson has simultaneously increased net revenue, increased student quality and decreased the overall discount rate.

In addition to the increased net generally associated with those on merit aid, Jefferson also depends upon a sizeable group of "full-pay" students. For the fall of 2003, Jefferson will enroll approximately 180 (20% of the new freshmen students) full-paying students. Generally these students cluster at the lower admission rating levels. Any strategy to achieve qualitative improvement that involves reducing the number of students admitted with low admission ratings will inevitably adversely impact overall net revenues.

Under the leveraging program, we have reduced support for those students with weaker academic profiles and retargeted the funds toward those students with stronger profiles. As a result of this effort, Jefferson has realized:

- Increased enrollment

- Increased net revenue

- Increased student quality, and

- Reduced discount rate.

As a result of Jefferson's cost management efforts, overall cost increases for the past several years have been at about the national average for cost of attendance increases. Today, Jefferson's published costs still place us near the top of the cost list when compared to our top competitors

A sample "financial aid leveraging matrix" is presented on the following page.

STUDENT
MARKETING
FOR COLLEGES
AND UNIVERSITIES

Financial Aid Leveraging Matrix (TE = Admission Rating)

	TE = 6.70 +		TE = 5.70 – 6.69		TE = 4.00 – 5.69		TE = 0.00 – 3.99		Total		
	To Date	Goal	To Date	Goal	To Date	Goal	To Date	Goal	To Date	Goal	Over/ Short
Need = $26,000+	**1**		**2**								
Applied	330	183									
Confirmed	93	46									
Yield	28%	25%									
Average Net	11,914	11,347									
Need = $20,000 – 25,999	**3**		**4**								
Applied											
Confirmed											
Yield											
Average Net											
Need = $11,000 – 19,999	**5**		**6**								
Applied											
Confirmed											
Yield											
Average Net											
Need = $1 – 10,999	**7**		**8**								
Applied											
Confirmed											
Yield											
Average Net											
No need merit	**9**		**10**								
Applied											
Confirmed											
Yield											
Average Net											
Full pay	**11**		**12**								
Applied											
Confirmed											
Yield											
Average Net											
Special Talent											
Applied											
Confirmed											
Yield											
Average Net											
Employee Benefit											
Applied											
Confirmed											
Yield											
Total											
Applied											
Confirmed											
Yield											
Average Net											

Sample data display ←

Target Area for Financial Aid Leveraging Strategies Using Need-Based Funds (Cells 1–6)

High Need/ High Ability

Target Area for Financial Aid Leveraging Strategies Using Merit-Based Funds (Cells 7–12)

Low or No Need/ High Ability

SAMPLE MARKETING PLAN

Admission Office Goals 2004 – presented to the academic deans June 6, 2003

- Recruit and enroll 950 traditional freshmen for the Fall 2004 class

  — Arts & Sciences   500
  — Business   200
  — Education   100
  — Health Sciences   150

- Increase the representation of African-American and Hispanic students to 15%

- Increase the number of out-of-state and international students

- Build an applicant pool of 6,000 for the Fall 2004 admission cycle

- Increase yield, particularly among highest ability students, to 30% (+1%)

- Accept 3,167 students for the Fall 2004 term

- Increase the SAT average of first-time enrollees by 5 points to 1190

- Recruit and enroll 125 transfer students for the 2004–05 year

- Make all recruitment plan information available to the entire University community for review, comment and revision

- Place continued and increased emphasis on the quality of Jefferson's academic programs and faculty in all recruitment activities and recruitment materials

- Provide faculty and staff with increased opportunities for participation in the admission and recruitment process

- Cap recruitment expenses at FY03 levels

- Evaluate effectiveness of our on-campus recruitment activities as they are executed and make adjustments, if necessary

- Recruit and enroll an additional 300 first-time, part-time undergraduate students

STUDENT
MARKETING
FOR COLLEGES
AND UNIVERSITIES

Recruitment Strategies – Categories & Tactics

Student recruitment is accomplished using a variety of recruitment strategies. The Office of Admission coordinates Jefferson University's full-time undergraduate recruitment program and is responsible for its design and execution.

Various recruitment strategies can be classified into several broad categories as described following.

Direct Mail Strategies – 2004

While direct mail strategies are employed during all phases of the recruitment program, these strategies are of primary concern during the inquiry and application pool building phases of the recruitment cycle.

Jefferson University utilizes the Student Search Service of the College Board, the Educational Opportunity Service of American College Testing (ACT), College Bound Student Search (CBSS) and the National Research Center on College and University Admissions (NRCCUA) to identify those high school students (high school sophomore and juniors) who might be interested in Jefferson. Jefferson purchased the names and addresses of approximately 207,550 "Prospective Students" from these sources. The names purchased represent those students whose academic achievement to date is consistent with our admission target market criteria. The total (207,550) is "segmented" by academic ability level (e.g. potential honors, etc.), year of study (high school sophomore or junior) discipline interest, geography, and/or ethnicity. Students on these segmented lists are recruited differently. Once these names are in hand, the Admission Office eliminates duplicates and initiates direct mail contact (as well as e-mail contact) with these individuals. Those individuals who express interest in Jefferson (i.e., respond to one or more mailings) are placed on our "Inquiry File."

Once the "inquiry" file has been built, a series of publications are mailed to the student over the course of the recruitment period. Some of the "direct mail" communications are summarized as follows. (A complete delineation of the communication campaign is included in the section of this plan labeled "Communication Plan" appended to this document.)

- Junior-Senior Communications
  - Undergraduate Prospectus
  - Fall Reception Invitation
  - Financial Aid Brochure
  - Admission Application
  - Financial Aid Sourcebook

- Sophomore-Junior Communications
  - Mini-Prospectus/Freshmen Class Profile
  - Fall Reception Invitation
  - "144 Reasons" Poster
  - "Art of Picking a College" Newsletter
  - College Planning Calendar
  - "The Financial Aid Game" Newsletter

The entire "family" of publications was redesigned for the Fall 2001 recruitment cycle. The new publications feature an entirely new graphic identity and have a greater emphasis on the unique academic aspects of a Jefferson University undergraduate experience. The theme *"Jefferson – The Wise Choice"* is intended to position Jefferson as a place offering rigorous academic experiences played out in a unique geographic setting distinguished by its cultural, commercial, environmental, urban, artistic, technological, architectural, and sociological character. Graphical elements are intended to make Jefferson stand out from the pack and to illustrate the basic theme – *Jefferson – The Wise Choice.*

In addition to three sources identified above, Jefferson also obtains names and addresses of selected populations of students from several other sources, including *Private Colleges & Universities* magazine, *The College Guide,* and *Peterson's Competitive Colleges.* These names are also placed in our inquiry file and rolled into a communication campaign designed for these individuals.

For the 2003–04 recruitment cycle, Jefferson has identified 31 separate market segments to be contacted during our initial outreach. Unless otherwise specified, the market segment includes men and women, sophomores and juniors, in all 50 states as well as APO and FPO Military addresses.

STUDENT
MARKETING
FOR COLLEGES
AND UNIVERSITIES

Source	#	Target Pool	Quantity
Inquiry pool	01	2002 Juniors	18,000
Total Inquiry			*18,000*
CBSS	01	Local juniors	3,000
CBSS	02	Local sophomores	3,000
CBSS	03	Health Science juniors	2,000
CBSS	04	Business sophomores	8,000
CBSS	05	Education juniors	9,000
CBSS	06	Education sophomores	5,000
Total CBSS			*30,000*
NRCCUA	01	Business juniors	5,000
NRCCUA	02	Health Science juniors	4,000
NRCCUA	03	Computer science juniors	1,000
NRCCUA	04	LAS juniors	20,000
NRCCUA	05	Education Juniors	5,000
NRCCUA	06	Business sophomores	6,000
NRCCUA	07	Health Science sophomores	6,000
NRCCUA	08	Education sophomores	4,000
NRCCUA	09	LAS sophomores	20,000
Total NRCCUA			*71,000*
PSAT	01	Business juniors	5,000
PSAT	02	Health Science juniors	4,000
PSAT	03	Computer science juniors	1,000
PSAT	04	LAS juniors	20,000
PSAT	05	Education Juniors	5,000
PSAT	06	Business sophomores	6,000
PSAT	07	Health Science sophomores	6,000
PSAT	08	Education sophomores	4,000
PSAT	09	LAS sophomores	20,000
Total PSAT			*71,000*
ACT–PLAN	01	Sophomores	15,000
ACT–PLAN	02	Local sophomores	5,000
Total ACT			*20,000*
Noel–Levitz	01	Declared juniors	2,000
Noel–Levitz	02	Declared sophomores	2,000
Noel–Levitz	03	Matched juniors	2,000
Noel–Levitz	04	Matched sophomores	1,500
Total N–L			*7,500*
Total Direct Marketing Mail Outreach			**207,500**

SAMPLE
MARKETING PLAN

Initial "outreach" letters are unique for each of the 31 market segments. All letters are personalized and appear to have been forwarded to the student via first class mail.

High School Relations Program Strategies

An effective recruitment campaign is dependent upon maintaining good relationships with the secondary school guidance community. The primary strategy employed to sustain and develop this relationship is the high school visit.

During the 2003–04 recruiting year, Jefferson representatives will visit some 350 high schools in 26 states. These schools are carefully selected on the basis of their location, quality, and record of referring students to Jefferson. Some of our feeder schools are visited every year while others are on a 24–36 month visitation schedule

In addition to school visitations, the Admission Office maintains an extensive file of secondary school counselors. Each year the Admission Office forwards a number of mailings to these individuals. The information distributed includes:

- Admission Applications

- Financial Aid Brochure

- Undergraduate Prospectus

- Undergraduate Course Catalog (printed every other year)

- Fall Reception Schedule

The Jefferson Admission Staff maintains active membership in the National Association of College Admission Counselors (NACAC), the American Association of Collegiate Registrars and Admission Officers (AACRAO), NAFSA: Association of International Educators, and the College Board. Regional representatives also maintain active membership in the regional affiliates of each of the national associations. During the annual meetings of each national and regional group, members of the Jefferson admission staff meet with and entertain targeted secondary school counseling personnel. Such events make it possible for us to reach several hundred additional college counselors on an annual basis.

Jefferson admission staff members serve as "faculty" for a number of summer training programs for new secondary school personnel. These training programs target new college counselors and afford us the opportunity to favorably impress counselors just entering the profession. During the 2003–04 academic year, Jefferson staff served as faculty at the College Board Summer Institute (Orlando), the Texas Association of College Admission Counselors Summer Institute (Houston), The Southern Association of College Admission Counselors Summer Institute (Atlanta) and "Dry Run" (North Carolina.)

Admission representatives sponsor counselor breakfasts and luncheons when traveling throughout the United States and abroad. Local secondary school counselors are often guests of the Admission Office at university athletic, cultural, and social events. In February 2004, Jefferson will host approximately two-dozen counselors from the selected geographic areas for a three-day fly-in Jefferson University program.

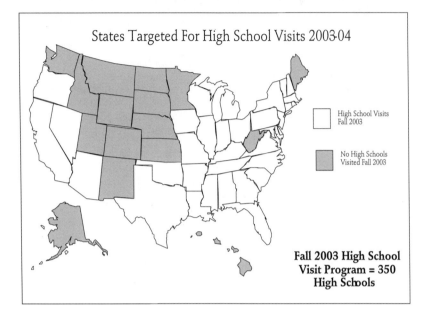

States Targeted For High School Visits 2003-04

High School Visits
Fall 2003

No High Schools
Visited Fall 2003

Fall 2003 High School
Visit Program = 350
High Schools

Off-campus Program Strategies

Since Jefferson can visit only a small fraction of the high schools in any geographic area, the Admission office has scheduled approximately 25 Jefferson University Admission Forums (JUAF) for prospective students from September through November and an additional 20 for accepted students during March and April. These weekend or evening meetings generally take place in hotels located in areas from which we draw significant numbers of inquiries and applicants.

Prospective applicants (fall programs) and accepted students (spring programs) are invited by personalized invitation to these receptions. The program format provides individuals with important information about Jefferson's academic programs, living environment, the admission requirements, and the financial aid program. In addition to admission staff, many programs also include as a guest speaker a member of the faculty. The goal of these programs is to encourage the prospective student to apply for admission (in the fall programs) or to enroll as a first-year student (spring programs for accepted students.)

College Fair programs take place throughout the year and provide opportunities for large numbers of prospective students to go to one location to gather information about a large number of colleges. A single high school, a group of high schools, or various professional associations can sponsor fairs.

Depending upon the location and sponsor of the fair, the participation may vary from less than 50 students to well over 20,000 students.

Representatives of the admission staff participate in as many of these fairs as possible given our available financial and personnel resources. These fairs draw large audiences with attendance sometimes in excess of 20,000 prospective students. Highest priority is assigned to three categories of fairs that are sponsored by different professional associations:

- National Association of College Admission Counselors (NACAC)

- National Hispanic Institute (NIH)

- National Scholarship Service (NSSFNS)

Fairs sponsored by individual schools or groups of schools from which we have historically received applications and fairs sponsored by Kennedy secondary schools are assigned to the second priority category. Other fairs are assigned to the lowest level and are attended only if resources allow.

In addition, members of the Alumni Admission Committee take a very active role in attending some of the fairs not covered by Jefferson staff. During the 2002–03 academic year, we anticipate that members of the admission staff will attend approximately 150 fairs. Recent graduates participating in Jefferson's Alumni in Admission program will provide coverage at an additional 250+/– college fairs.

Jefferson invites prospective students and their parents to attend Jefferson University information sessions. Each program lasts approximately 90 minutes and includes a presentation by an Admission Office staff member, the introduction of area alumni, a preview of the Jefferson video, and a question and answer session. The schedule for Fall 2003 follows. (*Indicates Pres. D. Smith will attend)

STUDENT
MARKETING
FOR COLLEGES
AND UNIVERSITIES

Program Location	Event Day	Event Date	Event Time
Alexandria, LA	Thursday	09/11/03	7:00 PM
*Atlanta, GA	Saturday	09/06/03	11:00 AM
Lolley, TX	Sunday	09/07/03	5:00 PM
Baltimore, MD	Saturday	09/06/03	1:00 PM
*Baton Rouge, LA	Thursday	09/04/03	7:00 PM
Birmingham, AL	Saturday	09/20/03	11:00 AM
Boston, MA	Sunday	09/21/03	11:00 AM
Charleston, SC	Wednesday	09/03/03	7:00 PM
Raleigh, NC	Wednesday	10/01/03	7:00 PM
*Chicago, IL	Tuesday	10/14/03	6:30 PM
Cincinnati, OH	Thursday	10/02/03	7:00 PM
Columbia, SC	Monday	09/28/03	7:00 PM
Dallas, TX	Sunday	09/14/03	7:00 PM
Denver, CO	Saturday	09/06/03	1:00 PM
Fort Lauderdale, FL	Thursday	10/16/03	7:00 PM
Hartford, CT	Saturday	09/06/03	11:00 AM
Houston, TX	Saturday	09/06/03	11:00 AM
Jackson, MS	Sunday	09/14/03	6:00 PM
Jacksonville, Fl.	Thursday	09/04/03	7:00 PM
Kansas City, MO	Thursday	10/09/03	7:00 PM
Lake Charles, LA	Tuesday	09/02/03	7:00 PM
Little Rock, AR	Sunday	09/14/03	5:00 PM
Long Island, NY	Sunday	09/07/03	1:00 PM
Los Angeles, CA	Sunday	09/21/03	1:00 PM
Louisville, KY	Saturday	10/18/03	11:00 AM
Memphis, TN	Saturday	09/13/03	11:00 AM
Miami, FL	Tuesday	10/14/03	7:00 PM
Mobile, AL	Sunday	09/14/03	5:00 PM
Montgomery, AL	Tuesday	09/16/03	7:00 PM
Nashville, TN	Wednesday	09/10/03	7:00 PM
New York, NY	Monday	09/22/03	7:00 PM
Oklahoma City, OK	Thursday	09/11/03	7:00 PM
Omaha, NE	Monday	10/06/03	7:00 PM
Orlando, Fl	Sunday	09/07/03	1:00 PM
Philadelphia, PA	Sunday	09/21/03	7:00 PM
Pittsburgh, PA	Saturday	09/20/03	11:00 AM
Phoenix, AZ	Sunday	09/07/03	1:00 PM
Portsmouth, NH	Saturday	09/20/03	11:00 AM
Providence, RI	Tuesday	09/09/03	7:00 PM
Richmond, VA	Sunday	09/07/03	1:00 PM
San Antonio, TX	Wednesday	09/10/03	7:00 PM
San Francisco, CA	Sunday	09/14/03	5:00 PM
St. Louis, MO	Tuesday	10/21/03	7:00 PM
Stamford, CT	Monday	09/08/03	7:00 PM
*Tampa, FL	Sunday	09/07/03	6:30 AM
Tulsa, OK	Saturday	09/13/03	1:00 PM
Washington, D.C.	Sunday	09/07/03	7:00 PM
Westchester, NY	Sunday	09/07/03	7:00 PM

SAMPLE
MARKETING PLAN

On-Campus Program Strategies

The Admission Office schedules a number of on-campus programs designed to provide prospective students with an opportunity to see and experience Jefferson University. These programs are held throughout the academic year and include:

- Inside Jefferson (2003: September 13, & October 4 & 18).

  These half-day (Saturday) programs are designed to expose the prospective student to Jefferson University. The program includes a presentation by the president, a panel discussion for students and parents, an academic forum, a campus tour, and complimentary tickets to a Jefferson football or volleyball game when the event coincides with a scheduled home game.

- Campus Tours (twice daily Monday through Friday, and once on Saturdays during school year)

- Overnight hosting of student guests (Sunday – Thursday evenings) by current students.

- Jefferson Days (2004: March 29 – to April 30 excluding spring break)

  Daylong (weekday) programs include a campus tour, an advising session, lunch with faculty, staff and students, and optional class attendance and special sessions, such as financial aid, student life, and the Honors program.

- Business Fridays (spring)

In addition, the Admission Office annually sponsors a "Counselor Fly-In." This program is "by invitation only" and brings a small number (18–24) of secondary school counselors to Jefferson and Kennedy for a three-day intensive visit. The program includes two full days on the Jefferson campus, evening social events, and tours of Kennedy.

Our on-campus program strategy cluster also includes our "video outreach" and telemarketing functions.

These strategies are explained in greater detail in the sections that follow.

STUDENT
MARKETING
FOR COLLEGES
AND UNIVERSITIES

E-Recruitment

Effective for the Fall 2001 recruitment cycle, Jefferson implemented a comprehensive "e-recruitment" business strategy. This category of recruitment activities includes:

- A new admission Web page series designed specifically for prospective students, applicants, accepted students, and secondary school counselors.

- An e-mail inquiry response and communication campaign

- Web-based "applications for admission" (Jefferson University server plus three commercial sites.)

- Voice response telephone system applications for checking application status

- Mediated "Chat Room" application for prospective students

- An e-correspondence campaign for prospective and accepted students. (In 2003–03, approximately 1,000,000 e-mails were sent to these individuals.)

- Server-based "just-in-time" publications describing every academic program and every academic support service provided by Jefferson

All aspects of the e-recruitment plan were fully operational by September 1, 2000 and expanded for the 2003–04 recruitment year

Throughout the year, the Admission office sponsors a number of chat room events for prospective students, applicants and accepted students. Each chat event is limited to a set number of topics and is mediated by institutional "experts' drawn from those responsible for the functions under discussion.

The revised (8/01/02) Admission Web Page map is outlined on the next page.

A. Prospective Students
General Information
   About Jefferson
Undergraduate Colleges
Academic Resources
   & Student Support
Student Life
Admission Profile
Financial Aid Programs
Applying To Jefferson
Information Request
On Campus Admission Events
Freshman Year Experience
Contacting Jefferson
Visiting Jefferson
Virtual Campus Tour
Regional Receptions
Transfer Students
International Students
Chat Room
Academic Calendar

B. Applicants
Applications For Admission
Application Instructions
Application Status
Financial Aid Status

C. Parents of Prospective Students
Campus Safety
Academic Calendar
Payment Plans
Shipping Things to Jefferson
Parents Association
Advising

D. Secondary School Counselors
Regional Receptions
Admission Profile
Admission Calendar
Contacting Jefferson
Applicant Roster
   by School Code
Application Status
Financial Aid Status

E. Jefferson Faculty
Admission Summary Statistics
Enrollment Status
College Roster – Applied
College Roster – Accepted
College Roster – Deposited
On Campus
   Admission Functions

F. Admitted Students
Jefferson Days
Regional receptions
Orientation
Alumni Admission Committee
Chat Room
Student Admission Committee
Time lines

G. All Persons
Information On Majors
Information on Colleges
Undergraduate Catalog
Financial Aid Publications

STUDENT
MARKETING
FOR COLLEGES
AND UNIVERSITIES

Fall 2003 Travel Schedule

Date	Day	Jones	Smith	Martin	William	Peter	Mary H	Kelsey	Tony	Bernard	Louise	Jesse
28-Aug	Thu											
29-Aug	Fri											
30-Aug	Sat											
31-Aug	Sun											
1-Sep	Mon	LABOR DAY	LABOR DAY	LABOR DAY	LABOR DAY	LABOR DAY	LABOR DAY	LABOR DAY	LABOR DAY	LABOR DAY	LABOR DAY	LABOR DAY
2-Sep	Tue				out	AR-L.C.				AR-LAKE CHARLES		
3-Sep	Wed					out	AR-LAFAYETTE			AR-CHARLESTON,SC		AR-LAFAYETTE +LACRAO
4-Sep	Thu						AR-BATON ROUGE	AR-SACRAMENTO	AR-ALBUQUERQUE	AR-JACKSONVILLE	AR-BATON ROUGE	AR-BR+LACRAO
5-Sep	Fri									LACRAO		
6-Sep	Sat			AR-HARTFORD	AR-MONROE	AR-BALTIMORE	AR-HOUSTON	AR-SEATTLE	AR-DENVER	AR-ATL		
7-Sep	Sun		So Consortium-IL	AR-LI/WESTCH		AR-RICH/D.C.	AR-LOLLEY	AR-PORTLAND	AR-PHOENIX	AR-ORL/TAMPA		
8-Sep	Mon		So Consortium-SL	AR-STAMFORD	AR-S'PORT+LACRAO	AR-E.BRUNSWICK, NJ	Lolley			TN		
9-Sep	Tue		So Consortium-DC	AR-PROV	LACRAO	AR-PARSIPANY, NJ	Lolley			TN		
10-Sep	Wed		So Consortium-PA		AR-ALEXANDRIA+LACRAO		AR-SAN ANTONIO			AR-NASHVILLE		
11-Sep	Thu		So Consortium-MA		Alex-Bfast+HSV		San Ant.		AR-OK. CITY	TN		
12-Sep	Fri						San Ant.		OK	TN		
13-Sep	Sat	INSIDE JU	INSIDE JU	INSIDE JU	INSIDE JU	INSIDE JU	INSIDE JU	INSIDE JU	AR-TULSA	AR-MEMPHIS	INSIDE JU	INSIDE JU
14-Sep	Sun		AR-SF		AR-JACKSON			TAMPA FAIR	AR-DALLAS/FW	AR-LITTLEROCK	AR-MOBILE	
15-Sep	Mon		So CA		MS		BR fair & BR lunch		Dallas	AR	AL	
16-Sep	Tue		So CA		MS fair		BR HSV + fair		Dallas		AL + AR-Mont	
17-Sep	Wed		So CA		MS fair		BR HSV + fair		Dallas		AL	
18-Sep	Thu		So CA				BR HSV + fair	ME/VT	Dallas		AL	PITT
19-Sep	Fri		So CA					ME/VT	Dallas		AL	PITT
20-Sep	Sat		AR-NWPT BCH					AR-NEW HAMPSHIRE	Dallas-fair		AR-BHAM	AR-PITTSBURG
21-Sep	Sun		AR-L.A.					AR-BOSTON			BHAM NACAC	AR-PHILADELPHIA

Date	Day	Jones	Smith	Martin	William	Peter	Mary H	Kelsey	Tony	Bernard	Louise	Jesse
22-Sep	Mon	AR–MANHATTAN		AR–MANHATTAN				NH			GA + fairs	PA
23-Sep	Tue	Manhattan		Westchester				Exeter/Andover			GA	PA
24-Sep	Wed	Manhattan		Westchester				NH	MN NACAC		GA	PA
25-Sep	Thu	Manhattan		Westchester				NH (S. NH NEACAC)	AR–MINNEAPOLIS	AR–DETROIT	GA	PA
26-Sep	Fri – RH	Manhattan		Westchester				NH (S. NH NEACAC)	MN HSV	MI	GA	PA
27-Sep	Sat – RH	ACT	ACT	ACT	ACT	ACT	UT v.JU	ACT	ACT	ACT	ACT	ACT
28-Sep	Sun – RH									AR–CLEVELAND		
29-Sep	Mon			Long Island	Prof Dev?		Houston	MA		OH	AR–COLUMBIA,SC	
30-Sep	Tue			Long Island	Prof Dev?		Houston	MA		OH	SC	
1-Oct	Wed			Long Island	Prof Dev?		Houston	MA		OH	AR–DURHAM	
2-Oct	Thu	NACAC		Long Island	NACAC		Houston	MA (NH NEACAC)		AR–CINCI	NC	
3-Oct	Fri	NACAC		Long Island	NACAC		Houston	MA (NH NEACAC)		OH	NC	
4-Oct	Sat	NACAC	INSIDE JU	INSIDE JU	NACAC	INSIDE JU	INSIDE JU	INSIDE JU	INSIDE JU	Out	INSIDE JU	INSIDE JU
5-Oct	Sun – YK	NACAC	ECIS	Fairs	NACAC							
6-Oct	Mon		ECIS/Fulbright		SF		AZ		ECIS – LAm	AR–OMAHA		CO
7-Oct	Tue		ECIS/Fulbright		SF		AZ		ECIS – LAm	NE		CO
8-Oct	Wed		ECIS/Fulbright		SF		AZ		ECIS – LAm	KC + fair		CO – DEN fair
9-Oct	Thu		ECIS/Fulbright		SF		NM		ECIS – LAm	AR–KANSAS CITY		CO – DEN fair
10-Oct	Fri		ECIS/Fulbright		SF		NM			KC		CO
11-Oct	Sat	SAT 1 & II	SAT 1 & II	SAT 1 & II	SAT 1 & II	SAT 1 & II	RMACAC	SAT 1 & II	CO – DEN fair	SAT 1 & II		
12-Oct	Sun											
13-Oct	Mon							MD	MD			
14-Oct	Tue	AR–CHI w/ A.C.	FL	FL+AR–MIAMI					MD	CT	AR–CHICAGO	CT–NC/D
15-Oct	Wed			FL			DC	W. MA	MD		AR–INDIANAPOLIS	CT–W/W
16-Oct	Thu			FL+AR FT. LAUDERDALE			DC	W. MA – Deerfield	MD		KY	CT – Gwich
17-Oct	Fri	N.O. LUNCH		FL				W. MA – NMH		N.O. LUNCH	KY	CT
18-Oct	Sat	INSIDE JU	INSIDE JU	INSIDE JU	INSIDE JU	INSIDE JU	INSIDE JU	NMH	INSIDE JU	INSIDE JU STL NACAC	AR–KENTUCKY	INSIDE JU
19-Oct	Sun											RI FAIR?

STUDENT
MARKETING
FOR COLLEGES
AND UNIVERSITIES

SAMPLE
MARKETING PLAN

Date	Day	Jones	Smith	Martin	William	Peter	Mary H	Kelsey	Tony	Bernard	Louise	Jesse
20-Oct	Mon		FL						STL	RI		RI
21-Oct	Tue			FL		VA	CT	CT – loomis		AR–ST.LOUIS		
22-Oct	Wed			FL. L NACAC			VA	CT – hotchkiss		STL		
23-Oct	Thu			FL	Chicago		VA	CT		STL		
24-Oct	Fri			FL	CH. NACAC			CT		STL		
25-Oct	Sat	ACT	ACT	ACT	CH. NACAC	ACT	ACT	ACT	ACT	ACT	ACT	ACT
26-Oct	Sun											
27-Oct	Mon		FL – Tampa & Orlando		WI NACAC				OR		Sport fast/lunch	NJ
28-Oct	Tue		FL		WI				OR		Sport	NJ
29-Oct	Wed		FL		Chicago				OR		Sport	NJ
30-Oct	Thu		FL		Chicago				OR		Monroe	NJ
31-Oct	Fri		FL		Chicago				OR		Bfast + Monroe HSV	NJ
1-Nov	Sat	SAT I & II	SAT I & II	SAT I & II	SAT I & II	SAT I & II	SAT I & II	SAT I & II	SAT I & II	SAT I & II		SAT I & II
2-Nov	Sun											LI NACAC
3-Nov	Mon		FL – Pan Handle						Spokane WA NACAC			
4-Nov	Tue		FL						WA			
5-Nov	Wed		FL						WA			
6-Nov	Thu		FL						WA			
7-Nov	Fri		FL						Portland OR NACAC			
8-Nov	Sat		JAX NACAC						Portland OR NACAC			
9-Nov	Sun								Seattle WA NACAC			
10-Nov	Mon						LC & LAF		Seattle WA NACAC			
11-Nov	Tue						LC & LAF					
12-Nov	Wed						LC & LAF					
13-Nov	Thu						LAF Fairs + reception?					
14-Nov	Fri						LC fair AM + LC lunch					
15-Nov	Sat											
16-Nov	Sun											

Recruitment – Personnel Resources

Mounting a worldwide recruitment program involves the entire University community. In order to expand market penetration and reach, while maintaining realistic recruitment costs, the Admission Office utilizes faculty, staff, students, parents, and alumni in its recruitment strategy. The Alumni Admission Committee and Student Admission Committee have been operational for many years.

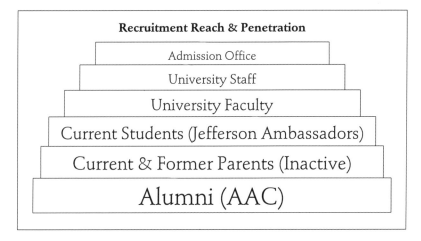

Recruitment Reach & Penetration

Admission Office
University Staff
University Faculty
Current Students (Jefferson Ambassadors)
Current & Former Parents (Inactive)
Alumni (AAC)

Jefferson Alumni Admission Committee (JAAC)

The Alumni Admission Committee has over 300 active members organized in subcommittees based on geography. Each subcommittee has a chairperson who is responsible for coordinating the activities of his or her subcommittee. The basic AAC responsibilities include:

1. Direct referral of prospective students to the Admissions Office

2. Participation in admission receptions in the fall and spring

3. Representing the University at college fairs and college nights not covered by University staff or faculty

4. Telephone contact with prospective students and parents

Jefferson Ambassadors

The Jefferson Ambassadors consists of currently enrolled students. The members are carefully selected from a pool of applicants. Approximately 100 participants are selected. The membership is called upon in a variety of tasks associated with recruitment. They represent a powerful recruitment force upon which the Admission Office relies heavily. Some of the tasks undertaken by students include:

1. Conducting most of the campus tours

2. Staffing telethon sessions

STUDENT
MARKETING
FOR COLLEGES
AND UNIVERSITIES

3. Serving as hosts and hostesses for prospective students wishing to spend a night on campus as part of their decision-making process.

4. Serving as student panel members for various on-campus programs (e.g. Inside Jefferson)

University Faculty and Staff as Recruiters

University faculty and staff have been and continue to be involved in the recruitment program. They perform the following functions.

1. Attend fall and spring receptions as featured speakers

2. Host (in their classes) prospective students who want to experience a college-level lecture

3. Visit local high schools and cover special programs in local high schools

4. Provide the Admission Office with specific descriptions of their majors and programs

5. Participate in the Case Management Admission Initiative (CMAI)

Admission Office Recruitment Staff – 2003–04

Joe Smith
Vice President for Enrollment Management
& Institutional Research (1993)

Undergraduate Manhattan College
Graduate The Johns Hopkins University M.S., M.S.
The University of Connecticut

Tom Benedict
Assistant Vice President for Enrollment Management/
Director of Admission & Recruitment (2003)

Undergraduate Ohio University, B.A.

Louise Jacobs
Associate Director (1988)

Undergraduate University of Vermont
Graduate Harvard University, M.Ed.

Michael Lolley
Assistant Vice President for Enrollment Management/
Communication & Budget (1999)

Undergraduate U of Miami, B.A.
Graduate Jefferson University, Freeman School
(in progress)

Kelsey Hammer
Assistant Vice President for Enrollment
Management/Operations
Assigned to project Matrix 2003–2005

Undergraduate Trinity College (DC)
Graduate Jefferson University, Freeman School, M.B.A.

Anthony Blake
Assistant Director of Admission (1996)

Undergraduate University of New Orleans
Graduate University of New Orleans (in progress)

Susie Franks
Counselor (2002)

Undergraduate Jefferson University, B.A.

Peter Terrey
Assistant Director of Admission (2000)/ Interim
Assistant V. P. for Enrollment Management/Operations

Undergraduate Boston University, B.S.M.

Joe Jones
Counselor (2003)

Undergraduate Providence College

Kevin Isaacs
Counselor (2002)

Undergraduate Jefferson University, B.A.

Lonnie Richards
Counselor (2003)

Undergraduate Duke University
Graduate University of California, Berkeley M.A.

Doreen Holoday
Counselor (2001)

Undergraduate Texas Christian University, B.S.M.

STUDENT
MARKETING
FOR COLLEGES
AND UNIVERSITIES

Francis Waters   Counselor (2002)

Undergraduate   Furman University, B.S.M.

Pat Diamond   Transfer Student Coordinator (2002)

Undergraduate   Jefferson University

SAMPLE
MARKETING PLAN

Staff Project Assignments 2003–2004

UNIVERSITY LIAISONS:

Alumni Affairs	Jacobs
Athletics	Lolley
Business School	Hammer
Computing Services	Blake & Franks
Development	Terrey
Financial Aid	Jacobs/New AVP
Honors Program	Waters
Housing and Residence Life	Franks & New AVP
Human Resources	Franks & New AVP
International Students & Scholars Center	Terrey
Multicultural Affairs	Lolley
Liberal Arts & Science	Waters
Health Science	Richards & Daley
ROTC	Terrey
Graduate Recruitment	Jones, Waters

RECRUITMENT:

Travel Planning & Reporting	New AVP
Admission Receptions Coordination	Isaacs
Guest speaker coordination for Admission Receptions	Richards
College Fair Coordinators	Jacobs
Transfer student recruitment	Terrey, Holoday
International student recruitment	Terrey
Alumni & Parent Admission Committees	Jones, Waters & Jacobs

COMMUNICATIONS: ISAACS

Communications mailing operations	Franks
Publications – Liaison with PUBLICATIONS Group	Isaacs, Richards & Franks
Video – Liaison with Videc	Isaacs & Hammer
Web – Liaison with PUBLICATIONS/TS	Isaacs & Franks
Direct Mail – Liaison with Royall & Co.	Isaacs
Publications mailing operations	Franks

ON-CAMPUS PROGRAMMING: TERREY

Counselor of the Day	Terrey
Counselor Fly-Ins	Waters & Terrey
Daily Visits & Tour Guides	Jones & Hammer
Faculty coordinator (Case Management) – yield events	Lolley
Inside Jefferson	Waters & Hammer
Multicultural Preview	TBA
Jefferson Ambassadors	Jones & Hammer

STUDENT MARKETING FOR COLLEGES AND UNIVERSITIES

Honors weekend . . . . Richards, Waters &
Daley
Student interns. . . . . Franks & Hammer
Jefferson Days . . . . Daley, Jones & Jacobs

FILE REVIEW/EVALUATION PROCESS: . . . . . . TBA

Common Application liaison . . . . Isaacs
21-Day Personal Applications. . . . . Isaacs
Institutional Interest/BGS . . . . Terrey
International review & credentials evaluation . . . . . . Terrey
Transfer review . . . . Holoday
Transfer credential evaluation. . . . . Holoday

SCHOLARSHIP PROGRAMS: . . . . TBA

Diboll, Dixon, National Merit, ROTC . . . . Terrey
Deans' Honor Scholarship . . . . New AVP
DSA & Founders . . . . Waters
Mayoral and Gus Mayer Scholarships . . . . Jacobs
Urban Scholars Award. . . . . Richards & Jones

STRATEGIC PROGRAMS: . . . . SMITH

Marketing Plan. . . . . All
Annual Report . . . . All
Target group recruitment strategy coordinators
  Education – target activities . . . . Jones
  Health Sciences – target activities. . . . . Richards
  Honors – target activities. . . . . Richards, Waters
  & Daley
  International recruitment – target activities . . . . . . Terrey
  Kennedy recruitment – target activities . . . . Lolley, Jones & Jacobs
  Multicultural recruitment – target activities . . . . . . Lolley, Richards, Jones
  & Terrey
  Transfer recruitment – target activities. . . . . Terrey & Holoday

TRAINING AND DEVELOPMENT: . . . . ISAACS, LOLLEY
& TBA

Admission Staff . . . . Smith
Operations Staff. . . . . Franks
Staff training session coordination . . . . Isaacs & Lolley
Staff search coordination. Terrey

BUDGET . . . . SMITH, ISAACS
& FRANKS

SAMPLE
MARKETING PLAN

Admission Communication Calendars

Detailed communication calendars for both print and e-mail correspondence are attached as appendices to this report. These are as of July 1, 2003 and are subject to revision as the recruitment year progresses.

STUDENT
MARKETING
FOR COLLEGES
AND UNIVERSITIES

SAMPLE
MARKETING PLAN

Admission & Recruitment Timeline

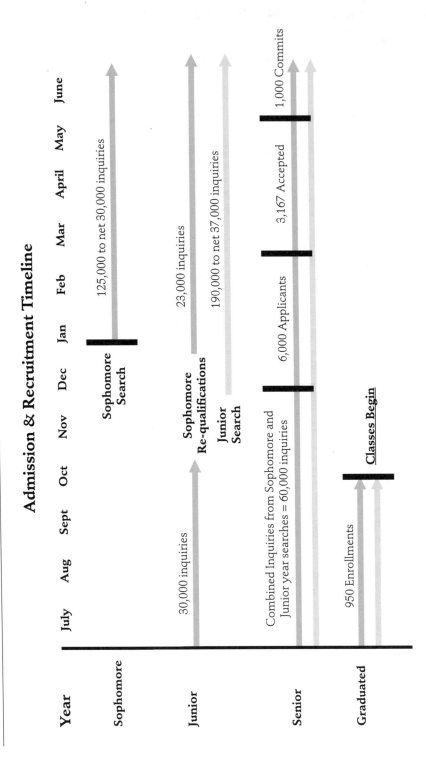

Year

July Aug Sept Oct Nov Dec Jan Feb Mar April May June

Sophomore

Sophomore Search

30,000 inquiries

125,000 to net 30,000 inquiries

Junior

Sophomore Re-qualifications

Junior Search

23,000 inquiries

190,000 to net 37,000 inquiries

Senior

Combined Inquiries from Sophomore and Junior year searches = 60,000 inquiries

6,000 Applicants

3,167 Accepted

1,000 Commits

Graduated

950 Enrollments

Classes Begin

Communication Calendar

COMMUNICATION	TARGET	CNSLR	VENDOR	RUN DATE	MAIL DATE
JULY					
President's letter	Conf	JA	WP	07/02/03	07/12/03
eQual	JR	JA	DIRECT MAIL	NA	07/08/03
Pre-Senior Newsletter: "How to Choose a College"	JR	PS	Publications		07/12/03
Pre-Fast App e-mail (incl. Focus LA & Sec. School)	SR	JA	DIRECT MAIL	NA	7/26/2003 0:00
Online Personal Application	SR	JA	DIRECT MAIL	NA	7/26/2003 0:00
Transfer Close-out letter (spring)	Apply	PW	WP	Rolling	07/26/03
Web Spur Card/URL addresses	SR	JA	Publications		07/26/03
Pre-Fast App letter (incl. Focus LA & Sec. School)	SR+	JA	DIRECT MAIL		07/31/03
AUGUST					
Personal Application	SR	JA	DIRECT MAIL		08/02/03
Admission Reception Evite (incl. AAC)	SR/JR	JA	DIRECT MAIL	NA	8/2/2003 0:00
Admission Reception – Fall	JR	JA	DIRECT MAIL	07/15/03	08/05/03
Admission Reception AAC Invitations, Fall	AAC	RA	DIRECT MAIL	0	8/05/03
Travel Piece/Just the Facts	SO/JR/SR	JA	Publications		
Kennedy Report/Booklet	HS	VT	Univ. Printing**		08/02/03

APPENDIX A

STUDENT
MARKETING
FOR COLLEGES
AND UNIVERSITIES

SAMPLE
MARKETING PLAN

COMMUNICATION	TARGET	CNSLR	VENDOR	RUN DATE	MAIL DATE
Inside Jefferson Evite	SR/JR	JA	DIRECT MAIL	NA	8/14/2003 0:00
Inside Jefferson	SR/JR	JA	DIRECT MAIL	07/15/03	08/09/03
High School Announcement poster	HS	PS	Publications		08/09/03
H S Announcement letter accompanying poster	HS	ST	WP		08/09/03
International Travel Piece	Travel–Intl	DS	Publications		
LACRAO Packets	HS	VT	In House		08/09/03
Prospectus 2003 (redesign)	INQ	JA	Publications	08/12/03	08/16/03
Common Application Supplement	SR	JA	Publications	08/05/03	08/16/03
Catalog of Undergraduate Courses (postcard)	HS	AA	Acad Affairs	08/06/03	08/16/03
Counselor Breakfast Invite	HS	ST	Counselor	08/06/03	08/16/03
AAC Handbook	AAC	RA	Univ Printing**	NA	08/16/03
Admission Reception E-mail Bump	INQ	JA	DIRECT MAIL	NA	8/5/2003 0:00
Admission Reception E-mail Reminder	INQ	JA	DIRECT MAIL	NA	8/5/2003 0:00
Early Decision Incentives announcement	SR	JA	DIRECT MAIL	8/19/2003 0:00	8/30/2003 0:00
Governor's Scholarship Application	HS	VT	Univ. Printing**	08/16/03	08/30/03
Mayoral Scholarship NO HS Cover Letter	HS	VT	Univ. Printing**	08/16/03	08/30/03
Counselor Breakfast Packet	HS	ST	In-house	08/16/03	08/30/03
Inside Jefferson Confirmation card	JR/SR	JA	DIRECT MAIL		08/30/03

COMMUNICATION	TARGET	CNSLR	VENDOR	RUN DATE	MAIL DATE
SEPTEMBER					
Urban Scholars application	SR	KG	Univ. Printing	08/01/03	09/03/03
Inside Jefferson e-mail bump	SR/JR		DIRECT MAIL	NA	9/3/2003 0:00
Urban Scholars announcement	SR		CRM	8/26/2003 0:00	9/6/2003 0:00
Application–Freshman	SR	JA	Mail House	08/19/03	09/06/03
Transfer Application and Brochure	Tran	DS	Mail House	08/19/03	09/06/03
Deans Letter to Inquiries Health Sciences	SR	KG	Mail House	08/19/03	09/06/03
Deans Letter to Inquiries Education	SR	VT	WP	09/03/03	09/06/03
LA Weeks letter – Fall	SR		Mail House	09/06/03	09/06/03
Fall Chat room announcement	SR		CRM	9/4/2003	9/9/2003
Inside Jefferson reminder	SR/JR		DIRECT MAIL	NA	9/10/2003
Mini Prospectus	JR	JA	Publications	09/03/03	09/15/03
Focus LA announcement	SR		CRM	9/6/2003	9/13/2003
1st Fall Chat room reminder	SR		CRM	NA	9/15/2003
Web application announcement with Royall URL link	SR		CRM	9/9/2003	9/15/2003
Just In Time Brochures (JIT)	SR		TIS/WP		09/20/03
National Merit High Scores	SR	CP	Publications	09/09/03	09/20/03

STUDENT
MARKETING
FOR COLLEGES
AND UNIVERSITIES

SAMPLE
MARKETING PLAN

COMMUNICATION	TARGET	CNSLR	VENDOR	RUN DATE	MAIL DATE
Deadline Reminder/EA/ED Spur Card	SR	JA	Publications	09/16/03	09/20/03
Inside Jefferson reminder	SR/JR		DIRECT MAIL	NA	9/24/2003
Benefits Piece	JR		Publications		09/30/03
OCTOBER					
LA Weeks reminder	SR		CRM	9/23/2003	10/1/2003
Health Sciences Newsletters – Fall 2002	SR	KG	Health Sciences	09/23/03	10/04/03
Transfer Newsletter – Fall 2002	Tran	DS	Mail House	09/23/03	10/04/03
Mayoral Scholarship NOLA Inquiries Cover Letter	SR	VT	Mail House	09/23/03	10/11/03
Mayoral Scholarship Application Form	SR	VT	Mail House	09/23/03	10/11/03
Governor's Scholarship LA High School Cover Letter	SR	VT	Mail House	09/23/03	10/11/03
Honors Program letter (to generate applicants)	SR	CP	WP	09/30/03	10/11/03
Inside Jefferson reminder	SR/JR		DIRECT MAIL	NA	10/15/2003
Financial Aid Brochure (sourcebook in 03)	*SR*		Publications		*10/15/03*
Admission Decision Letters, Fast App	Apply	JA	WP	Rolling	10/15/03
Admission Decision Letters, Freshman	Apply	JA	WP	Rolling	10/15/03
Admission Decision Letters, International	Apply–Intl	JA	WP	Rolling	10/15/03
Admission Decision Letters, Transfer	Apply–Tran	JA	WP	Rolling	10/15/03

COMMUNICATION	TARGET	CNSLR	VENDOR	RUN DATE	MAIL DATE
Accept Packet, Freshman	Accpt	JA	Publications	Rolling	10/15/03
Accept Packet, International	Intl	DS	Publications	Rolling	10/15/03
Accept Packet, Transfer, Spring	Tran	DS	Publications	Rolling	10/15/03
Accept Packet, Transfer, Fall	Tran	DS	Publications	Rolling	10/15/03
Merit Scholarship, DHS Spur Card	SR	JA	Publications	10/07/03	10/18/03
Deans Letter to Applicants – Education	Apply	VT	WP	10/07/03	10/18/03
Deans Letter to Applicants – Business	Apply	PS	WP	10/07/03	10/18/03
Deans Letter to Applicants – Health Sciences	Apply	KG	WP	10/07/03	10/18/03
Deans Letter to Applicants – Newcomb	Apply	CP	WP	10/07/03	10/18/03
Deans Letter to Applicants –Jefferson	Apply	RA	WP	10/07/03	10/18/03
Missing Document letter	Apply	JA	TIS/WP	Rolling	10/18/03
EA/ED e-mail reminder	SR		CRM	10/17/03	10/24/03
2nd Fall Chat room reminder	SR		CRM	NA	10/27/03
***Live chat with students	Accpt		CRM	10/28/03	10/28/03
NOVEMBER					
Financial Aid Brochure	*JR*		*Publications*	*11/12/03*	*11/08/02*
Q &A Curriculum Guide–AB Freeman School of Business	Apply	JA	Publications	11/05/03	11/15/12

APPENDIX A

SAMPLE
MARKETING PLAN

COMMUNICATION	TARGET	CNSLR	VENDOR	RUN DATE	MAIL DATE
Q &A Curriculum Guide–Education	Apply	JA	Publications	11/05/03	11/15/02
Q &A Curriculum Guide–Health Sciences	Apply	JA	Publications	11/05/03	11/15/02
Q &A Curriculum Guide–Newcomb	Apply	JA	Publications	11/05/03	11/15/02
Q &A Curriculum Guide–Jefferson College	Apply	JA	Publications	11/05/03	11/15/02
Q &A Curriculum Guide–University College	Apply	JA	Publications	11/05/03	11/15/02
Just In Time Brochures (JIT)	*JR*		*TIS/WP*		*11/15/02*
Sophomore Junior – eSearch	*SO/JR*	*JA*	*DIRECT MAIL*	*NA*	*11/22/02*
Search	*SO*	*JA*	*DIRECT MAIL+*	*10/20/02*	*11/22/02*
"144 Reasons" poster	*SO/JR*				
DSA & Founders letters for ED	*Acct*	*JA*	*WP*	*11/11/02*	*11/22/02*
Learning Disabilities Mailing	Accpt	JA	Mail House	11/11/02	11/22/02
DECEMBER					
Holiday Greeting Card	AAC/EA/ED	RA	Mail House	11/18/03	12/01/03
3rd Fall Chat Room reminder	SR		CRM	NA	12/04/03
DHS/merit scholarships e-mail reminder	SR		CRM	11/29/03	12/07/03
Pre Senior College Planning Calendar	JR	JA	Publications	12/02/03	12/13/03
Health Sciences Newsletters – Winter 2002	SR	KG	Health Sciences	12/02/03	12/13/03

COMMUNICATION	TARGET	CNSLR	VENDOR	RUN DATE	MAIL DATE
Financial Aid Workshop Invitations (Art Work)	SR	JA	FA	12/02/03	12/13/03
***Live chat with students	Accpt		CRM	12/05/03	12/05/03
Transfer Close-out letter – Fall	Apply	DS	WP	12/10/03	12/20/03
Afr Congress of Jefferson Pres Ltr to Afr Amer Inq	Accpt	KG	WP	12/10/03	12/20/03
Latin American Student Association pres letter	Accpt	KG	WP	12/10/03	12/20/03
Regular App Deadline e-mail reminder	SR		CRM	01/03/03	01/07/03
JANUARY					
Counselor Tour Invite	HS	ST	In House	12/30/03	01/10/03
***Live chat with students	Accpt		CRM	01/13/03	01/13/03
Email reminder to complete application	Apply		CRM	1/8/2003	01/15/03
Fulfillment (poster) & DVD/Video Requests	Soph		DIRECT MAIL		01/15/03
Fulfillment (poster or CD) & DVD/Video Requests	JR		DIRECT MAIL		01/15/03
Just In Time Brochures (JIT)	Accpt	KG	Mail House	01/14/03	01/24/03
Email reminder to complete application (2)	Apply		CRM	01/23/03	01/30/03
FEBRUARY					
On-line FinAid status announcement	Apply		CRM	01/27/04	02/02/04

STUDENT
MARKETING
FOR COLLEGES
AND UNIVERSITIES

APPENDIX A

SAMPLE
MARKETING PLAN

COMMUNICATION	TARGET	CNSLR	VENDOR	RUN DATE	MAIL DATE
On-line App status announcement	Apply		CRM	01/27/04	02/03/04
Too late to apply letter	Apply	JA	WP	01/15/04	02/01/04
LA Weeks letter – Spring	JR	VT	Mail House	01/02/04	02/07/04
DHS & LA Scholars non-winner letter	Apply	JA	WP	01/27/04	02/07/04
DHS appeal letter	Apply	JA	WP	01/27/04	02/07/04
Print all CO & IN Applications	Apply	AA	WP	01/27/04	02/07/04
Pre Senior Mardi Gras Postcard	JR	JA	Mail House	02/03/04	02/07/04
Admission Reception Evite – Spring	Accpt	JA	DIRECT MAIL		02/14/04
Admission Reception – Spring	Accpt		DIRECT MAIL	02/10/04	02/21/04
Honors Program Invitation	Accpt	CP	WP	02/18/04	02/28/04
Jefferson Days Program Invitation	Accpt	JA	Publications	02/18/04	02/28/04
Honors Weekend Invitation	HRS Accpt	CP	ON Campus	02/20/04	02/28/04
MARCH					
Admission Advisor: "Financial Aid Game"	Soph	JA	Publications	03/01/04	03/01/04
Admission Reception information	Accpt		CRM	2/26/2004	3/5/2004
Admission Reception e-bump	Accpt		DIRECT MAIL	2/26/2004	3/5/2004
Hotel rates	Accpt		CRM	3/3/2004	3/9/2004

COMMUNICATION	TARGET	CNSLR	VENDOR	RUN DATE	MAIL DATE
Airline fares (if possible or admission reception reminders)	Accpt		CRM	3/3/2004	3/12/2004
Admission Reception e-reminder	Accpt		DIRECT MAIL	2/26/2004	3/14/2004
Spring DVD	Accpt	RA	VIDEC	03/04/04	03/14/04
Jefferson Days Confirmation Card	Accpt	JA	Publications	03/04/04	03/14/04
Online Catalog e-mail	Accpt		CRM	3/12/2004	3/18/2004
First Year Experience from Provost	Acc.–Parents		CRM		3/20/2004
Health Sciences Newsletters – Spring 2003	SR	KG	Health Sciences	03/10/04	03/21/04
Letter to Counselors about applicant pool	HS	RW	In House	03/10/04	03/21/04
College Yield Piece (TC, NC, AR, EN)	Accpt	RA	Jefferson College**	03/11/04	03/21/04
Preview Conference Invite	Accpt	KG	Mail House	03/11/04	03/21/04
RJ/IN letter	Apply	JA	WP	03/14/04	03/21/04
JYA	Accpt		CRM	3/19/2004	3/26/2004
Religious Life (& announce live chat with student programs)	Accpt		CRM	3/24/2004	3/28/2004
APRIL					
Video Brochure e-mail	Soph		CRM		4/1/2003
Case Management	Accepts		TIS/WP		4/1/2003
Jefferson Days Thank you	Visitors	AA	On Campus	NA	04/01/03

APPENDIX A

STUDENT
MARKETING
FOR COLLEGES
AND UNIVERSITIES

SAMPLE
MARKETING PLAN

COMMUNICATION	TARGET	CNSLR	VENDOR	RUN DATE	MAIL DATE
***Live chat with Student Programs	Accpt		CRM	3/26/2004	4/2/2003
Sports at Jefferson	Accpt		CRM	3/26/2004	4/2/2003
Academic Advising (announce Wed. online chat with professors)	Accpt		CRM	3/26/2004	4/6/2003
***Live chat with professors	Accpt		CRM	3/26/2004	4/9/2003
President's "Annual Report"	Accepts		Publications		4/9/2003
Jefferson in the News	Accpt		CRM	3/31/2004	4/9/2003
After Jefferson (announce Wed. online chat with alums)	Accpt		CRM	4/9/2004	4/13/2003
Financial aid e-mail	Soph		CRM		4/15/2002
Governor's scholarship letters	Accpt	VT	WP	03/05/04	04/15/02
***Live chat with alums	Accpt		CRM	4/9/2004	4/16/2003
4+1 Programs	Accpt		CRM	4/9/2004	4/16/2003
NOLA e-mail (highlight FQ Fest) & announce online chat with students	Accpt		CRM	4/9/2004	4/16/2003
***Live chat with students	Accpt		CRM	4/9/2004	4/20/2003
Deadline reminder e-mail (one week left)	Accpt		CRM	4/24/2004	4/23/2003
WEEKLY CHATS W/PARENTS					
eQual (likelihood of enrolling)	Accpt		CRM		?

COMMUNICATION	TARGET	CNSLR	VENDOR	RUN DATE	MAIL DATE
MAY					
Mini-Prospectus	Soph		Publications		5/1/2004
Admission Advisor "How to Choose a College"	Soph		Publications		5/15/2004
Beat the Heat Online Application	JR				5/15/2004
Valedictorian letter (LA Students)	Conf	JA	WP	05/07/04	05/17/04
Confirmed Student Packets (some Jan 20 for EA)	Conf	AA	Univ Printing**	Rolling	05/23/04
Commit receipt letter	Conf	JA	WP	Rolling	05/23/04
Denied Wait list letter	Conf	JA	WP	Rolling	05/30/04
JUNE					
D & F letters	Conf	JA	WP	Rolling	06/06/04
Pre Senior Newsletter #1: "How did we get your name?"	SO	KG	Publications		06/07/04
Admission Advisor "How are Admission Decisions Made"	Soph		Publications		06/01/04
Beat the Heat Online Application	JR				06/01/04
JULY					
Just The Facts	Soph		Publications		07/01/04
Equal					**07/15/04**

STUDENT
MARKETING
FOR COLLEGES
AND UNIVERSITIES

SAMPLE
MARKETING PLAN

COMMUNICATION	TARGET	CNSLR	VENDOR	RUN DATE	MAIL DATE
OTHER					
Brandt Dixon Scholarship letter	Accpt	DS	WP	NA	NA
Frances Louise Diboll Chesworth Scholarship Ltr	Accpt	DS	WP	NA	NA
Pre Senior Private Colleges and Universities	Prosp	VT	PC & U	NA	NA
Pre Senior College Guide	Prosp	VT	College Guide	NA	NA
Peterson's Four Year Guide To Colleges	Prosp	JA	Peterson's	NA	NA
National Achievement Finalists	SR	KG	WP	NA	NA
National Merit Hispanic Finalists	SR	KG	WP	NA	NA
A Better Chance Program	JR/SR	KG	WP	NA	NA

BIBLIOGRAPHY

Aaker, David A. (1991). *Managing brand equity: Capitalizing on the value of a brand name.* New York: The Free Press.

Archibald, R.B., & BeVier, M.J. (1998). Imposing market discipline on public colleges and universities. (No. 3, pp. 1–15). Richmond, Virginia: Virginia Institute for Public Policy.

Birnbaum, R. (2000). *Management Fads in Higher Education: Where They Come From, What They Do, and Why They Fail.* San Francisco: Jossey–Bass Publishers.

Black, J. (1999). *Navigating Change in the New Millennium: Enrollment Leadership Strategies.* Washington, DC: American Association of Collegiate Registrars and Admissions Officers.

Black, J. (2000, October). The integration of enrollment management with the academic enterprise. *The Data Dispenser* [Online edition]. Available: www.aacrao.org.

Black, J. (2001, September). Fragmented marketing: Causes and cures. *The Greentree Gazette,* 24–26.

Black, J. (2003, May). Delivering the promise of the brand. *The Greentree Gazette,* 44–46.

Blackburn, J. C. (1980). Marketing admissions: A perspective on its use. *College Board Review,* (116).

Blackwell, R., Miniard, P.W. & Engel, J.F. (2001). *Consumer Behavior.* Orlando: Harcourt College Publishers.

Bolman, L. G. & Deal, T. E. (1991). *Reframing Organizations.* San Francisco: Jossey–Bass Publishers.

Bontrager, R. (2002). *Strategic enrollment management: An introduction to core concepts and strategies.* San Diego: AACRAO Strategic Enrollment Management Conference.

Brubacher, J. S. & Rudy, W. (1976). *Higher Education in Transition* (3rd ed., p. 6). New York: Harper & Row.

Bryson, J.M. (1995). *Strategic planning for public and non-profit institutions.* San Francisco: Jossey–Bass Publishers.

Buell, V. P. (1986). *Handbook of Modern Marketing.* New York: McGraw–Hill.

Burns, Robert (1904). *The Poetical Works of Robert Burns,* New York.

Chin, G. (2003, Fall/Winter). Empty promises? Restoring our commitment to access. *On Target* (23), 18–22.

STUDENT
MARKETING
FOR COLLEGES
AND UNIVERSITIES

247

Clark, C. R. & Hossler, D. (1990). Marketing in nonprofit organizations. In D. Hossler, J. P. Bean, & Associates (Eds.) *The Strategic Management of College Enrollments.* San Francisco: Jossey–Bass Publishers.

Collins, J. (2001). *Good to Great: Why Some Companies Make the Leap and Others Don't.* Harper Collins.

Conlin, M. (2003, May). The new gender gap. *Business Week,* pp.74–82

Covey, S. R. (1989). *The 7 Habits of Highly Effective People.* New York: Simon & Schuster, Inc.

Csikszentmihalyi, M. (1997) *Creativity: Flow and the Psychology of Discovery and Invention.* Perennial.

Csikszentmihalyi, M. (2003) *Good business: Leadership, flow, and the making of meaning.* Viking Press.

Cummings, T. G. & Worley, C. G. (2001). *Essentials of Organizational Development & Change.* Cincinnati, Ohio: South-Western Publishing.

Czerniawski, R., and Maloney, M. (1999) Creating Brand Loyalty: The Management of Power Positioning and Really Great Advertising. AMACOM.

Dey, E. L., Astin, A. W., & Korn, W. S. (1991). *The American Freshman: Twenty-five Year Trends.* Los Angeles, CA: Cooperative Institutional Research Program.

Dimun, B. (1998). *Educational Marketing: An Essential Tool for Managing Change.* Unpublished manuscript, Princeton University.

Dolence, Michael.(1993) *Strategic Enrollment Management: A Primer for Campus Administrators.* Washington, D.C.: American Association of Collegiate Registrars and Admission Officers.

Dolence, M.G. (1999). *The ABCs of SEM.* Paper presented at the Strategic Enrollment Management Conference of the American Association of Collegiate Registrars and Admissions Officers, Lake Buena Vista, FL.

Drucker, P. F. (1990). *Managing the Non-profit Organization: Principles and Practices.* Harper–Business.

Drucker, P. F. (1997). An interview with Peter Drucker. *Forbes Magazine.*

Ferrari, M.R. & Lauer, L.D. (2000). Vision of the future. *Currents XXVI.* (4), 19–22.

Gelernter, David. (2003). Apres Spam. *The Weekly Standard,* September 29, 2003, Volume 009, Issue 03.

Gibbs, P. & Knapp, M. (2002). *Marketing Higher and Further Education.* London: Kogan Page.

Goffman, I. (1961). On the Characteristics of Total Institutions. *Asylums: Essays on the Social Situation of Mental Patients and Other Inmates.* Anchor Books.

Green, K.C. (2000). First to the ballroom, late to the dance. In Katz, R.N. & Oblinger, D.G. (Eds.), *The "E" is for Everything: E-Commerce, E-Business, and E-Learning in the Future of Higher Education* (pp. 11–20). San Francisco: Jossey–Bass Publishers.

Hayes, T.J. (Ed.), (1991). *New Strategies in Higher Education Marketing.* New York: The Haworth Press.

Hertenstein, J., and Platt M. (2001). Valuing Design: Enhancing corporate performance through design effectiveness. *Design Management Journal,* 12 (3) 10–19.

Hossler, D. (1984). *Enrollment Management – An Integrated Approach.* New York: College Entrance Examination Board.

Hossler, D. (2000, Spring). The role of financial aid in enrollment management. *New Directions for Student Services* (89), 77–90.

Howe, N. & Strauss, W. (2000). *Millennials Rising: The Next Great Generation.* New York: Vintage Books.

Howe, N. and Strauss, W. (2003). *Millennials Go to College: Strategies for a New Generation on Campus: Recruiting and Admissions, Campus Life, and the Classroom,* AACRAO and LifeCourse Associates.

Huddleston, T. (1980). In consideration of marketing and reorganization. *The National Association College Admissions Counselors Journal,* 25 (1), 18–24.

Ihlanfeldt, W. (1980). *Achieving Optimal Enrollments and Tuition Revenues.* San Francisco: Jossey–Bass Publishers.

Kemerer, F., Baldrige, J.V., & Green, K. C. (1982). *Strategies for Effective Enrollment Management.* Washington, DC: American Association of State Colleges and Universities.

Kimrey, R. P. (2000). Enhancing recruitment with financial aid packaging. *The SACRAO Journal,* 15, 21–23.

Kirp, D. L. (2003). *Shakespeare, Einstein, and the Bottom Line: The Marketing of Higher Education,* Harvard University Press.

Kotler, P. (1975). *Marketing for Non-profit Organizations.* Englewood Cliffs, New Jersey: Prentice Hall.

Kotler, P. (1976). Applying marketing theory to college admissions. In *A Role for Marketing in College Admissions.* New York: College Entrance Examination Board.

Kotler, P. (1982). *Marketing for Nonprofit Organizations.* New Jersey: Englewood Cliffs.

Kotler, P. and Fox, K. F. A. (1985). *Strategic Marketing for Educational Institutions,* Englewood Cliffs, New Jersey: Prentice Hall, 1985.

Kotler, P. (1999). *Kotler on Marketing: How to Create, Win, and Dominate Markets.* New York: The Free Press.

STUDENT
MARKETING
FOR COLLEGES
AND UNIVERSITIES

Kotler, P. & Armstrong, G. (2001). *Principles of Marketing.* Upper Saddle River, NJ: Prentice Hall.

Kotter, J. P. & Schlesinger, L. A. (1979, March). Choosing strategies for change. *Harvard Business Review,* 19 (3), 74–83.

Kvavik, R. (2000). Transforming student services. *EDUCAUSE Quarterly,* 23 (2), 30–37.

Lauer, L.D. (2000). The status of integrated marketing in colleges and universities. *The CASE International Journal of Educational Advancement,* 1 (2), 101–112.

Lauer, L.D. (2000). Marketing and advancement. *Handbook of institutional advancement* (3rd ed.). Washington, DC: Council for Advancement and Support of Education.

Lay, R. & Endo, J. editors (1987). *Designing and using market research.* San Francisco: Jossey–Bass Publishers.

Lay, R. & Maguire, J. (1980). Identifying the competition in higher education. *College and University,* 56 (1), 53–65.

Levitt, T. (1986). *The Marketing Imagination.* Expanded Edition, Free Press.

Lewin, K. (1947, June). Frontiers in group dynamics: Concept, method, and reality in social sciences, social equilibrium and social change. *Human Relation,* I (I).

Litten, L. H., Sullivan, D., & Brodigan, D. L. (1983). *Applying Market Research in College Admissions.* New York: College Entrance Examination Board.

Litten, L. (1987). Viewing the world without ivy-colored glasses. In Lay, R. & Endo, J. editors *Designing and using market research.* San Francisco: Jossey–Bass Publishers.

Massa, R. (2001). Developing a SEM Plan. In *Strategic Enrollment Management Revolution.* Washington, DC: American Association of Collegiate Registrars and Admissions Officers.

McKenna, R. (1991). Relationship marketing. *Harvard Business Review,* January–February.

Merritt, S.R. (1999). *The Student Enrollment Challenge of the New Millennium.* Paper presented at the Strategic Enrollment Management Conference of the American Association of Collegiate Registrars and Admissions Officers, Lake Buena Vista, FL.

Michalko, M. (1991). *Thinkertoys: A Handbook of Business Creativity.* Ten Speed Press, Berkeley, CA.

Michalko, M. (2001). *Cracking Creativity: The Secrets of Creative Genius.* Ten Speed Press. Berkeley, CA.

Michelle, M.L. & Brent, C.D. (2001). *Integrated Marketing in Higher Education.* Research report prepared for Higher Education program in Texas Tech University.

Oblinger, D.G. & Katz, R.N. (2000). Navigating the sea of "E." In Katz, R.N. & Oblinger, D.G. (Eds.), *The "E" is for Everything: E-commerce, E-business, and E-learning in the Future of Higher Education* (pp. 1–10). San Francisco: Jossey–Bass Publishers.

O'Hara, Frank. *The Collected Poems of Frank O'Hara,* University of California Press, London, England, 1995.

Ohio State University (2000). *Marketing the Land Grant University* [Online committee report]. Available: http://cfacs.ohio-state.edu/products/documents.html.

Percy, L. (1997). *Strategies for Implementing Integrated Marketing Communications.* Chicago: American Marketing Association.

Peppers D. & Rogers M. (1996). *The one to one future.* New York: Doubleday.

Pride, W. & Ferrell, O. C. (1995). *Marketing* 9th Edition. Boston: Houghton Mifflin Co. .

Pride, W. & Ferrell, O. C. (1999). *Marketing 2000e.* Boston: Houghton Mifflin Custom Publishing.

Rogers, G., Finley, D. & Kline, T. (2001). Understanding individual differences in university undergraduates: A Learner needs segmentation approach. *Innovative Higher Education,* 25 (3), pp. 183–196.

Rudolph, F. (1962). *The American College and University.* New York: Vintage Books.

St. John, E. P. (2000, Spring). The impact of student aid on recruitment and retention: What the research indicates. *New Directions for Student Services* (89), 61–75.

Schein, E.H. (1992). *Organizational Culture and Leadership.* San Francisco: Jossey–Bass Publishers.

Schnaar, S.P. (1998). *Marketing Strategy: Customers & Competition.* New York: The Free Press.

Schiffman, L. G. and Leslie L. K. (2000). *Consumer Behavior,* 7th edition. Englewood Cliffs, New Jersey: Prentice Hall.

Senge, P.M. (1990). *The Fifth Discipline: The Art & Practice of the Learning Organization.* New York: Currency Doubleday.

Sevier, R.A. (1998). *Integrated Marketing for Colleges, Universities, and Schools: A Step-by-Step Planning Guide.* Washington, DC: Council for Advancement and Support of Education.

Sevier, R.A. (1999). *Much Ado About Something.* Stamats Communications, Inc. Web site [Online white paper]. Available: http://www.stamats.com.

Sevier, R.A. (2000). *Brand as Relevance.* Stamats Communications, Inc. Web site [Online white paper]. Available: http://www.stamats.com.

Sevier, R. (2001). *Thinking Outside the Box.* Hiawatha, Iowa: Strategy Publishing, Inc.

Seymour, D.T. (1993). *On Q: Causing Quality in Higher Education.* Phoenix, Arizona: Oryx Press.

Seymour, D.T. (1995). *Once Upon a Campus: Lessons for Improving Quality and Productivity in Higher Education.* Phoenix, Arizona: Oryx Press.

Siegel, D. (1999). *Futurize Your Enterprise: Business Strategy in the Age of the E-Customer.* New York: John Wiley & Sons, Inc.

Solomon, M. R. (2002). *Consumer Behavior: Buying, Having, and Being,* 5th edition. Prentice Hall International Series in Marketing.

Strauss, J. & Frost, R. (2001). *E-Marketing.* Upper Saddle River, New Jersey: Prentice Hall.

Stryker, S. (1997). *Strategic Planning: A Guide to Long-Term Organizational Viability.* Rockville, MD. Stryker Associates, unpublished manuscript.

Swenson, C. (1998). Customers & markets: The cuss words of academe. *Change,* 30 (5), 34–39.

The survey of college marketing programs – Management practices (Volume 1) [Numerical/quantitative data file]. (1998). New York, NY: Primary Research Group, Inc. [Producer and Distributor].

Tonks, D.G. & Farr, M. (1995). Market segments for higher education: using geodemographics. *Marketing Intelligence & Planning,* 13 (4), pp. 24–33.

Topor, R. (1997). *Marketing Higher Education: A Practical Guide.* [Online]. Available: http://www.marketinged.com/library/index.html#books.

Topor, B. (1998). *Developing a Higher Education Marketing Paradigm.* Topor Consulting Group International web site [Online white paper]. Available: http://www.marketinged.com.

Topor, B. (1998). *Relationship Marketing.* Topor Consulting Group International web site [Online white paper]. Available: http://www.marketinged.com.

University of Oregon (2000). *Three Market Orientations to the Changing Market of Higher Education* [On-line committee report]. Available: http://darkwing.uoregon.edu/~acadaff/change/5/changingmarkets.html.

National Enrollment Management Survey [On-line report available only to survey participants]. (2000). Littleton, Colorado: USA Group Noel–Levitz [Producer and Distributor].

U. S. Census Bureau (2000). *Census 2000 – Annual Projections of the Resident Population by Age, Sex, Race, and Hispanic Origin: Lowest, Middle, Highest Series and Zero International Migration Series, 1999 to 2100* [PDF file]. Washington, DC: U.S. Census Bureau [Producer and Distributor].

Von Oech, R., (1998). *A Whack on the Side of the Head: How You Can Be More Creative* (Third Edition). Warner Books, Inc., New York, NY.

Wallhaus, R. A. (2000). E-learning: From institutions to providers, from students to learners. In Katz, R.N. & Oblinger, D.G. (Eds.), *The "E" is for Everything: E-Commerce, E-Business, And E-Learning in the Future of Higher Education* (pp. 21–52). San Francisco: Jossey–Bass Publishers.

Winter, G. (2003). Jacuzzi U: A battle of perks to lure students. *New York Times,* October 5.

Zemsky, R., Shaman, S., & Iannozzi, M. (1997). In search of strategic perspective: A tool for mapping the market in postsecondary education. *Change,* 29, 23–38.

Zemsky, R. (July, 2003). CASE National Forum, Washington, DC.

BIBLIOGRAPHY

STUDENT
MARKETING
FOR COLLEGES
AND UNIVERSITIES

INDEX

STUDENT
MARKETING
FOR COLLEGES
AND UNIVERSITIES

STUDENT
MARKETING
FOR COLLEGES
AND UNIVERSITIES

INDEX

STUDENT
MARKETING
FOR COLLEGES
AND UNIVERSITIES

INDEX

Threats: 60, 61, 67, 176, 189

Traditional vs. integrated marketing: 174

Trust: 16, 135, 179

Turf issues: 172, 173, 176

U

Unfreezing: 178

V

Value: 6, 7, 8, 9, 10, 13, 15, 16, 28, 29, 31, 33, 49, 53, 58, 59, 91, 98, 100, 102, 103, 105, 127, 143, 150, 151, 156, 157, 164, 171, 172, 174, 175, 176, 181, 197, 248

Value exchange: 8

Value proposition: 6

Values: 4, 9, 13, 27, 47, 52, 95, 104, 105, 130, 175, 177, 179

Vision: iii, viii, 1, 4, 19, 20, 21, 22, 23, 26, 28, 29, 34, 40, 47, 49, 65, 105, 106, 109, 170, 173, 177, 178, 179, 249

Vision statement: 20, 26

W

Weaknesses: viii, 13, 26, 38, 41, 58, 60, 61, 67, 70, 72, 174, 176, 189

INDEX

262